David Urquhart, John Fife

Manual of the Turkish Bath

A Mode of Cure and a Source of Strength for Men and Animals

David Urquhart, John Fife

Manual of the Turkish Bath
A Mode of Cure and a Source of Strength for Men and Animals

ISBN/EAN: 9783337293253

Printed in Europe, USA, Canada, Australia, Japan

Cover: Foto ©Thomas Meinert / pixelio.de

More available books at **www.hansebooks.com**

Manual of the Turkish Bath.

Heat a Mode of Cure

and a

Source of Strength

for

Men and Animals.

From Writings of Mr. Urquhart,

Edited by

Sir John Fife, ~~M.D.~~, F.R.C.S.,

Senior Surgeon to the Newcastle Infirmary.

London, 1865:

John Churchill and Sons, New Burlington Street.

Introduction.

BY THE EDITOR.

IN introducing to the medical profession and to the public a work on the Turkish Bath, by an author not of the profession, it is necessary, in the first instance, to guard against any hasty conclusions, on the one hand; or, on the other hand, the rejection of statements that may seem at variance with the therapeutic science of men experienced in the value, and justly confident in the indications, which therapeutics afford.

As regards the use of the baths of the ancients in a sanitary point of view, or as an habitual luxury of cleanliness unattainable to the same degree in any other way, doubts will exist only in the minds of those who have not experienced the enjoyment produced by the operation, or the sensations of elasticity and vigour it leaves afterwards.

The same persevering confidence which enabled the author to effect the restoration to us of this Greek and Roman luxury may be well excused in regarding the Turkish bath as a panacea, because without such a faith in its powers no one could have laboured so long, or have made the sacrifices required to revive this institution, buried for nearly a thousand years.

The history of medicine shows how generally it is the fate of new remedial agents to be at first overrated, then undervalued, and at last forgotten; but such a destiny cannot reasonably be anticipated in a case where such a hold is gained upon the feelings and confidence of those who use it, even in instances of commencement in alarm, aversion, or prejudice.

In the year 1859, having previously satisfied my own mind of the efficacy of this process, I brought it under the consideration of the Pathological Society of Newcastle, and afterwards addressed on the subject the House Committee of the Newcastle Infirmary; who, encouraged by his Grace the Duke of Northumberland, well experienced during his Eastern travels in the value of the Turkish bath, entered energetically into the enterprise of constructing such baths for the hospital. The effect of this wise measure has been essentially economical, inasmuch, as by shortening considerably the necessary period of confinement within the walls of the hospital, less expense has been incurred in restoring many hundreds of working men to their habits of useful industry.

Great must be the value of a process which in a few minutes will secure a general diaphoresis, bring the circulation to the extremities, and equalize the arterial action, instead of permitting a disordered nervous influence to direct an undue flow upon one tortured part to the comparative deprivation of arterial blood to other and distant structures; a process competent to allay spasm immediately, in many cases which might resist all other diaphoretics, or exhibit their effects only in gastric and intestinal irritation.

It may be safe to conclude that it will prove of service in every case of internal congestion, and its effects are most remarkable in obviating disorders and palliating the diseases of the liver and the kidney; as it not only distributes a more equal circulation, but allays spasm in the excretory ducts—the passage of gall-stones, and the sudden relief of liver obstruction, occurring immediately on the use of the bath.

Spasmodic and permanent stricture of the urethra, enlargement of prostate gland, vesical mucous inflammation, albuminuria, and diabetes are palpably amenable to this bath; and in one of the most remarkable cases of strictured urethra of thirty years' duration that ever came under my notice, health was restored, and life, even in advanced age, rendered cheerful and comparatively strong.

In the treatment of the diseases of joints, as may be easily imagined, its efficacy is re-markable, whether they are of an organic and scrofulous character, or inflammatory and rheu-matic; indeed, in many cases of the latter de-scription, the bath, with ordinary attention to the digestive organs, will effect complete resto-ration, independent of many of those counter-irritants so painful in themselves and so often required.

It is in vain to hope for the same remedial powers from the ordinary hot water bath, which can seldom be borne much above 100°, which leaves behind it relaxation, debility, susceptibility to cold, and that moisture of the surface which is coexistent with coldness of the extremities.

I am unable to point out any class of cutaneous diseases in which the Turkish bath may not prove an effectual treatment or an important auxiliary, as the skin which has been long in an almost impervious condition, with obstructed pores and inflamed epithelium, entirely changes its character in a few minutes, and exhibits moisture on its surface, to the inexpressible relief of many uneasy sensations previously experienced.

In bronchial inflammation or laryngeal, the surface affected is instantaneously reached. A clergyman well known for his eloquence, having quite lost his voice for some days, accompanied me to a Turkish bath, which he entered with a whispering hoarseness, but which he quitted with a restored voice, and continued well enough to preach on the following day.

Instances of sudden relief from spasmodic or inflammatory obstruction of the viscera or their ducts, or gradual relief from chronic disorder, might be multiplied without end, but the Turkish bath is incontestably as valuable a remedy in many diseases as it is a luxury and a means of training in health.

We have yet to discover the degree to which our remedial process may be exercised as regards temperature, duration, and frequency; therefore I put to Mr. Urquhart the question, " What is the precise point in effectiveness and economy that may be attained in your belief by your plan of radiating heat, and ventilation by suction ? "

REPLY.

" The practice to which I have now reached is, on getting out of bed, to go in at 220° (up to 250°), for a period varying from five to ten minutes. I then plunge into cold water and come out to dress, saving at least half-an-hour on the time it would take me to dress without the bath. I repeat the operation at night on going to bed. This takes from ten minutes to a quarter of an hour. Should I require the bath on account of indisposition, incipient or threatened, I repeat the above operation, and continue doing so till the cause has ceased."

In the Newcastle Infirmary the number of

people sent into the Turkish baths amounted to about fifteen a day, according to the report of Dr. Bolton, our house surgeon; and most of these were under my care. This number does not appear great till it is remembered that there are four physicians and four surgeons, dividing thus the number of cases into eight parts: of these, many with organic diseases, or compound fractures, or requiring capital operations, could not easily enjoy this luxury or obtain its benefits; and a large proportion of such cases always fall to my lot, as to the share of the three other surgeons.

In an hospital of a more medical and less surgical character, though of less extent altogether, a wider field might be found for the trial of the Turkish bath; but from what I have witnessed of its effects in health for training, convalescence for enabling the valetudinarian to commence exercise, in disease as a remedy or a palliation, I am not afraid to stake my professional character, by declaring my belief in its efficacy.

JOHN FIFE.

Topics.

1.—Use of Heat in pre-historic times.
2.—The Bath an artificial climate.
3.—A Substitute for exercise.
4.—Its action in acute, chronic, and epidemic disorders.
5.—Arrests consumption.
6.—Prevents the diseases of children.
7.—Effects in insanity.
8.—Discharges poisons, animal and mineral.
9.—Relief in childbirth.
10.—Why man perspires.
11.—Relationship of perspiration to disease.
12.—Temperature of various diseases.
13.—Detection of disease by the smell.
14.—Disease incidental to the restriction by clothing of the discharge through the skin.
15.—Construction of public and private baths, and for asylums and hospitals.
16.—Radiant heat: its connection with solar rays, the source of life and motion.
17.—Muscular power increased, as shown in runners, wrestlers, boxers and RACE HORSES.
18.—Productiveness increased in regard to work, flesh, milk, and progeny, as shown in FARM STOCK.

Maladies.

PART II.—CATTLE.

Contents.

PART II.—ACTION ON ANIMALS.

APPENDIX.

ERRATA.

Page 30, for the title "Tendency of Blood to the Head and *Epilepsy*," read "and *Apoplexy*."

,,   65, line 4, for "*treating*," read "*heating*."

,,   92, ,, 2, for "*for since cure*," read "*cure*" (the words "for since cure" to be cut out).

,,   97, ,, 15, for "*Bath*," read "*Baths.*"

,, 117, ,, 3, for "*wasted*," read "*washed.*"

,, 119, ,, 6, for "*lightest* specific gravity," read "*highest* specific gravity."

,, 171, last line, for "*split*," read "*spilt.*"

,, 183, note, line 3, for "*tenticulari*," read "*lenticulari.*"

,, 206, line 3, for "*would*," read "*should.*"

,, 227, ,, 3, for "*facilities*," read "*faculties.*"

,, 235, ,, 19, for "*would*," read "*should.*"

,, 298, ,, 17, for "*somewhat* self-reproach," read "*severe* self-reproach."

Part I.

Action of the Bath on Man.

First Dialogue.*

Heat: how useful for Man, and how used by him.

July 27th, 1860.

Present, between 30 and 40 Medical and Professional Gentlemen, and others.

Mr. Witt.—How was it that in the East you took up the bath as a matter to be introduced into Europe, seeing that no other traveller had hitherto done so?

Mr. Urquhart.—I became an Eastern, and, therefore, I wanted it in Europe.

Mr. Erasmus Wilson.—Was it luxury or health which prompted you?

Mr. Urquhart.—First, as a luxury; secondly, as a necessity.

Mr. Wilson.—Have you experienced its application in disease in your own person?

Mr. Urquhart.—I have; I have saved my own life by means of it on four occasions.

Mr. Wilson.—Your acquaintance with the bath goes further back than recent years when you have tried it

* From short-hand notes.

B

for the purposes of health. You discovered it as the botanist discovers a new plant, as the physiologist, who has discovered some new function. What was it, in the first instance, that led you to consider that the bath was so necessary?

Mr. Urquhart.—I did not find, in the East, the bath used for the cure of disease. I only inferred that it must have that effect; and, therefore, when I was myself afflicted with sickness, I made use of it, and with success.

Mr. Wilson.—Will you give us an instance?

Mr. Urquhart.—I had been quail-shooting on the coast of the island of Scio. On my return to the town of Scio, on one of the hottest days of August, I received a stroke of the sun. I arrived in the port of Scio in a delirious condition, but yet so far master of myself as to require to be taken to a bath. I had great difficulty in getting myself carried thither, as the people believed it would kill me. I was placed in the hottest part, and continued there for six hours: then only did the perspiration break out.

Dr. Sibson.—They gave no reasons for their objection to the use of the bath?

Mr. Urquhart.—They have no thought of its use in this fashion.

Dr. Sibson.—It had never been tried.

Mr. Urquhart.—Apparently not there, at that time.

Mr. Wilson.—Then, as used by the Easterns as by the Romans, the bath seems to have been employed rather as a luxury and means of cleanliness than as a necessity?

Mr. Urquhart.—An answer would involve illustrations.

Mr. Witt.—If you please.

Mr. Urquhart.—Among the Romans, as amongst the Turks, the curative effect was unconsciously produced. It has been an old saying, that during five hundred years there was no medical man in Rome. It is the same to-day amongst the Turks. For the first time now, and in consequence of what has been done in England, the bath is dealt with in Turkey as a medical agent, as appears by a series of articles which has appeared in the *Turkish Medical Gazette.* The first time I entered a bath in Turkey, it was in company with two eminent physicians, now strenuous advocates of the bath. An expression of one of them on that occasion probably fixed my attention to the subject in an investigating fashion. Experiencing a feeling of faintness, the attendant dashed cold water over my feet: he exclaimed, " Those brutes of Turks!" I was, however, immediately relieved; and thus I first began to doubt the infallibility of European physiology.

Mr. Witt.—Are we to infer that the medical use of the bath has remained up to this time unknown?

Mr. Urquhart.—There can be no question that, in primeval times, so evident a provision of nature as heat could not have been, and was not, overlooked; and races who retain their primitive characters continue so to employ it. One instance will suffice. Here is a note I have just received from Captain Burton, giving an account of the medical use of the bath with herbs by the tribes of Mesopotamia.

(Note read.)

It will suffice to connect this still extant usage with the story of Medea, to establish an uninterrupted sequence during more than thirty centuries of this practice among primitive races in and surrounding the Caucasus, with whom the Greeks first, and subsequently the Romans, came in contact.

Mr. Wilson.—What could have first suggested to the mind of man the use of the bath ?

Mr. Urquhart.—Will you allow me to substitute for " bath" "heat ?"

Mr. Wilson.—Yes.

Mr. Urquhart.—I conceive heat to be the meaning in mythology of the "negative and the positive principles." These pervade all religions ; they are the groundwork of all ancient philosophy, whether in the Western or Eastern world. These are water and heat. The sun represents the one, the moon the other ; for the moon was held to be the emblem of water. This is the myth of the lotus. That plant dropping in a capsule its seed upon the lake Manaswara, expanding and growing without contact with the earth, nourished by the water and called up by the sun ; represents the conjunction of the two principles operating in the procreation, and for the development of the animal and vegetable worlds. They deified moisture and heat. Can there be a doubt, that having traced their action they had called in their aid ? Heat and moisture constitute the bath. The sun to the Egyptian was the "performer of miracles." They distinguish between *apparent heat* and *curative heat;* that heat that we seek when in sickness, that is to say in a state of deficient electricity—these direct rays being electrical. We are only beginning after thirty centuries to understand that meaning in the rays of the sun, which induced the Egyptians to symbolize them by the human hand. Before Galileo, the Egyptian definition of musical chords was incomprehensible. Until we had the scientific analysis of the rays of the sun, the distinction between a value attributed to the sun as rays and the sun as heat, was equally so. We know now that not only the rays of the sun have a power independent of heat, but that each subdivision of those rays possesses independent powers. We also know now that even the most recondite parts of our frame—the bones for instance—are dependent upon the action of the rays of the sun upon the surface for their very substance. This, therefore, gives us the value of those early instincts of man which have always been right, for they were based on observation, not formulas. What is essentially good is always so ancient that its origin is a mystery.

This use of heat has been so clearly an instinct, that it is not found in those regions of the earth where the temperature is so high as not to require it. In the torrid zone, and for some degrees north and south, accumulation upon and congestion of the skin is not a source of disease as in countries of a moderate temperature, where the body has been artificially covered up. In the latter the bath appears to have been almost universally a primeval institution. The whole of the north of Europe possesses it in one shape or another. The Red Indians of America have it ; the Swedes have

it; the Russians have it; the Fins have it; the Tartars, the Persians, have it; the Celtic races possess the
remnants of it in the Irish "sweating houses;" the
Gothic races originally had it too.   But when you
come down to the south it is no longer to be found.

Mr. ——.—I thought the bath was particularly
Mussulman, at least that it was enjoined by that religion,
and that religion had its origin in a very hot country.

Mr. Urquhart.—That is a common belief in Europe,
but like so many other beliefs, it is not only without
foundation, but the very reverse of the truth. The practice before Mahomet's time had spread from the Greeks
into Arabia, but was held to be an innovation on
early simplicity, and effeminate : consequently Mahomet
struggled vehemently against it.   He even risked his
credit by attempting to put it down.   He denounced it
as impure.   He coupled it with the grave-yard, using
these words : " In these two I have no part."   He was,
however, beaten, and had to give in, suffering its use
on a point which nearly touches the feelings of Easterns, and on which depends the perpetuation of the
human race.*   His proselytes held that by the agency
of the bath barrenness was removed, and the labour
and danger of childbirth diminished.   In confirmation
of this view some interesting particulars will be found
in the letters of Lady Mary W. Montague.†   Thus you
have it not in the islands of the Indian Archipelago ;
you have it not in Japan ; you have it not in China ;
you have it not originally in India ; you have it not in

---

* See note at the end, on " BARRENNESS."
† See note at the end, on " CHILDBIRTH."

Arabia, nor among the primitive tribes of Africa, although its earliest type is perhaps that of the city populations of Morocco, as derived from the Iberians. It has, however, to be observed that it is not unknown in intertropical regions, but it is there *only used in case of disease.* * Thus in whatever region of the earth the bath was requisite, it was invented and applied by the ingenuity or the instinct of primitive man.

Mr. Witt.—You say, speaking of the action of the sun, that it was known and understood by the ancients. Pliny, in both his country-houses of Florentinum and Tuscum provided special walks with evergreen clipped hedges, where he could take his walks naked and bare-footed daily in the sun.

Mr. Urquhart.—When I speak of antiquity, Rome sinks to the level of London. You first called my attention to that passage where Pliny describes himself as preparing a field for his own exercise; so that the breezes of heaven and the rays of the sun should come upon him. He must have understood that it is the sun which more especially gives us length of days, and strength to enjoy them. I have myself successfully treated a case of consumption solely by the rays of the sun.

In America, where *Actinism* has been peculiarly studied, they now look upon the handling the rays of the sun as an item in the Pharmacopœia. We do not turn science to account for our bodies. Look at electricity

---

* See note at the end, on "THE USE OF THE BATH IN SICKNESS BY INTERTROPICAL RACES."

and animal chemistry: what have these and all other
sciences done for our health, our food, and our houses?
What have they done for our dress?—what for our
habits?

Mr. Wilson.—As to the influence of caloric upon the
surface of the human body, there are just one or two
little illustrations that occurred to me: they may be
interesting to you. I have always attached, from my
earliest days upwards, the greatest value to any practical hint; and I have frequently had to admit that the
old woman was more powerful than the most learned or
scientific man. Accompanying a country medical man
in his rounds, he told me he had made a great discovery
in the treatment of sprains. We all know there is
nothing more painful or more serious than a sprain of an
ankle: it will lay a man up longer than the fracture of
a bone; and he may recover with a very weakened
joint. Now, the orthodox treatment of the sprain of an
ankle is this: firstly, a number of leeches are to be
applied to it—possibly to abstract that which does not
exist, but which may come—inflammation; secondly,
cold applications very largely, and the part to be as
nearly frozen as possible. But my friend said, " I find
that that is all wrong; and the way I cure a sprain is
this: I take some lard; I warm it, and rub it into the
sprain half or three-quarters of an hour; I then take
some cotton wool, and wrap around the joint, and put
on a light bandage. That sprain which would have
taken many months to get well, gets well in a few days
—certainly in a few weeks, without any ill effects or
after consequences." " Well, but," said I, " what is

your theory?" "Why," he said, "it is caloric : the old system abstracted the caloric ; I retain the caloric, and even add more to it." A few days afterwards, a friend of mine in Hanover-square slipped from his horse, and had a sprain. I put my country friend's treatment into use ; and after I had once packed the joint, my duty as a physician was at an end. He got well, and in a few days was walking about his room on this seriously-sprained joint; whereas, on a previous occasion, when he had a sprain, he had been laid up for months. Another illustration of the effect of caloric upon the surface I had myself to-day. I was in Mr. Rolland's bath, enjoying a temperature of 160 degrees for some time ; and then I was invited into a temperature of 170, the heat of which was rendered still more appreciable by its being moist air instead of dry. When I made an attempt to go in, I stepped back. My friend, however, said to me, "Go in ; you will bear it :" and I went in ; and then I was astonished to find that the part of the body that was most sensitive to the influence of the heat was just the part of the body which, according to previously-considered theory, should not have felt it. It was my face and my hands which felt burnt, and not the rest of my body. Whereupon I was obliged to say, " The least sensitive part of my body is that which is covered by my clothes;" and I acquired the knowledge that the exposure of my face to the air had given the skin an appreciation of temperature which the rest of the body was incapable of, and which, in point of fact, indicated that the rest of the body was, to a certain extent, in a paralyzed condition. Those are the two remarks which I had to make.

Mr. Pollard.—The observation of Mr. Wilson with respect to the practice of the sprain by the country practitioner explains the success of Dr. Scott, of Bromley, with diseases of the joints. I had occasion to attend his practice with his patients, which consisted in spreading over the joints an ointment—the mercurial ointment with it, but only in small quantities—of putting a plaster on it, and wrapping it up as you describe the country practitioner to have done with a loose bandage; and it is astonishing the success which I have myself both seen and experienced. Dr. Scott made an enormous fortune by his treatment of these diseases. I never heard an explanation of it before this evening.

Mr. Urquhart.—The part of the body that was less painfully affected by this amount of temperature, was it not that part of the body that had been painfully affected by a lower temperature?

Mr. Wilson.—Yes.

Mr. Urquhart.—There are therefore two distinct kinds of sensation of the skin, since it can become sensible in one respect and less sensible in another, and *vice versâ?*

Mr. Wilson.—Yes.

Mr. Urquhart.—Therefore there must be two natures involved in the transmitting power of the nerves between the surface and the brain?

Mr. Wilson.—Yes.

Mr. Urquhart.—Shall we pursue this point?

Mr. Wilson.—Certainly.

Mr. Urquhart.—Well, I have asserted the state of our skins as resulting from our habit of covering up the body, and so excluding air and light, to be morbid. The sense of pain is a matter of degree; but taking the average sensation of pain that we endure from average causes, these, I say, are symptoms of disease, not conditions of health.

Mr. Wilson.—Clearly.

Mr. Urquhart.—I have myself found from experiment made upon a child, by bringing him up with his body exposed to the action of the light and air, and subject to the extremest alternations of heat and cold which our climate affords, that he presented the opposite phenomena, namely, sensitiveness to pleasurable impressions and insensibility to unpleasant ones. I arrived at a subdivision of the fibral nerves. The same conclusion has been microscopically arrived at, I understood, at Berlin. Thus we have engendered a state in ourselves which when we examine it, as that of nature, disqualifies us for understanding the physiology of man.

Mr. Witt.—What is your experience as to the value of the skin?

Mr. Urquhart.—The results of my experience are, that I have the consciousness of possessing entire command over all organic disease by means of the skin, and can command the skin by heat. A man comes to me with a disease of the heart, the lungs, the liver; if he is still able to move about, I am certain as to the result. I can arrest the further progress of the disorder: if

the diseased organ still affords him the means of life, he
can then live on.   The skin becomes the medicine for
the other organs.   That it is so, should be inferred
à priori upon these grounds; that it is the only organ
in contact with the world.   This case keeps you within
yourself, through it you touch surrounding bodies,
through it you receive all external impressions.   You
can therefore handle it or manage it.   It moreover is
the means through which you cast out a portion (in
composition at least) of the disintegrated tissues,
whilst it is the principal means by which you expel
the poisons produced by the very operation through
which life is generated during every second of time.
If that organ is not kept in due working order, the
whole frame must suffer; suffering, and yet life not
being extinguished, to restore the working order of
that engine is to relieve any other overpowered organ
whatever it may be.   Now, as this organ is with us
invariably in a morbid state, and as its restoration to
healthy activity is easy, it follows that the first curative effort must be directed to this end.   It occurs to
me daily and hourly, and without failing, that all diseased organs obtain relief when I have got the skin to
act.   Incontestably this is the subject matter of medical science, yet it has not been dealt with as such.
Medicine when it has touched the skin has touched it
specifically with reference to its own disease.   But as
the means of acting upon the skin is not by chemical
agencies, but by external heat, and as medicine never
so much as articulated that word, it follows that by
medicine the means of cure have been entirely neglected,

and that no experience derived from ordinary medical treatment can be quoted on the other side.

Mr. Wilson.—It is a bold as it is a broad assertion that all diseases can be remedied by the use of heat. If we glance at some of the more common phases of disease we shall see the extent of this declaration. We have scrofula. Is it to be cured by heat? We have a host of diseases originating in the stomach, which go by the name of indigestion, rheumatism, gout, neuralgia. Are they all curable by the agency of heat? We have a series of diseases which originate in poisons—poisons which are received into the body by contact, or through the agency of the air; are these to be treated by heat? Mr. Urquhart has taken a very strong position, and a very bold position as a non-medical man; he declares that which will make the whole medical profession shudder, that all these diseases are to be cured by heat. Now, I am very much inclined, from what I have seen, to agree wholly with Mr. Urquhart. I will explain to you why. Let me give an illustration which has just occurred to my mind. Suppose that I had a complex piece of machinery with an aperture at one end by which I was enabled to introduce a power that would work that machine—all its wheels, and all its various contrivances—so that I could bring about an infinity of results from the proper working of that machinery. That machinery is concealed from view. Now, my difficulty is this: I can supply the material which gives power to the machine, but somehow or other the machinery will not always work rightly. There is something or other in the material which I supply to it that does not go quite right. And yet the machine is a most perfect one in itself. I say, if I had any power by which I could regulate that which gives an impulse to this machine, I could manage all its actions in such a manner as to produce perfection. This machine is the human body. That which I introduce into the machine is food. Food is the sustenance of the body. Food necessarily consists of a great variety of substances which in different combinations are calculated to cause disease, and which must be removed from the body, or if not removed they will interrupt the harmony of the functions. Now, there is no power by which the proper direction of nutrition can be attained excepting through the skin, and that I believe to be the explanation of the extraordinary results which seem to flow from the use of the bath. The bath does no more than regulate the nutrition. Scrofula is imperfect nutrition : cancer is imperfect nutrition ; indigestion, rheumatism, gout, neuralgia, are imperfect nutrition. Give a power by which nutrition can be regulated, and you can immediately control these various diseases. Then if you take the other class of diseases originating in poisons : they have to be removed. The skin is the agent by which they are to be removed, either primarily or secondarily. The skin is perfectly equal to the removing of any poison that may be taken. There is another class of poisons which act as a yeast, or ferment ; but this again is removeable by the agency of the skin, and you have only to combine with it some internal remedy which would control the fermentation of this material to correct this disease at once. There is no great difficulty in understanding how the bath, or how heat applied to the surface of the body so as to create perspiration may cure diseases which originate in poisons; because it is clear that the perspiration mechanically carries the poison out of the body; and neither do I conceive there would be any difficulty in comprehending how the bath would equally regulate nutrition, and consequently those diseases which in their essence are mal-nutrition, or as we technically call them, mal-assimilation: you have only to take a scrofulous child and give it good food, plenty of air, plenty of oxygen, plenty of exercise, and you cure the scrofula. But you necessarily have to work against considerable difficulties, all of which difficulties would be removed if you could regu-late the distribution and the supply of the nourishing matter which you give to the child through the agency of the skin. You can by perspiration make the body take up nutritive matter more actively than it ordinarily does. By withdrawing from the body a certain quantity of moisture you make it more ready to imbibe into its tissues moisture which is taken into the stomach, and which moisture at the same time carries with it the nutritive matter. I want to know whether I have sufficiently clearly explained my view with regard to this mode of application of the bath to the skin. I want to show that it is not simply the action of the bath, the action of heat upon the skin itself directly, but that it is the indirect action upon the source of nutrition, con-sequently upon the whole mass of the blood. If you can regulate nutrition, which I apprehend you can through the agency of the bath, you are then in a position to cure all diseases which are at all dependent upon nutrition.

Mr. ——. —Is there any action of the air through the skin upon the blood ?

Mr. Wilson.—Yes. I have not the slightest doubt of the action of the air upon the blood through the agency of the skin, although I must confess that I have been very much surprised latterly in meeting a gentleman, a companion of the bath—Mr. Witt's bath—and a physiologist of great celebrity, who doubted the action of the atmosphere upon the blood. Why he could have doubted it for an instant, I cannot comprehend, because we are all physiologists enough to know that the lungs are nothing more than a bit of skin turned in, just as the internal surface of the lung would become skin if it were exposed externally : that there is no special structure about the lung which enables it to be the special respiring organ, beyond its being a moist membrane, whereby oxygen passes in, on the one hand, and carbonic acid gas passes freely out, on the other ; and assuming that the skin is thus made moist, an active respirative current will be established in both directions, inwardly and outwardly.

Mr. Urquhart.—I should like to follow up what Mr. Wilson has said. I find that in the bath, persons suffering from disease of the heart obtain instant relief, although the number of pulsations is increased. It is just as in the case of a steam-engine going down an inclined plane : the piston works more rapidly, because the work is done for it. The skin comes to the aid of the heart and lungs. Again, in a very high temperature, you lengthen your respirations. Up to a certain height you are oppressed, say at 110, 120, 130, 140. The sense of enjoyment begins to manifest itself at 155, as if from that upwards there was a relief afforded to the heart.* Now, as the object of the action of the heart is to bring back the blood, and to pour it into the lungs, in order that it may there lose its poison or carbonic acid, and regain new life, or oxygen,—that is to say, undergo the chemical operation of decarboniza-tion ; if that operation should take place partially throughout its course and at the extremities, the heart by this chemical subvention is mechanically relieved. The counterpart of this reasoning explains disease, whether of the liver, the kidneys, the lungs, or the heart,—namely, that the skin being coated with a varnish more or less impervious, the decarbonization of the blood does not take place so freely, and an effort is thrown upon the lungs and heart to drive it through, or upon the kidneys or the liver, for the elimination of

* In July, 1863, a friend, who has a bath of his own, wrote to me :—" My mother, who is seventy-five, has suffered from .organic disease of the heart for years, and often goes into the bath so ill as to find her way with difficulty, but after lying a short time in her hammock she falls asleep, to waken free from pain and oppression, and walks to the house with a step more elastic than many younger women. The tonic effect of heat in this case is remarkable. The bath never fails to restore strength, and is never taken under 140°, 160° being preferred."

In January, 1864, in answer to a letter urging him to obtain a higher degree of heat, he writes :—" I have been able to raise the heat to 180°, but cannot get it beyond that point. My mother prefers it at that heat, and experiences greater relief from it. After the bath at 180°, the irregularity of the beats of the pulse entirely ceases."

foreign matter, beyond that which is allotted to them; and so, being called upon for extra toil, they are over-powered, and become disordered. Weakness ensues; then the patient is confined to bed, and thus the cura-tive effect of rest is called in. The balance is thus partially restored; and unless death ensues, the patient is rendered capable of recovery. When this happens, it is attributed not to rest, but to the method of treat-ment, which consists in administering poisons for the infliction of comparative disturbance on the less suffer-ing organs, as a means of relieving the more oppressed ones. If you varnish the skin of any animal it will die. The cause of death would be suffocation, not because his mouth was closed, but because his skin was closed, as in the case of small-pox. We have a very remarkable instance on the accession to the pontificate of Leo X., when, to represent the golden age, a child was gilt: it died in the course of a few hours. Therefore we are always living through the skin. It stands to reason, that a piece of mechanism never would have been formed, if it was not to be of use. Every portion of the surface of our bodies is pierced with fountains., These fountains will run with foul water, so long as there are impurities within the man, and with distilled water from the moment that these are expelled. Thus the nauseous effluvium that belongs to impurity is given us as a warning. The impurities of man come from within; the cleansing power of man comes also from himself. Disease is only filth.

Mr. Witt.—Therefore you do not think that perspi-ration is weakening?

Mr. Urquhart.—I could understand a bird saying " perspiration is weakening."* I could also under-stand any but an Englishman saying " perspiration is weakening,"- considering that we are occupied in the training of horses. You are here to-day, for the first time in the metropolis, thinking about a practice which has already spread throughout the country amongst the working men. The reason is this : that the working man is not like the educated man ; he does not talk nonsense. Talk to a working man about perspiration being " lowering :" he will laugh in your face. His bread is earned by the sweat of his brow. In Central Asia, the groom tests the perspiration, in order to find out the condition of the horse. They do it in two ways ; the one by taking it so, between the finger and thumb, for the purpose of seeing if it is sticky. So long as it is sticky, the horse is not in condition. The other mode is by tasting it ; so long as it is acrid, the horse is not in condition. You see there what the purpose of training is, it is simply to cleanse by perspiration. The adipose matter that has filled up the apertures of the skin has to be removed, that the acrid matter that runs from the blood may escape. I myself regulate the bath for myself by my eyelids. So long as the perspiration running into my eye causes it to smart, I continue in. I am not clean till it ceases to be acrid. Your notions of cleanliness have reference to that which, philosophically, is not filth. My sense of cleanliness is chemical. Your idea

---

* Referring to the analogy of perspiration and urine.

is washing a sponge on the outside; my idea is taking
and compressing that sponge.

You train a horse that he may be enabled to pass over
a certain space of ground in a certain time; you do not
propose to supply muscle, but wind. Wind is supplied
by the decarbonization of the blood otherwise than by
the lungs. That and health is the object of training.
The winner of the Oaks was not trained in the ordinary
way, but in a Turkish bath. At Sheffield, there are running matches and wrestling matches still extant; and the
men no longer train as formerly, by toil, but by frequent-
ing the bath.* You have got two means by which this
may be attained—one by training, the other by the
bath. Both are great operations. This is the country
of training. Probably not one in this room can tell
how it is done. It is a mystery and an art in itself.
The trainer's art is a great achievement.

Mr. Wilson.—It is medicine.

Mr. Urquhart.—But it beats your application of it.

Mr. Wilson.—It is medicine. My "medicine" applies
as well to the beef-steak as to the black-draught.

* CHAMPION BELT OF ENGLAND WON BY THE TURKISH
BATH.—[From *Sporting Life*, Dec. 2nd, 1863.]—" While training for the race under notice, he (William Lang) broke down,
one of his legs giving way, and Mr. Martin, his backer and
mentor, was at one time fearful he would not be able to come
to the scratch to contend for the belt which, having twice won,
he had almost within his grasp. Acting upon advice, he had
recourse to Turkish baths, and by local application, almost
daily, he was soon as ' sound as a roach,' and on Monday he
appeared in splendid condition; indeed, so confident were his
friends and the public generally of his success that odds of 2
to 1, and ultimately 3 to 1, were offered on him."

Mr. Urquhart.—Supposing the whole of England underwent training, you would have a people of a superior order, physically ; and, as you can obtain for the horse equal if not greater results, by another process, it follows that there are two processes by which this condition of men and animals can be attained. Either will develope the powers ; each will be a safeguard against disease ; by each every man will be made lighter, stronger, more alert to take up any work, and more able to accomplish it, and with a less quantity of sleep and food.* Both, therefore, are remarkable results as obtained in particular cases by individuals or by entire nations. Now, suppose both these processes conjoined, what a wonderful people you would have. Look at that handful of Greeks, who made for themselves a name that is like the sun in the heavens : look at that little collection of Italian outlaws, who gave laws to the world, and whose name remains synonymous with noble ! The distinctive character of Greeks and Romans, was that they combined the Gymnasium and the Bath.

Sir W. Topham.—Is extreme perspiration weakening? —is very profuse perspiration weakening?—because that is the objection that is raised by people who are ignorant.

Mr. Urquhart.—No substance goes out from you by perspiration, except the noxious matter that you ought to get rid of ; and you might as well ask if the dinners of a city might not be diminished were its sewers overflushed.

Mr. Wilson.—A man's greatest enemy is his stomach.

* See *postea*, the Chapter on " THE FARM."

A man would be a god if it were not for his stomach. Now, as there is no possibility of preventing man from destroying his health and strength by food, the bath comes in as the remedy. It not only diminishes his appetite, but it takes away all that excess that has been taken into the man's stomach, and which, by over-loading his system, produces loss of rest, sleeplessness, incapacity. We shall never be able to invent any contrivance which will act as a check to the quantity that a man will put into his stomach. We have the glorious resource of the bath, which controls, and regulates, and diminishes, and abstracts that which has been taken in excess; because I suppose that, even in the instance of training, the reception of food is a very important item. While you take away the old matter by your bath and perspiration, you are supplying good and wholesome matter for the purposes of nutrition by the stomach.

Mr. Witt.—I think there are many here who would rather that the conversation should go upon the bath proper. What is the difference between the cleanliness of the East and that of the West? We English esteem ourselves a clean people.

Mr. Urquhart.—As health can be appreciated only by disease, and disease by health, so it is with reference to cleanliness and filth. Those only who have gone through the bath can say, " Now I know how filthy I have been." But until you put a man through that process, he will be offended if you render him the service of telling him that he is filthy. Not only in the East, but in all antiquity, throughout the whole human

race down to our times, and in our European districts
of the world, there has been a standard of cleanliness—
a standard in the mind applied to every action of man,
and to every circumstance of life.   The instinct of
early society always pointed to the construction of a
standard.   So soon as a doubt arose men said, "Let us
solve this doubt;" consequently the simplest rule was
adopted.   If you go to the British Museum and look at
the Elgin marbles you will see a standard of measurement
in a bas relief representing the bust of a man with outstretched arms.   In the same way there was a standard
of colour; you have now all sorts of colours, but having
lost the standard you have no colour.   There was blue,
red, and yellow ; these are now words only, the discri-
minating sense having disappeared.   So, in like manner,
of right and wrong.   There was therefore a standard
of cleanliness.   Nothing has cost me more than the
attempts to convey such an idea to a European.   I take
a person into a suite of rooms belonging to the bath,
and I say to him, "This is ' the clean,' and that is ' the
dirty.' "   I have had printed cards docketed " clean "
and " dirty," in order to fix attention thereby.   What
we are examining now is no longer the bath of the
East, but our own minds or our own bodies.   The standard of cleanliness was religious no less than social.   The
Jews had not the bath : the Mussulman ablutions are
distinct from the bath—the five canonical washings
were not superseded by the bath.   These ablutions came
from the fire-worshippers, who again did but copy.
All religious, and consequently all political institutions,
were based upon the ceremonial of cleanliness.   Clean-

liness was incorporated in the sacrifice to the Manes
or the Ancestral worship. The oblation could not be
made by an unclean person. The abdest is a washing
only of the five organs, the hands, the feet, and the head,
and it was with pure running water. Yet these have
not of necessity to be repeated three or four times in
the twenty-four hours. I may take my morning abdest.
I then go on till night without another, if in the meantime nothing has occurred to pollute me—that is to say
if I have not been exposed to one of the five impurities
from within, and if I have not been touched with any
moist or unctuous matter, any external object which
adheres to my skin. When pollution has occurred,
the man can be restored to intercourse with his fellow
man only after purification has been performed, which
consists in washing first, and then rinsing; an idea
which is wholly incompatible with our notion, which
is putting a dirty limb in a vessel of clean water and
so polluting it. The clothes are washed in the same
way, so also the room you occupy. Once polluted,
purification is imperative, on the penalty of *ipso facto*
excommunication. There is not a member of the
Hindoo, of the Bhuddist, or Mussulman religions who
from the moment of his birth to that of his death has
ever once deviated in that respect. Christ on earth
followed the ceremonial of the Jews. Open the Old
Testament; you will now see how incomprehensible to
you have hitherto been all words connected with pollution and purification. They must remain so until you
acquire the idea of a standard. The two principles
have never stood in contrast or opposition except in my

own residence. They can only be in opposition to
struggle, or if not to struggle, to be the one conquered
by the other ; because I say, whenever they have come
for a moment into open opposition, cleanliness has gone
down before filth. You see it is just as the bath itself.
The bath has been possessed through uncounted ages,
through nearly all the races and varieties of mankind,
and there never was an article in a paper written
about it ; there never was a sheet of print about
it ; there never was a word of talk about it ; it was
possessed and known, and could not be talked about.
Where not possessed, it could not be written about. So
of cleanliness. Where the rule of cleanliness exists,
of course it cannot be spoken about. By those who do
not practise it, again, of course, it cannot be spoken
about. The two have come into contrast for the first
time now and here ; and when you put to me the question how it was that I had thought of introducing the
bath when no other European had done so, I was on the
point of giving you this answer : "The first time that I
saw water poured over the hands in washing, instead of
being accumulated in a basin to be dabbled in, I adopted
that rule, and I have never since once deviated from
it. I said to myself, This is my nature and not the other,
and I practised it accordingly, and from that time to
the present I never have washed my hands in dirty
water. No other European has done the like, and therefore no other European has introduced or could introduce the bath." The Sikh abjures community with
mankind ; he is the renegade and outcast of all human
classes and sects, and he establishes his war with the

human race by taking water and washing his hands in it, drinking it afterwards.   You may imagine the loathing and disgust that a European creates in the East; and you can now imagine what Easterns will become when that loathing disappears.   "Civilisation" has driven the bath out of Greece.   The last time I was at Constantinople I could not get a bath, at least such as it used to be.   Cleanliness is a matter of self-examination, not of external seeming.   You must acquire the ideal standard of cleanliness before you can acquire the habits of that refined people from whom you are endeavouring to adopt this practice.

Mr. Wilson.—But, admitting cleanliness to be good, I am afraid that we must have a stronger argument than cleanliness to make the bath popular with the inhabitants of Great Britan.

Mr. Urquhart.—Unless you introduce simultaneously with the bath the habits which belong to such a people as the Romans or the Turks—because they are exceedingly alike—you will not have the bath long, if you have it at all, in England; and you will have it disappearing, and leaving a noxious vapour behind,—you will have it vulgarized, debased, demoralized, ridiculous, and hateful; and it will pass by as a vagary which a practical nation had the taste to detect and the sense to reject.

Mr. Wilson.—But how are we to become Romans or Turks?

Mr. Urquhart.—I was saying to a gentleman, a little whilo ago, "The bath is going on too quickly." As Lamartine said, " Time only respects that in which he

has himself a part." It is not an easy operation. You
have had the bath in Europe. It belonged to the Celtic
races. It was introduced, if not found, by the Romans.
It was then introduced, by the Crusaders, against the
plague. It was in use in the last generation universally in Ireland. If then it is capable of going out
merely by the want of discrimination, how much more
so if you do not introduce it with all its proper conco-
mitants? How is it to be introduced? Who will be
the undertakers? Tradesmen of one sort or another.
Gain, and gain only, will be the object. If the bath
is to be introduced, we must have a model institution. The capital must be raised, not for dividends;
and there must be no pandering to the public taste
or to common notions. I should be quite prepared to
undertake—on condition of not being interfered with—
not only for the architectural part, but also to instruct
men in shampooing, so that the double and heavy expense
and delay would be saved of sending out an architect to
Constantinople, and bringing from Constantinople a
staff of shampooers, &c. There can be no bath without
shampooers. The luxury, the enjoyment, the curative power of the bath are inseparable from the shampooing. If we had time, I could give you details of
cures—marvellous cures—effected; but I should always
have to bring in shampooing as the operative part. I
will only give you one instance. A medical man came
to me yesterday from Torquay, Dr. Toogood. He had
been for years bent, and unable to convey his food to
his mouth, from a contraction of his fingers. He had
two good hours of it, with shampooing; he stood erect

before he left the bath, and used at dinner his own
knife and fork. Shampooing is a peculiar service, a
delicate operation. But it, too, is going out. If I
were going into a bath at Constantinople, I would have
a crowd of Turks round, to see the operation properly
and elaborately performed.

Mr. Wilson.—I am afraid that you are assuming such
a standard of perfection, that we can hardly hope to
reach it, and that it hardly accords with the character of
Englishmen to take such a holy view of the subject
as you have just suggested. And I think that if one
Englishman gets rid of his gout in the bath, however
imperfect the bath may be, he will induce others to
come, and be equally relieved.

Mr. Urquhart.—The medical men have not found
it out as a cure, nor have the philosophers discovered it
as a social element, nor the antiquaries renewed it as an
adornment of life. Have they given you a single idea
upon the subject ? Have they led any man to desire
its benefits, or to comprehend it ? Not the least. But
the Turks have preserved it, and they practise it to this
day. You can get the knowledge of its existing life
from them, and you can transplant it from them just as
you would transplant a lettuce. A standard being thus
established, there will be no difficulty in extending the
practice. If you commence wrong, you will not go
right afterwards : if you commence wrong, you will
certainly go wrong afterwards. Establish it as an institution for the land, as well as a means of cure for the
invalid,—give to it its attractions and its real and solid
value, by bringing it to bear upon the morals of the

people, by introducing habits of politeness, by affording a field for the meeting of the different classes of society, by giving man an idea of what man is, by enabling one man to see another man without his artificial covering of clothes,—then it will have re-formed a new standard of what is desirable and what is enjoyable in cleanliness.

Mr. Witt.—You remember a medical man at your house the other day, who was desirous to establish a bath in the West of England, and his first observation was, " I wish to build a bath for the rich, and another for the poor." I remember you expressed your extreme disgust at such an idea.

Mr. Wilson.—It is a very English idea, nevertheless.

Mr. Urquhart.—That separation of class into class, which you do not observe because it is your state, but which is so painful anywhere else, because even persons from the Continent are struck with it, is the great misfortune which every individual undergoes. That " tuft-hunting," that seeking the society of people above them, destroys half the value of life for every man. Whatever tends to destroy this false appetite, and to restore man to himself, is a blessing to the land and each of its inhabitants. I belong to England, but I belong to the Turks equally; and I can, therefore explain to you the cause of the difference in this respect between them and you: you are not polite, and you are not clean. When politeness is wanting, it is impossible for different classes to meet. In the East, I can make my servant sit down at table with me. The code of etiquette is so perpetually occurring, that intercourse

never engenders familiarity: indeed, vulgarity is quite
a modern invention, and only to be found with "march
of intellect." Etiquette is there always, and marks the
distinctions, whatever they are, and fixes those distinctions. Here it is a different rule. The other is a
rational and a real one, because the distinctions between
man and man in their grades depends upon the age of
a man, the wealth of a man, the talents of a man; all
these so combined, that in every room there is always
one man who is fixed upon as superior: no two men
are considered equal for a moment. That being established, then, the form of etiquette is established: we
all meet together ; it is nothing but for the pleasure of
intercourse ; no derogation takes place ; the beggar
comes and he sits down at the same table with the
prince. Again: that free intercourse could not take
place, unless cleanliness were equally common to all.
Supposing that, by reason of a code of etiquette, the
workman from the streets could come and sit down at
table here, the state of his hands would prevent it. It
is utterly impossible to have free—let me say, human—
intercourse among a people, unless those characteristics
belong to all and each—namely, politeness and cleanliness. But if this distinction is drawn, and the enjoyment of intercourse with our fellow-creatures is limited,
then what ensues ? You put something else in the
place of your enjoyment ; you lose the natural gratification in intercourse from the qualities of the individual:
the something else which you put in lieu of this is your
own self-love. The present Grand Vizier was formerly
ambassador here. I put the following question to him :—

" What strikes you as being the essential contrast between your people and mine ? " He thought for a moment and said : " It seems to me the chief contrast is this : that we visit one another because we like it ; and you visit one another that you may be seen in certain places."

To politeness and cleanliness another quality has to be added to make a people happy, and that is sobriety. Sixty million pounds a-year are expended upon stimulants alone in this country. The desire is unquestionably, in part, superinduced by anxiety of mind and suffering of body, to which may be afforded, in many cases, instantaneous relief. Look at the aliments for disease thus furnished—the amount of drugs, the loss of valuable time, the expenditure of needful means. The enterprise is too simple, it is too easy, it is too great : there is the difficulty.

Mr. Pollard.—Can you explain how, after the bath had been in such universal use among the ancients, and was found of such remedial advantage, that it fell into disuse, and appears to have been lost in Europe soon after the introduction of Christianity, and only kept up in the East among the Mahomedans ?

Mr. Urquhart.—I think I can : mankind is very stupid.

Mr. Wilson.—Is there any project before us for such an institution as that which you mention ?

Mr. Urquhart.—I am not aware of any actually formed. I wish to revert to the word " bath : " in it resides the great obstacle. The application of external caloric to the frame is a very simple idea, but it is imperceptible behind the fog of the word "bath." Boiling water is poured over my feet; I prevent a blister from forming; and next day I put on shoes and stockings, as if nothing had happened. There is no medical means by which to prevent the blister, to relieve the pain, and suddenly to restore the foot to its pristine state. A medical man observes the incident: he says, "The bath has done it." Now, if he said, "Heat has done it," it would be impossible for him to resist a return upon himself, and say, "Have I, then, up to this hour disregarded at once the simplest and the most powerful of all the agencies of nature?"

As many persons have questioned the accuracy of the statement I made in my lecture at Brompton, respecting the degree of heat to which I had been subjected at Berlin, when there recovered from the jaws of death, I wish to recur thereto, as there are now in this room four persons present who were eye-witnesses. The malady was rheumatic fever, accompanied with spasms and local congestion. I was beyond all medical treatment, and sinking rapidly under the most excruciating tortures. The facilities of the German stove enabled those who attended me to heat a room. By keeping up a constant fire in the stove, the room was got up to 150 degrees. This was persevered in for a whole afternoon, and the ensuing night; the greater portion of the next day the same. It relieved me from pain, but it did not touch the malady. The next day, the 25th of August, there was a consultation at half-past three o'clock, and a telegraphic message, indicating a fatal termination, sent thereon to

London. Then it was that, as by a last mental effort, I caught at the idea of *more heat*, and proposed it in a whisper. The sofa was brought close up to the stove, blankets placed all round, and so the heat was got up to 175º. At eight o'clock that evening I was brushing my own hair with my own two hands! I expressed myself in these words: " I cannot understand how I could have been ill." The medical man, coming in, stood aghast in the middle of the room ; he trembled, stuttered, and walked away. To have said a word would have been to admit a miracle : he was terrified. Talk of miracles, you could not have anything more like a miracle than this. Now, had the additional twenty-five degrees not been obtained, this would have been an experiment triumphantly to quote in proof of the delusion of the influence of heat.*

Mr. Wilson.—Mr. Urquhart comes before us in a twofold sense as a discoverer ; he not only discovers the bath, but he discovers an application of the bath which was not known before, which originated in his own instinct. It was necessary to be in the state in which he was, and to have his mind to be able to suggest probably that it was not a temperature of 150º that was suitable

---

* At this time I attributed the result to the difference between 150º and 175º. I have since seen that the difference lay much deeper : having been brought close up to the stove merely for increase of heat, an unexpected effect followed. The body was exposed to the *rays of heat.* These rays have distinct properties from transmitted heat, as I have since discovered. This may be termed *active heat,* as contrasted with *passive heat.*

to him, but that it was a temperature of 170°. But we have known nothing of heat as a treatment of disease. I do not know any work where it has been referred to in the most distant manner. Here a new mode of treating disease has been introduced by Mr. Urquhart. A short time since I saw a gentleman now present suffering under a well-known disease, exima,— a disease which is generally very intractable, which requires careful treatment by means of medicine, and is a long time before the constitution is able to throw it off. I saw that gentleman going into a bath at a high temperature, and remaining in it for many hours—a whole night for example, I think, or living in it almost for two days, and it struck me that there was an experiment going on which was very interesting to see, and I should like to know the result of it. I made an inquiry as to the result to-day, and I find that the result was a most perfect cure in a short space of time. I am ashamed to say, in a much shorter space of time than I could have effected it, and the agent of cure was the application of caloric to the surface of the body in the way detailed to-night. Was there any modification of food?

Mr. Witt.—The point was the temperature of 160° as compared to that of 120°, the temperature as stopping fermentation.

Mr. Urquhart.—After what you witnessed in 1852, when you treated me and saw me recover, under the action of the bath, after considering my case desperate, I made sure of you. I was certain that some day you would come back to me.

Mr. Wilson.—You are mistaken. That incident made no impression on me. I only considered it a case of extraordinary endurance. I said no other man would go through with the like. How could I do otherwise, I was *doctus*, you were *indoctus*. How could I be taught by you?

Mr. Urquhart.—But I have not finished my Berlin story yet; indeed the most instructive part is still to tell. I thought myself cured. That is on the 25th August. Half a dozen friends took tea with me, some of whom are now present. I was put to bed in the cold room. I was seized again during the night; before I could get the other room heated several hours elapsed, and the malady had returned in all its violence, at least of pain. Then the struggle came on between heat and disease. It lasted for ten days. It was like the pumps working against a leak. I was only able to get back to England by having a room heated beforehand ready for me at each hotel as I arrived. They made no difficulty about it, and would made no additional charge. At Dusseldorf the room was large and lofty, and the heat was up to 190°. Mr. Wilson has spoken of my "instinct." It was no instinct. I am slow and patient at my work. It was a conclusion worked out. In Turkey the large attendance at the baths, and the opening and shutting of the doors causes a lowering of the temperature during the day. If you go at a late hour it is full of vapour. Often in travelling I slept in the bath; and was led to this in part from the enjoyment I derived from the dry air which you get at early morning. I had thus my mind fixed upon the dry air to

begin with, as contrasted with steam, and soon after
began to employ the bath as a medicine, or in lieu of
medicine.

Mr. Witt.—At the lecture that you gave at Brompton
you spoke of "Nature's thermometer," to the effect that
at particular points of the scale there were operations
effected on the human body with the same regularity
and certainty as in chemistry, metallurgy, &c. Will
you enlarge on this point?

Mr. Urquhart. — My starting point was that fever
had a standard degree, just as boiling water,—the one
being 212°, the other 112°. Why was it not 111° or
113°? I have worked at that while riding along
moors and toiling up hill-sides. I finally answered
myself thus: "If it were 113° it would no longer be
fever." If water boiled at 213°, the whole economy of nature would be upset. I then saw that the
fever was not the disease, but the effort of nature to cure
the disease. So I looked deeper for the disease. The
next formula was, "Help nature over the 112°." This
came out true. My first stage, then, was 112°. It was
long before I reached the second, 160°. This was fixed—
not merely on account of coagulation and fermentation, but because it puts you safe beyond that at which
the sebaceous glands are emptied,—that at which
gummy matter is dissolved, together with the solution
of some active chemical agents. But the stage of 160°
is not final, for to reach it you must go far beyond
it. You do not raise the temperature of the body
to that of the medium in which you place.it. This
medium must rise far above 160°, to give you

the effect of 112° ; and this again is only practicable through the extraordinary facility presented
to this very end, as I suppose, by the circulation of
the blood. That blood, at the extremity of its course
flies, as it were, in air, from one system of vessels to
the other. A certain portion of it is thus constantly
presenting itself on the surface of the skin; so that
with the bath say at 200°, you may get a portion of
the blood operated upon, so as to take inflammation out
of it; and as all the blood will successively pass in like
manner—perhaps in half an hour, certainly in forty-
five minutes—the whole blood of the body will be subjected to a similar action. The cholera might have been
arrested with as much certainty as I feel in dealing with
any ordinary disease. A man in the Midland Counties—
by an absurd process of reasoning, it is true—fell upon
the idea of heat as the cure, and they shut him up in a
madhouse. I have amongst these papers the pamphlet
he published at the time. He used to put them before
a hot fire, with blankets ; and he cured, as he states,
every person he undertook. I am myself an instance
of a cured relapse in cholera. It occurred at Gibraltar.
Dr. Dumbreck, now chief of the London staff, attended
me. On the occasion of the relapse he was not within
reach. I got down four men from the Arsenal. I
gave one limb to each. I was put in hot-water,
blankets were put round me, and I told the men to hit
me as hard as they could, to relax the congestion. Dr.
Dumbreck used these words :—" Your determination
has saved your life ; there was no other chance." It
was not the determination, but the reasoning.

Mr. Wilson.—Mr. Urquhart has certainly shown us
some very important matters to-night. He has shown
not only the good effects of caloric upon the body, but
he has also shown the manner in which heat may
be brought to operate upon the body. It is known
to all physiologists, that the interior of the body
does not become elevated in temperature, however
high the temperature may be to which it is exposed ;—
that a man with a thermometer in his mouth may be in
a temperature of 400°, and the thermometer will keep
the same temperature as if he were in a temperature of
60°. Therefore, at first sight, it might be a little
difficult to understand (the temperature being 90°) how
these high temperatures could act upon the body at
large ; but it is quite clear that the surface of the body
must be super-heated : and if all the blood of the body
is brought to the surface of the body, within a certain
number of minutes, it is clear that the whole of the
blood of the body must be super-heated, and must be
placed in a perfectly new physiological condition to that
in which it was placed before. In fact, it must be in
a state we can scarcely comprehend, possessing the
power of destroying poison, resisting poison, putting
the morbid changes altogether in a new point of
view, and explaining that which otherwise is somewhat
difficult to understand—the extraordinary power which
heated air has on disease. It has lately been discovered that sulphur and india-rubber being subjected
to a very high temperature, they combine in such a
manner as to produce a substance totally different from
both—a substance possessing extraordinary and very

valuable qualities—which goes by the name of vulcanite, and which is now applied to supply materials for artificial gums. It is indestructible, impermeable to moisture, exceedingly light, smooth, not altered by use, inexpensive, and may be melted into moulds, and not requiring the mechanical process which the preparation of plates for the mouth before required. So that it has become the means not only of supplying teeth, but of preserving the mouth when the teeth have been actually lost. I mention this as an illustration of the way in which heat acts chemically upon two substances brought together, which opens to us a new field of research as to the mode in which the blood itself might be influenced by a very high temperature. Of the value of the bath, there can be no doubt, as all those who have been in it must be witnesses to. Some of us have seen its influence upon disease. I have seen gentlemen who have had the gout dissolved out of their loins. A short time back a medical man applied to me, who was suffering from a very terrible and annoying complaint called prurigo. I recommended him to pay Mr. Witt a visit. He came here; he had a bath, which he enjoyed very much, and he left his complaint behind him. That gentleman went away to his own town, and has there established a bath; and I have no doubt that he there hopes to be most useful to his fellow-men, as his fellow-men have been of use to him here. Therefore those of the medical profession who have been fortunate enough to see its good effects, I think will not lose sight of them. For my own part, I intend, as soon as I can, to fit up a bath. The great question of all is the institution of the bath in Great Britain. I think that is the subject to which Mr. Urquhart has been endeavouring to draw our attention.

Mr. Urquhart.—I have always expected to be met with the objection that the temperature of the body could not be raised. I never had to give the answer which I have now given, because the objection was never put ; and probably if Mr. Wilson had not been sitting beside me I should not have thought of doing so now. I felt that though not making the objection, it would have occurred to him afterwards.

[After a pause.]

Mr. Urquhart.—I had intended to be concise in answering, but that required consecutiveness in questioning. You have been rather discursive, and I consequently diffuse. I am therefore desirous to sum up more methodically. We have spoken of—

1. *Bringing the skin into action,* and so evoking its latent powers, as the means of reinvigorating the constitution and throwing off disease.

2. Of *heat independently of that of the skin,* and its effect upon the morbid condition of the blood.

These are the two salient ideas which I have to present, affording the means of cure severally for chronic and acute disorders. But we have not touched upon—

3. *Endosmose and Exosmose,* or that law of nature by which the contents of a vessel are interchanged with the contents of an external medium. This is now practised in tanning. Instead of laying, as formerly, skins and tan alternately in layers, now they sew up the skin and put the tanning matter

outside. You would suppose that if you put the tanning matter on both sides of the skin it would be the best means of impregnating the skin, but it is not so ; and what formerly took months to effect is now done in a few hours. This is by endosmose. This law of nature is the source of vegetation. It is also the motor in those mysterious functions of our frame where we are unable to trace organic instrumentality. If you take a bladder and fill it with water, adding some foreign matter, such as vermilion, and if you put that bladder in a vessel of water, presently you will see the water all around coloured. The foreign matter will find its escape out of that bag the moment you immerse it in water. The same will happen if you employ thin slabs of marble. If you will look at the human body as a bladder, and expose it to the same action by giving it an external medium, and if you facilitate the transmission by a high temperature, you will see how, by the bath, you can extract from the body its foreign and incidental contents. Exosmose generally acts from the denser to the less dense medium, as if in order that more should benefit thereby, and discharge the matter which is contained within ; say that the body contains mercury which may have lain there for years, apply the external medium and you can draw it out, and that too whilst the perspiration pouring out facilitates its exit. I was led to connect endosmose with the action of heat by one day seeing a butcher strip the skin from off a sheep. It came away snow white, without tincture of blood ; yet the blood circulates in the skin. A word calls the instantaneous colour to the cheek—the tell-tale blood.

Endosmose, then, enters into the mechanism of the circulation, and it is at the moment of this mysterious flight
that the perspiration is dropped. This is a third branch.

4. *Electricity.* You know what it is to isolate a chamber
for the purpose of making experiments. You never isolate
a chamber for the benefit of your bodies. I have got an
isolated chamber, and if I am fatigued, I go into it, and
am relieved, and in a few minutes fit to resume my
work. I will not talk of negative or positive electricity,
but this is sure and certain, that when a man is not in
condition he is short of electricity ; he is a machine and
is worked by means of it; he produces it for his need,
and what he does not keep for himself goes off to others.
I defy you to distinguish between animal heat and electricity. At one time I had all the mattresses and
cushions stuffed with silk, but I have found that marble
is a sufficiently good non-conductor, and as my principal bath is a chamber of marble I obtain the results of
isolation. Nor is it only that the electricity in course
of generation is not extravasated, does not fly off to
the nethermost parts of the earth, and aid a Tartar to
mount his horse, or a Chinaman to use his chop-sticks,
but the supply is increased with a diminution of the
drain of vital power. There is heat supplying what
your unaided chemical process had hard labour to get.

5. *Actinism,* historically and constructively. The type
of the bath ascends to primitive and unartificial societies.
Therefore it was confined and dark. The Turkish bath
is dark and gloomy, no sun comes in. The Roman bath
originally was dark: at a later period it was light ;
they had plate glass, but there was no idea of letting the

sun in. They had the idea of the sun playing on their naked person which indeed superseded his utility in the bath. The only thing I have ventured on in the way of innovation has been to let in the sun, and that has arisen from having been the first to introduce the practice to a race which had it not without the concurrent introduction of the normal building. You will see in my bath in the garden a slab of glass let into the wall, so that when reclining on the couch in the hottest part the sun streams in full upon you.

6. *Cleanliness.* This can be obtained by no other process; and this alone is probably equal in curative effects for the sum and generality of maladies to the whole contents of all the apothecaries' shops in the three kingdoms.

With these six distinct means of action, what a command is not acquired over the whole of the phenomena of human life!

I have not spoken of medicine, for it is foreign to the subject. Medical science has perceived none of these means of cure. What I say has no connexion with vulgar and general abuse of the profession. I myself am too happy to profit by the knowledge and science of the physician when I require such aid; but while I respect his science of physiology, and within limits of pathology, I have no respect for him in reference to the means of cure.

Mr. Wilson.—We claim the bath: it belongs to us; it is a great medicine.

*Mr. Witt.**—The moment that any patient speaks to

* Mr. Witt is a retired medical man, having had for many years an extensive practice at Bedford.

a medical man about the bath, he has but one answer : "It is a capital thing, but "—pointing to his individual patient—"it will not suit you." He first of all tells what is not true, saying he understands it; and then he goes on to flatter the self-love of his patient.

Mr. Wilson.—When Mr. Urquhart first spoke to me about the bath, I thought I knew as much about it as he did. I am ashamed to say that I took no notice of his invitation to see it, till somebody said to me one day, "There is a gentleman living in Prince's-terrace, who wants you to go and see his bath. You must not put it off, because it is a thing to be seen; but if you agree to go, you must look upon it as a religious act, and not fail," and then I came to Mr. Witt's bath, and since then I have ceased to be myself. I am now a disciple of the bath.

Mr. Urquhart.—My statement was that medical science had not possessed itself of these means ; and as they are the most simple and the most effectual—as they are of undoubted benefit in many diseases in which medicine has no pretension to interpose between patient and disorder, it follows that when a medical man perceives this new light, he also perceives his own previous darkness, so that there can be no acceptance without recantation. And thus it is that the matter has been viewed by the body of practitioners. Their instinct tells them that there is that in it which is incontrovertible ; and that instinct is true. But they have another instinct which is not true, which is that they will lose their individual patients. The medical man with a foundation of practice, and a superstructure of capacity, who will frankly accept and boldly act upon these new perceptions, will have the profession at his mercy, say for instance, Abernethy. Their tremulous state is by nothing better exhibited than by this : that there has appeared in the course of this long discussion but a single exception to that timorousness that will neither accept nor deny. The incident may be an appropriate close to this evening's discussion.

Dr. Corrigan, holding a professorship in Dublin, and so instructing the minds of the young, whilst operating on the bodies of the old; a journalist, too, and proprietor of a review, has taken up the defence of medical science against the bath. By the aid of this science he has learned that that temperature which many of those present have enjoyed and benefited by, parches the skin, inflames the blood, convulses the heart, smites the brain, and drives distracted spleen and liver, stomach and kidneys. In fact that in 140° man becomes a cinder. I could not be indifferent to the means of instruction and correction thus afforded me, and I being, as Mr. Wilson has said, not *doctus*, and he being very *doctus*, I addressed myself to him craving for enlightenment in regard to some of the incidents of my daily life. I hold in my hand a copy of a letter which I wrote to him. Would you like to hear it ?

Mr. Wilson.—By all means let us hear it.

" Riverside, Feb. 15, 1859.
" SIR,—A few days ago I saw a controversy on the Turkish bath in an Irish paper, and glanced at the concluding paragraph of a letter of yours, to the effect that heat (140°) was injurious

and dangerous to the human frame. I therefore take the liberty of submitting to you my domestic experience of the last four-and-twenty hours, trusting that you will be so good as to set me right in regard to the explanation of the phenomena.

1. Yesterday forenoon, I being absent from home, my child, aged four and a half, playing before the drawing-room fire, lost his balance, and saved himself by falling, with his right hand closed, against the bar of the grate, inflicting a severe burn across the upper part of the hand. The servant in charge applied spermaceti, but in consequence of the agony which the child suffered, he was, after some time, taken into the bath, at about 180°. The pain was immediately allayed, and from that time he experienced none until the time that I returned, late in the evening, when I had the bath heated up to about 230° in the hottest part : kept him in it, varying the heats, for about an hour and a half. This morning he was in at the same heat, but for a longer period. The blister which had risen over the whole injured surface has collapsed, except in one corner. From my experience, I am satisfied that had he been submitted to the action of heat immediately on the occurrence of the burn, the injured part by this time would have exhibited no traces of the accident.

I have now to submit to you,—First, how a temperature of dry air at 230° did not produce on this child the consequences which you state to be inevitable even at 140° ? Secondly, how it was that in this case the pain ceased within ten minutes of his being subjected to a high degree of heat, and that recovery has been the rapid result ?

2. A lady resident here (six months *enceinte*), and in the habit of taking a bath every morning, complained yesterday of suffering much at night from oppression in the region of the stomach, palpitation of the heart, inability to lie on the left side. I recommended her to try the bath at night as well as the morning, and also to subject herself for a longer period of time to the highest temperature. She consequently did so last night, and her report this morning is that she passed an excellent night, suffered from none of the causes of uneasiness, and was able to sleep on her left side. She had formerly found benefit from taking the bath at night, but never to the same extent.

But on those former occasions it was a vapour bath which she had taken, and not a dry-air one. She further observed, with respect to last night, that when sitting in the hottest part, the palpitations seemed rather increased than diminished; but that while conscious of the rapidity of motion, she suffered no inconvenience or mental uneasiness: the weight seemed to be taken off.

Hot air being injurious to the human frame, the results in in this case also require explanation.

3. Although the incident I am about further to add has not occurred within the twenty-four hours, yet it is one so simple and striking that I venture to trouble you with it. At the time I sent for the medical man at Rickmansworth, to be witness should the accuracy of my statement be questioned. I had returned home late one night, had got on my dressing-gown and slippers, and was seated before the fire. The candles not having been lit, and wanting a cup of tea in a hurry, the servant placed the teapot on the rug beside my foot, and in pouring the boiling water into it he missed the teapot, and poured it over my foot. Without the delay of a moment I was carried into the bath, remained there, exposing it to the extremest heat I could endure, for a couple of hours. I repeated the operation early next morning. In the afternoon of that day there were no traces whatever of the scald except a few small blisters on the other parts of the leg, where sparks had fallen, but which spots had not been subjected to the same heat as the scald itself. You will understand that a jet of hot air was directed upon one particular part of the foot. The sparks on other parts not having been observed were not so treated.

Here I have to submit how a scald from boiling water was not aggravated by hot air, and how it was cured except by the hot air, seeing that no other means were applied to it?

Although 230° is the habitually highest temperature at present used, that is by no means the limit. Two medical men from St. Thomas' Hospital came down recently to inspect my bath. It was raised that day to nearly 300°, much to their enjoyment and benefit (both of them being themselves invalids).

I cannot close this letter without thanking you for boldly

raising for the first time as a medical man the question of the action of heat on the human frame.

> I have the honour to remain, sir,
>
> Your obedient servant,
>
> D. URQUHART.

To Dr. Corrigan, Dublin.

Mr. Wilson.—I shall be curious to hear the answer to that letter.

Mr. Urquhart.—I am sorry I cannot gratify your curiosity, for no answer has as yet reached my hands. (Exclamations of surprise.)

Removal of Barrenness.

(Note to page 6.)

AT first, I of course believed, in common with every other European, that the bath was a Mussulman institution. When an old sheik told me the reverse, and added that one of the reasons which constrained Mahomet to give in to its use was, that it produced fruitfulness in women, I passed the notion by as trivial or fantastic. It was only on hearing from the writer of the paper on the Farm (inserted elsewhere), of the effect on cattle, that the statement of the old sheik returned upon me.

On the farm in question the case had been brought to a test perfectly satisfactory, viz., the same individuals, male and female, being tried, first without the bath, that is before it came into use; and then tried with the bath; failure being the result in the one case, success in the other, all other circumstances remaining unchanged.

After the statement of such results, I reverted to the tradition preserved of the opinions prevailing twelve hundred years ago among the women of the East, as to an indication of great value, and a conclusion founded on experience.

Indeed, it has only to be stated in order to carry conviction with it—that, as on the health and vigour of the parents depend the vigour of the offspring, so on the same qualities of the would-be parents must it depend, whether they have offspring or not. As the bath invigorates for all purposes, so must it invigorate for

E

each purpose. It will be seen elsewhere that the effect on the stomach is to promote, alike desire and performance—that is, gives appetite and facilitates digestion.

But, independently of this general cause, there is a special one. Some functions are peculiarly electrical, and this process of the application of pure heat calls forth an electrical intensity in the body, which is not dispersed as it would be were the heat accompanied by moisture, or the subject of it encumbered with clothing. Nor is this all. The activity of secretions must depend on their purity. The purity of these must depend on the general purity of the blood.

Nor in regard to the delicate matter under review, and consequently so difficult to handle, is the purity of the exterior of our bodies to be overlooked. It is the imagination alone that can here take upon itself to be the expounder to the individual mind, of the arcana of physiology.

That it should have required the case of these cattle to call my attention to a point so grave as the propagation of the species, through a practice which I am introducing among my countrymen, is to me both strange and humiliating; and the more so, as particular instances have not been wanting which sufficed to awaken the attention of the most indifferent; such as *three children at a birth* by the bath mistress at Bristol, and within the week, *four children at a birth* by the bath mistress at Liverpool. All these children have done well, as have their mothers. They were both in the bath up to the hour of their confinement. These women had been for a considerable period, as also their husbands, in the bath daily, acting as shampooers. It is to be hoped that ladies going in periodically only, and then only to be shampooed, would not run the risk of so large a fertility. However, it is perhaps fortunate for the bath that the career of Malthus was cut short, before it came on the carpet.

Ease in Childbirth.

(Note to page 6.)

In respect to childbirth, there can be no question as to the solid reasons possessed by Mussulman women, in the time of Mahomet, for coercing him in regard to his violent prejudice against the bath. That the use of it during gestation relieves the worst symptoms, and prepares the body for its severe trial; that the use of it immediately afterwards allays incipient fever, and relieves in very grave cases of lactation, is established beyond question by numerous cases that have occurred in England within the last few years.

As evidence of action on that order of functions and complaints, I would refer to its beneficial effects in that malady, as dreaded by women as cancer, *ovarian dropsy.*

I subjoin some passages from Lady Mary·W. Montagu, who did introduce vaccination from the Turks, but who did not introduce the bath :—

January 4.
What is most wonderful is the exemption they (Turkish women) seem to enjoy from the curse entailed on the sex.

They see all company the day of their delivery, and at the fortnight's end return visits, set out in their jewels and new clothes. I wish I may find *the influence of the climate* in this particular. But I fear I shall continue an Englishwoman in that affair.

Lady Mary Montagu was in the habit of going to the bath after her confinement. She writes :—

March 10.

I don't mention this as one of my diverting adventures, though I must own that it is not half so mortifying here as in England, there being as much difference as there is between a little cold in the head, which sometimes happens here, and the consumption coughs so common in London. I returned my visits at three weeks' end, and about four days ago crossed the sea which divides this place from Constantinople to make a new one.

The following is from a lady who, reporting the case of another, reports also her own :—

I wish you had been with me during my last visit to Ireland, or that I could convey to you what I saw; for I am sure it would remove both doubts and objections, and induce you to make use of the means which I have myself found so very agreeable for the alleviation of the great trouble and penalty of our sex.

A lady in a house where we were staying was near her confinement. They had a bath, but only just completed. Consequently she had only been using it for a short time. She looked anything but well, and was not able for much exertion. We returned to the same house in about a month; I never saw such a change in any one. She looked perfectly fresh and well, and told me that she felt a different creature. She had been using the bath both night and morning ever since.

Now, then, this is what I have to tell you; and it is only the repetition of what I have already told you in my own case: but there is a virtue in repetition. When I recollect that formerly I could do nothing without my walk, my drive, or my gallop, and now that I write a great deal, seldom walk, and am never on horseback, I think I have given you the proof positive, and shall expect you to thank me for this in the way that will please me best : that is, by sending for a builder, without a moment's delay, that you may know the benefit of the bath even yet before your trial comes on : at least, have it for afterwards. Having this unexpected and blessed means placed within one's reach, I should be guilty of a crime if I did not endeavour to obtain it for those I love. For you, too, it is not less so, to put it lightly aside.

The following instructive curiosity is from a savage people :—

CALIFORNIAN MIDWIFERY.

[From the " Medical News," Sept. 5, 1863.]

The mother now (after the birth) remains quiet for fifteen or twenty minutes, when she goes to the nearest spring or pool of water, in which she bathes herself thoroughly. She is next caused to undergo a species of steam-bath, which is prepared by digging a hole in the earth, in which are placed hot stones, which are covered with sticks, over which are placed herbs ; next water is poured upon the stones, the patient, meanwhile, being placed over them in such a manner as to be exposed to the vapour thus generated. She is exposed to this *medicated* vapour bath, wrapped in blankets, *for half a day*, and thus returns to her hut, from which I have often seen her come forth, in two or three days afterwards, in comparatively good health, and resume her ordinary avocations.

Effect of the Bath on the Milk.

Letter from Mr. Crawshay.

Tynemouth, Feb. 1, 1863.

Dr. Bramwell, of North Shields, when here to-day, seeing the children, who are in the first stage of whooping cough, said he was curious to see what would be the course of the complaint with the use of the bath. He expected it would be much modified. He had found the bath had a strong tendency to increase *all* excretions ; and he concluded, therefore, it would assist in the throwing off the mucous substance, on the getting rid of which recovery depended. He has himself had a bath for some time. He had never tried the bath upon whooping cough, not having had a case in his house ; but a lady, during the period of lactation, had found that the use of the bath increased the milk very considerably without causing any fatigue or exhaustion. He had most carefully questioned her as to this. Since he had discovered this, other ladies among his patients had tried his bath for the same purpose, and in all cases with the same result. The usual heat of his bath is 150° to 160°.

From Dr. Bramwell.

North Shields, Feb. 22, 1864.

I have found the Turkish bath have a decided influence in two cases in promoting an increase of the secretion of milk. One lady stated that she felt a decided rush into the breasts while in the bath, and that she always found after a bath taken in the evening that there was a much better supply of milk for the child during the night. The other case I purposely requested to use the bath, with the object of increasing the flow of milk, which was exceedingly scanty; and I found a good result: but the lady had not opportunity to continue the use of the bath sufficiently frequent to have any permanent effect.

March, 1864.

A lady who had been obliged to wean her child, from deficiency in the secretion of milk, asked my permission to have a Turkish bath, about ten days after having weaned her child. She informed me that while in the bath the breasts were so stimulated that they filled with milk, even to running out. She considered that there had been no milk in the breasts for at least a week previous to taking the bath.

Ovarian Dropsy.

Dr. Toulmin to Mr. Urquhart.

Turkish Baths, Brighton, Feb. 22.

Sir,—I have been honoured by the receipt of yours of this morning respecting a case of ovarian dropsy under my care. I expect you met with it in " Public Opinion " of Nov. 7, which was a spontaneous effusion of gratitude on the part of the patient herself. The case is not yet completed, and therefore I have refrained from publishing it. At present the facts are these :—

She took six baths without my knowledge in the beginning of May last, when, finding herself the better for them, she placed herself under my care, and came into my house. She was then unable to walk, and as large as she could be, without endangering her life. She had then been tapped three times.

Before resuming the bath, I drew off eighteen quarts of fluid; and from that time to Dec. 4th I kept the disease at bay—that is, kept deposition balanced by absorption.

This was accomplished jointly by medicinal treatment, great attention to diet, and her taking a bath *daily* from May to December last; during which period she daily improved in health and strength, was capable of walking six miles a day, and was looked upon as the model of female health and vigour in my family.

On December 4, circumstances compelled her to return home ; and I am fearful, with the loss of her bath, the deposit of fluid may have regained the ascendant : but time alone will show this.

There is, however, another disease over which the bath has *complete control*, even in its later stages, viz., tubercular consumption ; and inasmuch as its altar is stained with the blood of the largest number of victims, it is the most important disease to which humanity is subject.

I have the honour to be, Sir,

Your most obedient and obliged Servant,

A. TOULMIN.

David Urquhart, Esq., &c.

The Use of the Bath in the Tropics.

(Note to page 7.)

Our fellow subjects have been transferred to the regions of the yellow fever in the New World, of putrid and
intermittent fevers in the Old. Our medical men have
been transported likewise to Jamaica and Sierra Leone.
Every inducement was thus supplied to profit by the
experience of the aboriginal populations: but hitherto
in vain, as the subjoined examples will show.

Africa.

From *Daniell's Medical Topography and Diseases of Guinea*, p. 119.

European practitioners in any degree conversant with the
medical customs of the negroes of intertropical Africa, cannot
fail to be deeply impressed with the marked attention paid by
the native doctors to the due action of the cutaneous tissues,
and their encouragement of this as a means of relieving disease.
The Mahomedan code of laws, whose sanitary injunctions are so
well adapted for the advancement of the moral and physical
condition of the barbarous pagan tribes in Central Africa, strictly
enjoins not only abluent but other hygienic measures for the
promotion of cleanliness, and the proper discharge of the
cutaneous functions. The inhabitants of most of the maritime
localities in the Bights are fully acquainted with the importance
of these views, and treat the remittent and other fevers to
which they are subject by endeavouring to excite a long-con-
tinued and copious exudation of sweat by the aid of heated
sand and hot water. In some countries the patient is placed

close to a large fire, whilst in others he is held over it, water being slowly dropped thereon, so that the steam as it ascends may act on the affected portion of the body. After a careful observation of the good effects of this remedial system, I was led to pay more particular study to the utility of its application, and at length to try a modified adaptation of it for the cure of those adynamic remittent fevers so destructive to European life. I have no hesitation in asserting that not only myself but many others who have experienced its efficacy by the speedy restoration to health, can vouch for its superiority over the ordinary practice of venesection, saline purgatives, and large doses of calomel, &c.

America.

From *The Ten Tribes Historically Identified;* Appendix, p. 363.

Among the means employed by the Mexican physicians for the preservation of health and cure of distempers, that of the bath was most esteemed. The Mexicans and other tribes of Anahuac made frequent use of the vapour bath or Temazcalli. This bath is formed of bricks. The form of it is similar to that of a baker's oven, but with this difference, that the pavement of the Temazcalli is a little convex and lower than the surface of the earth, whereas that of ovens is plain and a little elevated for the accommodation of the baker. Its greatest diameter is from eight to nine feet and its greatest height six. The entrance, like the mouth of an oven, is wide enough to allow a man to creep in with ease. In the place opposite to the entrance, there is a furnace of stone or raw bricks, with its mouth outwards, to receive the fuel from without, and a hole above it to carry off the smoke.

The part which unites the furnace to the bath, and which is about two feet and a half square, is shut with a dry stone of Tetzoutle, or some other porous stone. In the upper part of the vault is an air hole, like that to the furnace.

When any one goes in to bathe, he first lays a mattress

within the Temazcalli, a pitcher of water, and a bunch of fragrant herbs. He then orders a fire to be made in the furnace,
which is kept burning until the stones which join the Temazcalli
and furnace are quite hot. The person who is to use the bath
enters accompanied by a domestic; he is either nude or slightly
covered. As soon as he enters he shuts the entrance close, but
leaves the air-hole at the top open for a few minutes to let out
the smoke, should any have collected in the vault. When it is
all out he stops up the air-hole. He then throws water on the
hot stones, from which immediately arises a thick vapour to the
top of the Temazcalli. While the person lies upon the mat,
the domestic drives the vapour downwards, and with a bunch
of herbs gently beats the patient on the ailing part. The herbs
being first dipped in the water which is by that time a little
warm. The patient falls immediately into a soft and copious
perspiration, which is increased or diminished at pleasure, according as the case requires.

When the desired evacuation has been obtained, the vapour
is let off, the entrance is cleared, and the sick person clothes
himself, or is transported on the mat to his chamber, as the
entrance to the bath is usually within some chamber of his
habitation.

The Temazcalli has been successfully used in various disorders, especially those connected with the digestive organs.
The Indian women use it frequently, and always after childbirth ; *as also persons who have been stung by some poisonous
reptile.*

It is undoubtedly a powerful remedy for all such as have
occasion to carry off gross humours, and certainly it would be
very useful in countries where rheumatism is prevalent. When
a copious perspiration is desired the sick person is raised up
and held in the vapour ; as he perspires the more the nearer he
is to it.

The Temazcalli is so common that in every place inhabited
by the Indians there are many of them.

Asia.

Letter from *Captain Burton to Mr. Urquhart.*

As regards the hot-air bath, the people of Makran and Belochistan generally use it to induce perspiration during the algid state of fever.   It is simply effected by sitting under a large woollen or camel hair cloak, called by the Arabs Abá (or Abáyah), and by the Beloch Choghah.   Fire is placed upon a potsherd, the favourite fuel is "braise," the smaller branches of tamarisk well charred.   In fever a little frankincense (lubar) or bdellium (mukl) is added.   No cold affusion or exposure to the air follows the operation, the patient after perspiring is left to sleep.

Second Dialogue.

The Medical Society at Riverside.

RIVERSIDE, RICKMANSWORTH.

Feb. 25, 1861.

Dr. Druitt.—Celsus advises people, when they come in fatigued, to be anointed. He makes much more of anointing than of the bath.

Mr. Urquhart.—The skins of the Romans were subjected to much wear, and oil was therefore of use for them. *

Dr. Druitt.—My question is, whether in Rome anointing was not coincident with the bath? It is difficult to separate the one from the other in Celsus.

Mr. Urquhart.—I know the Turkish bath, and can tell you about it. I never was in a Roman bath, and consequently can tell you nothing about it. I have searched again and again in Celsus, and have found nothing on the subject to quote. You see what he is by the passage which has just been quoted from him. No one is ignorant as to the use of oil for anointing by the Romans. In the Turkisk bath no oil is used. To a Turk the very idea is abhorrent: it is pollution;

he goes there for purification. To occupy our time with the Roman bath, its practices or origin, would be to lose that time, as well as the occasion for understanding that which has brought you here, and which I take to be the means placed by nature and Providence within our reach, for the preservation of our health and the cure of our disorders.

Dr. Thudichum.—Still, would you be kind enough to give us your views on that point—the origin of the Roman bath?

Mr. Urquhart.—Well—since you desire it. The Romans commenced on a given day, and as bandits: they were not a race. All that was possessed by Rome she borrowed. There is nothing original, whether in constitution, ceremonial, or architecture. She drew everything from the Etruscans, the people of Latium, the Sabines, the Samnites. The bath does not appear in any Etruscan shape. We shut off, then, the bath from the beginnings of Rome. The bath is introduced unobtrusively; we find it, but how it came is never mentioned. It is spoken of as old in the time of the Cæsars, and as having been small, dark, and hot. We must assume common habits and institutions in Magna Græcia and Sicily. Therefore, as we know that it flourished in the latter,* we may assume that the Romans found it when they extended their operations

---

* At the siege of Syracuse by Marcellus, about a century and a half before Christ, the bath was in such common use, that in mentioning the neglect by Archimedes of the usages of life, it is said that his friends had to take him to the bath, as well as to the dinner-table. When there, he began to draw lines *in the ashes.*

to the South, and especially in the war with Pyrrhus.
Yet, had it been then a novelty, it scarcely would have
been passed by without notice, seeing the number of
writers on that period.   Besides, the bath as known to
the Greeks was neither small nor dark.   We may,
therefore, refer it to an earlier period—that of their
conquests in the North.   The Gaulish tribes had the
bath, small, dark, and hot, as preserved in Ireland to
this day in the "sweating houses," and in general use
up to the last century.   Still, this is not the type of the
Roman bath, which was not an independent and detached building, but a heated floor.   The bath of the
Celts is an oven swept out, and a man put in just as
a batch of bread might be.   The bath of the Romans
was a room over an oven, like the bath of Morocco.
The one practice being established among a people, they
would not change to another.   I do not suppose the
Romans copied the Moors or ancient Iberians; but the
same type, in a more constructive and primitive form,
exists to this day in Europe among races who do not
change.   I will now mention the incident which suggested to me the derivation of the Roman bath.

One winter's night, entering a cottage on the Balkan,
I observed that, after my supper had been cooked, a
stone was removed from the back of the fireplace, and
the embers were then shoved in behind.   I asked,
"What is that?"   They said, "That is the stoba."   I
said, "What is the stoba?"   They said, "Come and
see."   I was taken behind to a room raised about two
feet above the level of the first, being over the oven,
behind the hearth.   This is the hypocaust of the

Romans. This form of domestic architecture is the Northern adaptation of the primitive scheme of the Southern latitudes, where the cattle occupy the lower level. This mode of treating an apartment and a house is so economical alike in structure and in fuel, and so admirable, that it could not be seen without being adopted by a judicious people. Now, the peculiar character of the Romans was their judgment in selecting whatever was useful among their neighbours, allies, and enemies. This does not, indeed, give us the bath; but it gives us the hypocaust, or *under-heat*. This form of apartment the Romans did employ for common purposes : thus storehouses were so constructed in the North. I will show you presently beautiful Roman flour, from which bread has been baked after a lapse of 1,300 years, and which was found in a similarly con-structed building. What more natural, than to slip from a *warm* to a *hot* room ? Instances had, no doubt, occurred of benefit from some accidental great heat, and the bath so introduced would consist in one super-heated chamber adapted to each house. The apart-ment which I have described receives the name of stoba, which is our word *stove*, and the French *étuve*,—applied, indeed, by us to the fireplace, not to the apart-ment : the Greeks have στοφα ;—showing a common derivation throughout Europe from this primitive source. Throughout Tartary the name remains to the apartment. In Poland the large pottery stove is swept out and used for the bath, as in the Irish sweat-ing houses. Whether as used for ordinary purposes or for sweating, the advantage of this early practice is equally apparent, and presents a painful contrast with our open fireplaces and straight chimneys, by which 23 out of 24 parts of the fuel is wantonly wasted, besides the loss of an equable temperature, and all the filth and trouble of open fireplaces.* Besides, the Romans never had a type. A Turkish bath is an idea in stone. It is as remarkable in its completeness and in its thought as the mosque itself. In the thermæ of the Romans there is no parallel. It is merely a palace; porticoes and halls, marbles and paintings—an accumulation of these, and that is all.

Dr. Thudichum.—Do you think that certain adaptations of the bath might have been introduced from Asia to Rome; or do you think that the introduction of the bath into Rome was of a much earlier date?

Mr. Urquhart.—Certainly, the latter. The Greeks, like the Romans, were without the bath at the beginning. We need not go beyond the terms of their language for the proof. Their word was "washing,"— *loutra,* or *heracleia loutra.* The ancient vases display the process,—streams of water at the height of a man, under which they scrub themselves. The word "hot," *thermai,* belongs to a late period. It was also adopted in Rome. Lucian speaks of the genius required in the architect for such a building. A Turk would not so speak. He has a type, and the structure is normal. The practice became universal in Greece as in Rome. After the Macedonian conquests, and the Roman extension southward and eastward, there was, of course,

* See note at the end on "WASTE OF FUEL IN ENGLAND— ECONOMY BY THE BATH."

interchange and imitation in all things : then the habits of the East would be introduced, and the practice of both in regard to the oil-bottle and the strigil become identical with what we see in the tombs of ancient Lycia, especially at Myra. The most remarkable incident of the whole is the present Pantheon at Rome, anciently the Apodyterium of the Baths of Agrippa, identical with the Turkish Mustaby, and which stands by itself in classical antiquity. It is without parentage and offspring : neither Rome nor Greece afforded the model, and there has been no imitation of it.

Mr. Rolland.—That view of the case is confirmed by a dialogue in "The Clouds" of Aristophanes. The bath is mentioned in such a way as to show that it had nothing to do with *hot air.* The discussion wholly hinges upon the relative merits of cold and hot water to wash with ; the one being mentioned as the ancient and vigorous, the other as the modern and effeminate practice. Commending the first, one of the speakers says : " We wash in Hercules' Baths (*Heracleia Loutra*)." The bath was, therefore, not known in the time of Pericles.

Mr. Urquhart.—There would be much to say even on these points, were we to occupy our time with them. I will, however, crave your permission to touch on the one point in connexion with Rome and Greece which I conceive to be instructive for ourselves. Their clothing excluded neither light nor air. It did not maintain a permanent and general warmth round the person. It was of such material, and so interchangeable in form, that friction was obtained for the skin. The soles of

F

the feet alone were protected from too much wear ; in
other respects they were naked. The head had no special
covering, a fold of the toga being thrown over it at
times.   The costume thus adapted to the need of the
body, and open to the agencies of nature, was at the same
time easy for the person, graceful to the eye, developing
noble motions in the wearers, and investing the race by
which it was used with attributes of majesty. We
cannot carve a statue not repulsive to our own sight,
without reverting for our inanimate images to that
drapery of Rome which we will not employ for our live
selves.   The ruins spread over the earth testify to the
energies of that race.   This, then, is the lesson we have to
learn ; and if we cannot change our costume in the mass
or in ordinary life, let us examine into the difference, in
order that, understanding what effects the contrary habits
produce,—namely, our habits,—we may individually,
that is, each of us here present, know how to escape
from these consequences, at least when suffering from
disease.   Now, I consider the bath as having (for persons in health) only a negative value ; as recovering those
benefits which the Romans already possessed in their
costume, and in escaping from the effects of our cos-
tumes : for health cannot be maintained if you exclude
light and air, if you prevent changes of temperature,
and if the skin is not exposed to friction.   I have·found
but one modern writer who has indicated a trace of
thought on this most essential of all considerations, and
that is Robertson.   Speaking of the commerce of
Bactria, he says that the introduction of fine stuffs—
cottons, silks, and muslins—which form so large an item

in our trade with the East, was not of the same importance to the Greeks and the Romans, because the vesture
of these people being woollen, supplied all their wants.
Then he goes on to remark that it was probably in consequence of their frequent use of the bath that they did
not seek those pleasurable sensations from softer textures
which we find in linen. No application, no deduction
follows.

There is, indeed, another reference to the subject in a writer of authority and celebrity—Gibbon;
but the citation would scarcely be in place, except in an
exposition (an invaluable work when written) of the
obliquity of modern philosophical and historical vision.
In a panegyric of modern times, he says, "The common
labourers of England command luxuries that were
unknown to the Emperors of Rome. Augustus had
neither glass to his window, nor a shirt to his
back!" What chance is there for the young man here
in our times to know anything of his own nature, when
he is dropped into unnatural habits from his birth; and
then, with sensations rendered artificially morbid, he
passes to the regions of instruction only to receive perverted maxims?

But Rome, that had been great, became little: that
is, she underwent change, and change in all things.
Already at the period of Roman greatness a great
change had manifested itself in the introduction of the
under garment or tunic. The evidence is, however,
preserved of the one garment in the obliged clothing
of the candidates for the curule offices. He was called
candidatus, because his toga was white, that is, without

the red stripe of his order. But this was not all; it was the *only* garment, as an explanation of it allows us to perceive: for that explanation was, that the candidates exhibited to the people their honourable scars. On one occasion, mention is made of exhibiting the absence of posterior scars in a way to leave no doubt as to the total absence of all interior clothing, just as among some of the tribes of Mauritania of this day. The toga was woollen, but not flannel: that is, the yarn was hard-twisted or hard-laid. I can show you a Moorish *haïc* exactly such as the Romans wore. This not only gave it an immense durability, but also realized the great end, the friction of the body.

Coming to a later period, another change presents itself. Tertullian, in the third century, says, " the dead alone wear the toga." The drapery of the true Roman had become the winding-sheet of the false one. They had fallen into something approaching our *integumental clothing*. That most wonderful phenomenon among human aberrations arose amongst us from copying the military dress—the case of armour. When that was thrown aside, the vestment remained adapted to its form. One man, Petrarch, recorded it at the time. He referred, indeed, particularly to that strange process, with which you have become too familiar to notice, of encasing the feet. This change of costume in Rome, arising precisely from the same cause—the adoption of the military *sagum* by the whole people—was coincident with the rage for the bath, and with the great light and intense heat to which it was raised under the Emperors. The people had so recently shut out nature, that they sought once in every twenty-four hours to give their bodies the benefit of light, air, and heat.* I have said, when first treating of this subject, that "Rome owed her conquest of the world quite as much to the strigil as to the sword." At that time I had not considered the points just stated. Nevertheless, the words are correct, because the bath had already been established in a greater or less degree before the first conquest eastward took place—I mean the Macedonian conquest, the consequence of the struggle with Carthage. As conquests advanced, so did the bath; so that the period of the greatest military eminence of Rome coincided with that of the largest enjoyment of this luxury. Then observe that the clothing up of the body took place first among the soldiers of Rome. The Romans were as sedulous as the Turks to-day in supplying means of bathing for the soldiers. We have recently got some remarkable evidence on this head,—a camp in the neighbourhood of Homburg, where a body of men was placed in observation in the midst of a hostile country—that region from which the storm broke which overwhelmed the West. The post, which could not contain more than 1,000 men, had no less than two baths, these baths sufficing each for the bathing of forty-five persons at a time; so that they had provided the means of bathing daily for each soldier in garrison.

If, therefore, it be disputed that Rome owed her

---

* Until the end of the Republic, the population of Italy worked naked in the fields in summer. In winter they wore one coarse garment. This we know, because of Cato's habit of working with his slaves. Up to this time, also, they had but one meal a day.

conquests to the strigil no less than to the sword, it
will scarcely be denied that to the strigil she owed
their retention. When you come to the period of their
decline, the Romans had lost their bath; they lost it
as the Turks are losing it to-day, and just as I have
myself seen the Greeks lose it. Men run into one
excess, and then they run into another excess. The
human race, when it has got a good thing, is always
in a hurry to lose it (at least, so soon as they begin
to reason about it) : there is nothing words will not
smother. Already has the same course of decay manifested itself here before even the birth has taken place.
Bath is heat. Reduce the heat, where is your bath?
Some one gets up and says, as you medical gentlemen are now saying, " You must regulate your heat—
extremes are dangerous." Unreasoning men judge by
the effect. No longer obtaining the advantages of the
proper practice, the fashion goes out; and so the
Romans at the time of their decline had so completely
lost the bath, that at the later period of their literature
it is only mentioned to be sneered at.

Dr. Druitt.—I want your opinion on the point, how
far anointing is adverse to the oxydating theory of the
bath, and your experience on the virtues of anointing
per se. Let me add, that I have seen wonderfully good
results from the latter in my practice, in consumption
and atrophy.

Mr. Urquhart.—I cannot say more than I have
already said : the daily use of the bath, the contest of
the palestra, the absence of close-fitting garments, the
constant friction of the woollen toga and pallium, ex-

posed the skin of the Romans and Greeks to the very contrary evil of that from which we suffer—namely, excessive abrasion.

Dr. Thudichum.—As you have touched upon the question of heat, I may venture an important evidence on the heat of the bath in the East. Yesterday, Dr. Wollaston says, in a letter in the "British Journal," that at Constantinople he was in the habit of taking his thermometer with him into the bath, and he found the heat always ranging between 150° and 160°. This sets aside all the talk which we have lately heard of the baths in the East not being heated to that temperature, which you have advised.

Mr. Urquhart.—We must fix the heat for ourselves. In reference to this "Roman Bath," I have said you cannot explain so much as the words you use ; you cannot tell the heat of *calidarium* or *tepidarium.* At the Asiatic Society, the other evening, we had a singular illustration of this dilemma. Mr. Redhouse, during his lecture, was constantly speaking of the "cold room," it being clear that he was meaning a hot room. He was translating a Turkish word without explaining it, or even mentioning it ; that word being *souk havlut,* which certainly *means* cold room, but which *is* a hot room.

Dr. Thudichum.—You have mentioned that the Tartar couriers, after a long and severe journey on horseback, come from the hot bath new men and able to continue their journey. The Cossacks, when crossing Germany in the French war, used to cause the common baking stoves of the peasantry, which are two or three feet high and very large, to be heated, and pushing boards into these stoves, then crept in. We should be happy to hear what you have to say on this reinvigorating power.

Mr. Urquhart.—You invite me on a great and untrodden physiological field. It is one on which 500 years hence something may be known. The newly-invented term *myalgia,* or muscle-pain, points in that direction, as inviting inquiry into pain itself, independently of the disease or cause producing it. What an assistance in the examination of its nature would be the discovery of a relief for it! Now we have that relief, and it is equally common to fatigue. We may, therefore, assume a relationship between the two. The relief is again twofold, being heat and friction, or rather blows. By giving blows, you produce pain in your arms; by blows received, that pain is relieved. An Arab camel-driver in the desert is exhausted and unable to proceed. He rolls himself in the hot sand; one of his fellows comes up and tramples on him, or beats him. He jumps up ready to resume his journey. So, cold will give the pains of rheumatism; blows will in like manner take those pains away.—But I hold that myalgic pain will not be produced when the surface is exposed. The muscles of the face may suffer from neuralgia, or pain of the nerves,—that is, general pain; but they are not subject to myalgia, or pain of the muscle,—that is, local pain. You have never rheumatism in the face; and that is the only part of our bodies constantly exposed to the air, to the light, and to cold. Our life is electrical no less than sanguineous. When it is exhausted, the muscle suffers, and the symptom is pain. Restore the vital current and develop a larger amount of electricity, and the symptom disappears, and the muscle thereupon resumes its power of continued action ; so that you obtain the results that would otherwise have to await a prolonged cessation from labour, and the intervention of the restoring influence of sleep. I come in exhausted—have pain accompanying that exhaustion. I should have to lie for hours before the refreshing took place ; I should have to sleep upon it again in order to obtain it. But I go into the bath, wherein, in addition to heat, I have manipulations, and blows if necessary. I come forth again fit for my work, and relieved from suffering. This is what one can only call miraculous. I have been on horseback four days and five nights without resting. I had two intervals which I might have employed in sleeping ; but, instead of sleeping, I went into the bath and started afresh. In such a case as this, no disorder with its nomenclature intervenes to confuse the sight. You have merely life diffused by the effect of its own superaction ; you throw in a new element and restore it. What is that element ? The simplest, the most self-evident that human ingenuity could devise, if human ingenuity based itself on getting back from art to nature. These results have not come by progressive experiments in a science of which you are to-day continuing the line, and for the future triumphs of which you are accumulating the materials. Nor are they the achievements of some brilliant epoch of past investigation over which the tide of barbarism and oblivion has swept. They are the simple expedients and instincts of unlettered and untutored man, who, in the operations of his mind, when not distorted, presents a subject of inquiry of an interest analogous to that which we feel in examining the laws of nature in inanimate objects.

Dr. Leared.—Do you think the bath is adapted to a climate like ours ?

Mr. Urquhart.—What do you mean by "adapted" to a climate ?

Dr. Leared.—Whether the bath is as well adapted to our cold, moist climate of England, as it is to the dryer climate of the Levant, where it has become naturalized : because, after all, we find that people adopt fashions and customs as much from instinct as from anything else.

Mr. Urquhart.—You adapt a shaft to a mine, an arrow to a string, or a saddle to a horse's back ; but I do not see how you can "adapt" a bath to a climate. If you had a "bath" and a "climate" in each hand to fit into one another, as a handle into a brush, then I could understand the word "adapted." Your climate is one that, more than a dry one, assists disease. If you had a dry climate, the bath would be of less service. Having superinduced a morbid sensitiveness to cold and engendered a liability to catarrh, you go on heaping on bedclothes, shutting out air, and swaddling up your bodies, in consequence of the variations of your climate and its moisture. Much of this, and the consequent suffering and malady, you could escape if your climate were dry : therefore the bath is peculiarly adapted to your necessities. Again, you contrast our climate as a moist one, with that of the Levant as a dry one. Constantinople, the metropolis of the bath, has a climate far more variable than ours. In the middle of winter, summer is wafted by a south wind to the Bosphorus; and in the middle of summer, Boreas will bring down winter from the Black Sea. You have superadded so many things to climate, that climate, being no longer to be seen, becomes a pitfall. Those other things are feather beds, window glass, open fireplaces, fleecy hosiery, close-fitting clothes; then the dark colours of your outer garments, the soft texture of your inner ones, and the leather cases for your poor feet. These, then, make your climate, as well as your consumption, your cancers, your scrofula, and the morbid sensitiveness of your bodies, whether as to cold or as to pain. You have just discovered that the climate of Russia is good for consumption : but the Russians have taken your open fireplaces, and so consumption has invaded Russia also.* It is everywhere the same thing: Europe, talkative and scientific, pollutes whatever she touches, and she will handle everything. Clothing, not sky, is climate.

Dr. Rogers.—It is believed that the open fireplace is desirable.

Mr. Urquhart.—Examine, then, into that belief.

Dr. Druitt.—There is one effect I have heard ascribed to the bath, but I do not know whether it be true or not. Some ladies who have taken it, fancy that the hair comes out quicker than it did before. Have you any fact that bears upon that ?

Mr. Urquhart.—Your question reminds me of a small

* The Samovar, that most admirable of machines for getting hot water, and the name of which combines the sacred words for fire and water of the Sanscrit and the Zende, has been adopted by the Russians from the Tartars. A friend offered to bring me one from St. Petersburg. A Cockney tea-urn came.

incident which has produced upon me a lasting impression. Some ladies were in this room conversing on the improvement of their hair. A medical man from Rickmansworth, Dr. Garlick, came in. He said, " Now, if there were any virtue in the bath, it would show itself in the hair ; whereas we know it produces exactly the contrary effect." The exclamations which immediately burst forth warned him that he had dug a pit for himself. Last week, one of these supposititious cases as to injury from the bath was brought to issue between two medical men now present : I mean Mr. Spencer Wells and Dr. Thudichum.

Dr. Thudichum.—Some time ago, Mr. Spencer Wells communicated to me a case which had been under his own observation. A gentleman with thick hair, whiskers, and moustache, after one or two baths lost his hair in handfuls, particularly from his beard. Mr. Wells expressed his apprehension that he would become bald. Upon that, I stated the case to Mr. Urquhart, and asked him to supply me with his experience upon the point. In reply, I received a letter from Mr. Urquhart's secretary, who for four or five years has been among all classes of bath-men, and seen as much as any man, I believe, in this country. He stated that not only had he never known any case in which the hair had been lost in consequence of the bath, but that, on the contrary, it had been constantly observed by bath-men (meaning the attendants in the baths) how much more the hair grows in consequence of the new habit. I sent that letter to Mr. Wells ; and he had the kindness to state in reply that, from further information obtained from the case in question, it appeared that no permanent damage had been done. I may refer to Mr. Urquhart's chapter on the Bath in the "Pillars of Hercules," where he says that the Eastern ladies who constantly take the bath, and who remain in the bath for many hours, and expose the hair particularly to the influence of the heat,—that the hair of these ladies is celebrated for its luxuriance, and for the beautiful silky and curly condition of its fibre.

Mr. Urquhart.—Is that sufficient as to the hair ?

Dr. Druitt.—I put the question because it has been put to me. I should like to ask whether it is better to go into the bath with the hair wet or dry. A gentleman got his hair partially singed. The temperature was 180°: he did not wet his head.

Mr. Urquhart.—I have felt, when the temperature has been very high, alarm about the hair: I could not touch it, it was so hot. As I did not care about losing my hair, I continued the experiment to the extremest point of endurance, covering my knees, shoulders, and feet, and leaving my hair exposed: no injurious effect followed, as you may see. The hair is then highly electrical, giving off sparks and crackling. Take it as certain that we have never seen a case of injury to the hair. What we have seen, is grey hair recovering its natural colour. The vitality of all the parts are, of course, increased. But this may also be referred to the electrical currents. The hair being treated almost as vilely as the feet by Europeans, any change will be beneficial. It is constantly greasy. The hard brushing destroys the texture of the skin. When a man goes into a bath, the first thing to deal with is the head. I have to explain to him why the head is put upon his shoulders, and why the hair is put upon the head—that it may afford the means of getting lather for the body. This is, in fact, the only unalloyed use of the head. The hair, when subject to a new excitation, will contain a mass impervious to that action; and the first impulse will be to throw that hair off, in order that fresh young hair may come out.*

Mr. Druitt.—May I interpose one question as to the electricity of the hair?—whether that electricity in the hair may not be owing to its dryness? Patients always find that the hair sparkles when they dress it at night; but that state disappears when they are well.

Mr. Urquhart.—If the hair of sick persons gives off electricity, and that of healthy persons does not; then the first lose it, and the second retain it. I do not see the connexion between that and the superabundance of electricity to which I referred. Dryness does not develop electricity. But in the bath, as I have it, when there is both heat and dryness, the heat excites it and the dryness retains it, until an escape is found. If you mean the question as controverting what I have said, I beg to reply that in this case, were you successful, you would be controverting, not me, but the

---

* A friend thus writes:—" A man of sixty-two, powerfully built, who had been completely broken down by hard living and excessive work as a navvy, came to the bath, suffering from emaciation and inability to eat. His head was entirely bald. After four baths, appearances of hair showed themselves, in tufts. These increased, and the intermediate spaces filled in, till he had a head of soft brown hair, like a boy."

established and recognized laws of electricity and pathology.*

Dr. Leared.—I should like to ask if it is true that the bath tends to corpulency ? The Turks are noted for their stoutness, particularly the Turkish ladies.

Mr Rolland.—The Turks fat !

Mr. Urquhart.—If by corpulence you mean fat, I answer that it has directly the contrary effect. I have here a letter from Mr. Banting, who is the type of obesity. He says—

" I believe the restoration of the bath the greatest blessing which has fallen upon man for the last 1,000 years. It is like manna distributed to the Jews in the wilderness, according to Scripture history. To me they are most invigorating. I have striven against obesity for near twenty years unsuccessfully. Through the baths alone (thirty-seven in three months), I am reduced in girth many inches, and in weight 5 lbs.; besides being positively and unquestionably invigorated in body and mind—physical power to take exercise, and mental to enjoy it."

Five pounds are distinctly set down, but there must be some mistake. It must be 35 lb. I think I heard it mentioned that he had been reduced that amount.

* " As vapour and water are good conductors of electricity, they must exhaust the living body of its due supply, and debilitate it ; while hot air, being a non-conductor of electricity, is well calculated to regenerate and retain it within the system. Sir James Murray ascertained in Belfast, years ago, that in a moist, low locality, where an electrical machine could not be excited, and the power of the magnet to raise a weight was reduced from 50 to 10 lb., the inhabitants there were severely scourged with the prevailing epidemics, as if, being unduly exhausted of their animal electricity, they became an easy prey to pestilential poisons."—DR. TUCKER, of Sligo.

The deposit of fat indicates a morbid condition. By restoring the healthy action, you must remove that deposit. You will have one man diminishing in bulk and weight, and you will have another man increasing in bulk and weight; the same cause producing the contrary results. In the one case the fat is dissolved, in the other the fibre is increased.

Mr. Rolland.—Since I have had a bath of my own, taking it daily, I have not increased my usual amount of exercise, nor altered my diet; and yet I am four inches less in girth: my weight has been brought down from 14 stone to 12 stone 7 lb. But in regard to the use of dumb-bells, to fencing, and tennis-playing, there is not the slightest comparison as to what I can perform before and after I have had the bath.

Dr. Thudichum.—Let any one go to the baths and ask questions there. He will find dozens of persons attending them for the very purpose of reducing their obesity. Thirty-six pounds is the highest I have heard of from the person who has experienced it. But if a man goes to the bath and feeds like a pig all the time, it is quite clear that that person will increase in fat. Therefore, if a person will live properly, there is no doubt that the bath will increase the fibre, and decrease the dead matter which we call fat.

Dr. Leared.—I had in mind the popular notion that the fatness of the Turk is due to the bath.

Mr Urquhart.—The assumption that the Turks are fat is as groundless as that their climate is dry. The safe rule in all such cases is to take the contrary of a popular notion. The Turks are singular in this, that they combine slothfulness and energy. I am not speaking, of course, of the labouring population. The value of the bath, in a military point of view, can be estimated from the health and endurance of their army. The Duke of Wellington reckons ten per cent. to be deducted for sickness from the effective force of the English army, which is supposed to be in the best possible condition. Through the last Russo-Turkish war of 1828—9, as you will find by a statement added as an appendix to " Molkte's Campaign," the number of the Turks in hospital was set down at five per cent.—this in war time, and these raw levies. In what you call the Russian war of 1854, there was a French expedition to the Dobroja. It was absent a fortnight : it consisted of 14,000 men. Seven thousand only returned, not a man having been lost before the enemy. There was no enemy where they were sent. The Turks engaged with them had only their average proportion in hospital.*

I had looked to the co-operation of the army surgeons, whose interest it is to stop disease, but hitherto in

---

* " Thanks to their excellent state of health, cases of illness are rare in the Ottoman armies : ' To such a degree,' says Mr. Skene, ' that on one occasion, when 50 men out of 3,450 were in the hospital, the circumstance appeared so alarming that an extraordinary consultation was held. One sick man in seventy is not an extraordinary proportion in the military hospitals of Great Britain. While the Russians occupied the Principalities conjointly with the Turks, it has happened that the same day, after a parade, 300 Russians had to go into hospital, out of whom 160 died in a few days ; while there was not a single case of death in the Ottoman army.' "—UBICINI, *Lettres sur la Turquie,* p. 370 ; 1853.

vain. However, the idea has at last arisen of introducing the bath into the British army: so, at least, I infer from a letter I received two days ago from Lord Herbert.

Dr. Rogers.—You spoke of the changeableness of the climate of Constantinople as requiring a bath. May I ask if it has taken root in Egypt, where the climate is so dry that we look upon it as a model one?

Mr. Urquhart.—I did not say that it was desirable on that account: I was merely clearing away groundless objections. I need not say groundless, for all objections are from their nature groundless. If a proposition be not established, the evidences have to be called for; if false, its falsehood has to be shown. A witness is examined and cross-examined; he is not objected to. Whether the climate be dry and hot, or wet and cold, the bath will be in use, or not in use, according to the sense or senselessness of the people, or of their ancestors.

Dr. ——.—The objection to the introduction of the bath is the fear that our frames could not endure the transition from 160° or 170° to one which may be as low as 30°. The skin, becoming sensitive, would rapidly cool down, and be unable to retain its normal temperature.

Mr. Urquhart.—Really, this is perplexing. The objection that I have had hitherto to meet, was that the heat in the bath would kill. So soon as that monster is put down, its shadow starts up. Now it is, "the cold without will destroy." Let me put your objection in the form of a proposition, for otherwise

I cannot deal with it:—"*Alternations of temperature are injurious to man.*" I place against it the proposition, "*Alternations of temperature are ordained for the confectioning of the human frame.*" * We must first put some limits to the term "temperature." Doubtless, you will accept as such the extremes of our own climate. I will therefore add, "The alternations of our climate may be borne without clothing." If I succeed in establishing both propositions, I will then expect you to admit two consequences,—the one physical, the other metaphysical: the first, that we have engendered in our bodies a morbid condition; the second, that the morbid condition of our bodies has passed to our minds.

To prove my case, I have to address myself, not to your ears, but to your eyes. The proof stands before you in flesh and blood. Look at that child: observe his complexion, feel his muscle, try if you can hurt him by pinches or by blows. Well, that child only wears clothes for company. If you saw him twelve hours hence, it would be sleeping naked on the floor, with the window open. He has no more sense of cold than of pain. If you ask him if he is cold, he feels himself to find out.

Dr. Druitt.—What is the temperature of his skin under these circumstances?

Mr. Urquhart.—Hot in the central regions, but so cold in the limbs as to make me shiver on touching him. He had been brought up in the ordinary way until the fourteenth month. The process of weaken-

* See at the end of this Dialogue, "BATH OF THE FINNS."

ing had produced in him more than ordinary results, so that it was a misery to see him. He had a flaccid face, the cheeks hanging down like those of Louis-Philippe : the incessant crying was unbearable. I sat down and considered what could be done; and it occurred to me to operate upon the mind through the body, so that by hardening the one I might fortify the other. The process of tempering metal is that which I followed. That process is mere alternation of temperature. A little later, and it would not have been commenced at all; because I should have perceived the morbid sense of pain, and I should have desisted.

Mr. Rolland.—Having observed the experiment, I can testify. He was then about fifteen months old. The experiment had been commenced about a month. It was in the cold winter of 1856. I was staying at St. Anne's. I met Mr. Urquhart carrying the child, absolutely naked, through a wood. The temperature was about 10° above zero. He had just come out of the bath at 170°. He passed from 170° to 22° below freezing point without any consciousness of the difference. Large stalactitic icicles were hanging from the rocks. I took one of these and rubbed him from head to foot, and pressed it against him. He took it,—played with it, looked at it and amused himself with it. I, in my winter clothing, was glad to drop it.

Mr. Urquhart.—That is my case, and I hold I am entitled to a verdict, — namely, that he who holds alternations of temperature to be injurious to man, has superadded to a morbid skin a diseased mind.

[The bath was here announced as ready. The conversation was continued, but the shorthand notes were resumed only between two and three hours later.]

Dr. Druitt.—Will you tell us how children should be treated so as to enable them to go without clothing in our climate?

Mr. Urquhart.—Take off their clothes.

Dr. Druitt.—But, as a question of fact (for on such questions all *à priori* reasonings go for nothing), will you tell me the facts upon which you built your observation?

Mr. Urquhart.—The results I have obtained depend upon the *à priori* conclusions. "Fact" means "thing done."

Dr. Druitt.—Well, what led you first to make the experiment?

Mr. Urquhart.—It would be more to the purpose if I were to ask you on what ground you had come to the conclusion that clothes are necessary in our climate, or why you have not given up a notion which you now own is erroneous. To tell you the process of reasoning and observation I passed through would take hours, and would shut out entirely the subjects for which you have taken the trouble to come down here, and with a view to which your reporter is taking notes,—viz., that the Medical Society should be able to pronounce an opinion on the medical value of the bath. Nevertheless, I will give you what you will call a "fact," but which I do not pretend to designate otherwise than a "narrative."

In 1846 I was boar-hunting in Morocco. It was in the month of January. I had gone there in the lightest of summer clothes, and never in my life did I suffer more from cold. I had to remain for several hours shivering at my post, while the man beside me, leaning with his gun over a rock, allowed his toga-like drapery (the *haïc*) to fall away as if he did not know what cold was.

Dr. Leared.—Darius, in his expedition against the Scythians, is reported to have seen some who had no clothes. One was taken prisoner, and he was asked how it was he went with his body uncovered. In turn, he asked his captor how he went with his face uncovered. He said he was used to it; upon which the Scythian replied, "So am I : I am face all over."

Mr. ——.—There is the case more in point of the ancient Britons, as it happened in our climate.

Mr. Urquhart.—The wearing clothes has nothing to do with the power of being able to dispense with clothes. It is narrated of the Irish by a French writer of the fifteenth century, that, being in the house of a chief, he was told to put himself at ease, meaning that he was to throw off his clothes, as the chiefs did when the external ceremonial was over. They clothed themselves for company. The ancient Britons, in like manner, were clothed ; but on certain occasions they unclothed themselves. A person may be clothed during the day like every one else, and yet at night, when sleep exposes him to the influence of cold much more than in the day-time, when the cold also is more intense, he may wear none. A gentleman in Ireland who witnessed this experiment from the beginning tried it on himself, and in the course of a fortnight brought himself to dispense with clothing during the greater portion of the night (that must have been in November and December), to the great relief of his complaint, a chest disease, and the manifest improvement of his appearance.*

Dr. Druitt.—Will you tell us the *modus operandi*—how you set about training this child ?

Mr. Urquhart.—After great difficulty with the nurse, I got one blanket removed, and then I got a second

---

* One of those present having applied to the gentleman in question for a statement of the case, received the following reply :—

" 28th January, 1864. MY DEAR SIR,—I have no objection to answer your questions. Horrified at the reports I heard of Mr. Urquhart's cruel treatment of his son, I went to Blarney, determined to urge Dr. Barter to take legal steps to put an end to it. I took every opportunity of examining the child, and I was compelled to admit to myself that he was not only in robust health, but enjoyed a flow of spirits not often met with. Arrived at this, I began the experiment on myself, sleeping at night without covering. This I have now continued without one omission for three years, with the window open. I did not at first pass the whole of every night thus, but I always remained on the outside of the bed till I had gone asleep. Some time previous to this, I had had a severe attack of bronchitis, which rendered me liable to a recurrence ; and on catching cold, I often doubted whether it were wise to risk the chance of a second attack for the sake of the experiment. However, I continued, and never suffered from a cough : colds passed away rapidly. The muscles became firmer, and the power of enduring fatigue increased.—Yours sincerely, J. E. SCRIVEN."

blanket removed. The removing of the third blanket required the preliminary operation of removing the nurse : I did so, intending to supply her place with a rational woman. After several experiments, I discovered that such a person was not to be found. I was thus left with the child on my own hands, and had to become nurse. We had arrived at the last blanket in the month of October of the very cold winter of 1856. The bedroom was to the north, without fire ; the windows open. The child was on a rug on the floor : I began by laying the last blanket half over his loins ; he did not creep under the warm part.

Dr. Druitt.—Did you find the effects correspond with the object for which you commenced the experiment ?

Mr. Urquhart.—I did. The experiment, however, was not as to whether a child could endure the cold of our climate, but whether the cold of our climate could be of service to correct a fractious disposition.* I do not wish the subject to close without pointing out the economical view of the question. On my becoming nurse, a reduction of 10s. per week was effected in the washerwoman's bill. It is much for a child, but I suppose other people are not more economical. There was further a great saving in clothes, and of labour in the household—a child so brought up giving little or no trouble. In this case one servant was saved. We reckoned, at the time, the saving at

* The incident is recorded in a paragraph in a Cork paper, headed "The Wonderful Child," which was repeated in all the papers at the time. See note at the end,—"CLOTHING UNNECESSARY IN OUR CLIMATE."

between £70 or £80 a year. Look at the difference, then, in a family of five or six children. Say that the saving amounts but even to a tenth, and let that be again noted according to the varieties of grades, and see what the difference will amount to as regards the public wealth. Or put it the other way — see what you squander in the process you employ to diminish the strength and the enjoyments of the young population.

Mr. ——.—There are two boys, the sons of a German doctor at Brighton, who some years ago hearing you speak on the subject, brought up his sons accordingly.

Dr. Leared.—The earliest of our race, so far as we have any historical record, clothed themselves. What would be the process of reasoning that would have induced them to cover their bodies as we do at the present day?

Mr. Urquhart.—What! Adam and Eve. Singular illustration you have chosen. When they did put on clothes—and, after all, a fig-leaf—it was not because they were cold. You yourself just quoted the example of the ancient Britons the other way. You ask why men have put on clothing, implying thereby that it can only be because they were cold. "Pride knows no cold," says a Scotch proverb. Clothing is finery; clothing is false taste; clothing is vanity. Clothing is pride;—the African savage parading under a burning sun in an old uniform coat. The history of clothing is the history of the weakness of man's character in the first instance, of his frame in the second, and of the perversion of his intellect in the third. You have reached to the most ungainly costume that has ever been devised, and the most perverted ideas of your own nature that have ever been attained to, until at last you have justified yourselves in the shame which you feel for the noble form in which God has created you. You are now inflicting on your horses all your own disorders, and by the same process; covering them with clothes, enclosing them with window-glass, and feeding them four times a day. A groom is frightened at a breath of air for an animal whose race has sprung in Tartary and the Himalaya, and has descended in all his vigour from above the level of Mont Blanc. There is a charming little ode of Pignotti instituting a comparison between the fig-leaves of our primitive forefathers and the words of our modern philosophers, ending with—

> "Le Parole così, sono le fronde
> Con cui la propria nudità nasconde."

Dr. Rogers.—Does he suffer from chilblains in the winter?

Mr. Urquhart.—Not at all. He does not suffer from anything : that child has not had, and will not have, hooping-cough, measles, or any of those ailments of modern children.

Mr. Rolland.—The Nubians, men to whom old age does not come until they have turned their hundredth year, living in the tropical desert under a bright sun, are in like manner insensible to cold. When exposed to cold, as they are also to pain, those who have gone

up to the second cataract will all testify to this. The
work of Mr. Parkyn contains remarkable instances.

Mr. Urquhart.—I had a dinner-party of travellers
from all parts of the world at Manchester during the
Exhibition. They had been testing what I told them
of this insensibility to pain, and inquiring the explanation. I said it was because he slept naked. Upon
this each in turn exclaimed—" This explains why the
Patagonians are insensible to pain," " why the Abys-
synians," &c.

Dr. Druitt.—Now, I want to ask you a question of
practical use, because my daily life is spent in solving
questions like these. I have known a case of an infant
five weeks old, that has been blue with cold, miserable,
husky, and troubled with difficulty of breathing; and
I know that by wrapping it warmly in fleecy woollen
clothing, it will be restored to health. Let me put the
case in a practical point of view with regard to a young
infant; and let us suppose the case of a prematurely
born infant. What course would you take?

Mr. Urquhart. — A Turkish Reis Effendi being
exposed to a variety of questions from an English Ambassador in reference to what he would do in certain
hypothetical cases, answered thus :—" It is not the
custom of the Mussulmans to give a name to a child
before it is born and the sex known."

Dr. Rogers.—Still, you start with the elements of
health, when you speak of making such a change in
the constitution of the child.

Mr. Urquhart.—It is you who make a change in the
constitution of the child. It is I who propose to leave

his nature unchanged. I seek to retain the element of
health : you destroy it. You invent disease by your
ingenuity, without having the ability to cure it by your
science. Solomon said, long ago, " God made man
perfect, but he has found out many inventions."

Mr. ——. —You, then, conclude that the heat of the
bath does not produce any injurious effect by reason of
a superinduced sensitiveness of the skin to the cold of
our climate?

Mr. Urquhart.—The question should come from me,
as to whether you perceive the groundlessness of such
assumptions.

Dr. Druitt.—You said just now that your boy's food
was milk. What quantity will he consume?

Mr. Urquhart.—About two quarts a day. Medical
men, both here and on the Continent, have earnestly
remonstrated with me on the insufficiency of food. To
live on milk was an idea bewildering to them.

Dr. Druitt.—Does he take no solid food ?

Mr. Urquhart.—His diet is milk. I have reduced
him from five meals to two meals a day. The change
was an immense relief, nature not having to throw off
the superfluous food. He is now in the condition in
which a human being ought to be.

Dr. Thudichum.—In that remarkable case in which
you treated consumption by the means of the rays of
the sun, you mention, I see, by the notes of your
lecture at Brompton, that you had recourse to other
means—dietetic and others. Was milk one of those
means ?

Mr. Urquhart.—Most certainly. I should never think

of treating any disease without a return to nature. As I connect disease itself with habits, for since cure, that is *care*, must consist in rectifying them. I must begin with relieving the patient as much as possible from hampering clothes, and by supplying to him the nourishment of his childhood, the only nourishment which is prepared in the body of one animal for assimilation in the stomach of another.*

Mr. Rolland.—May I ask for specific cases, as more to the purpose than general speculation?—that case of the old man at St. Anne's.

Mr. Urquhart.—That was the first morning the first bath was opened. I was going in, about nine in the morning, when I met this old man coming out, supported by Mr. Rolland and Mr. Scriven. He had been in already an hour and a half. He was a man with a remarkable countenance; the magnitude of his frame in its past existence was evidenced by his skin hanging about him like a sack. He had been suffering for fourteen years from rheumatic gout, with thickening of the joints. I induced him to return with me. The heat was 170°. I shampooed him, not in the ordinary way, but applying the whole of my strength; hitting him as hard as I could, and standing on his chest and limbs. In the intervals, I subjected him to alternate rushes of hot and cold water, as he lay flat on the floor to get its full weight. After three hours, he walked away erect. The chains of fourteen years were broken in a single operation.

* See note at the end, on "MILK DIET."

Mr. Rolland.—His own expression was, "I went in on all-fours, and I went away on wings."

Dr. Druitt.—May I mention, as a matter of fact, two circumstances which I have known of injury resulting from the use of the Turkish bath? I mention them simply as matters of fact.

Mr. Urquhart.—Say, of inquiry.

Dr. Druitt.—The first was a young lady about nineteen or twenty, the daughter of very conspicuous people. She took the Turkish bath.

Mr. Urquhart.—This was in Turkey?

Dr. Druitt.—She took it at Dr. Barter's. What the details of that bath are I cannot say, but I know the result. The skin, which was remarkably fair and nice-looking before, was scorched : she was for some weeks afterwards sunburnt. The other case is of a gentleman who took the bath at Mr. Witt's. The hot air so scalded his trachea, that he was not able to speak above a whisper for a fortnight afterwards.

Mr. Urquhart.—You have now given us two narratives, and these rumours only, for you do not say that you saw the persons and examined them. Medical men do not accept cases on hearsay. How are these introduced? An authenticated case had just been stated of restoration from one of the most grievous of maladies which afflict human nature, and especially in our climate ; one in which all medical means had been tried in vain for fourteen years.* The science of medicine, if anything, is the science of cure. Are you not glad

---

* See note at the end, on "MEDICAL TREATMENT OF RHEUMATISM."

that a means of cure should be discovered?—do you not desire to extend the knowledge of it? It cannot be that it has no interest for you; and yet a rumour of a burnt face or a scorched throat as happening somewhere to somebody makes you forget it. I am here at your service to answer questions connected with my own experience : you are here, as I understand, to question me on those points. But if questions wholly irrelevant are put by one individual, while the rest are sincerely anxious to examine into the subject to which they have devoted a day of their time, I should be acting most unfairly and uncourteously to them if I allowed myself to be drawn away either into supposititious cases or into futile discussion.

Doubtless, there is great liability to injury from those heated cellars and suffocating rooms called Turkish baths. But these "facts" do not belong to this category: for they are alleged to have occurred in the baths of Mr. Witt and Dr. Barter, where the only inconvenience that can arise is in cases (eczema* for

---

* See p. 34, what Mr. E. Wilson says as to the high heat requisite for the treatment of this disorder. I would mention that a patient brought to the bath in Golden-square a note from an eminent practitioner, saying that he was not to be subjected to more than 130°. The manager, in his perplexity, came down to consult me. I told him that 130° would only irritate, and that relief would only be experienced after that point was passed, and that he should let the patient feel his own way to the higher temperature. Next day the medical man came in while his patient was relating the two experiences, which fell out exactly as I had said. The 130° is, in fact, the PONS ASINORUM.

instance) where a low heat only irritates, and does not relieve.

Dr. Druitt.—Then how are we to distinguish between the true and the false?

Mr. Urquhart.—Ah! there is, then, a true one? I can afford little time to this matter, yet I gave eight months to Dr. Barter: my task I considered then completed. Unless some one of you who are here now should happen to be a man of genius, or unless I am successful in putting you in the right way, so that your self-love will be on that side, I shall also have to regret that I ever called your attention to the subject. By past experience, I have learned that in every man who takes up the bath with the view of turning it to profit, whether as a builder, a practitioner, a speculator, or a patentee, I have to reckon ultimately on a bitter enemy. On these grounds I have refused to undertake any building in London, except on the condition that there shall be no architect.* The bath which you have seen, elaborate as it may seem to you, was built without architect, or builder, or even marble cutter. I taught myself the common bricklayers to cut and polish the marble. So in this neighbourhood, at least, the bath and I will have made no enemies.

* The name of Mr. Somers Clarke does appear as architect to the Jermyn Street Company, but these conditions were nevertheless carried out, as will be seen by the terms of his acceptance of the appointment when writing to me in December, 1860 : "Mr. Rolland has requested that I would communicate with you as to an appointment I have to make with you at Riverside, in connection with my acting as practical and professional *adviser* (*sic*) under you to the Turkish Bath Company."

Dr. Druitt.—I am exceedingly grateful to you for mentioning this, because I had not the remotest idea but that Dr. Barter's was an orthodox establishment.

Mr. Urquhart.—The bath is putting England on her trial. I never knew what the Turks were till now, by the contrast with us. Seeing that it was good, they accepted it without an emotion of self-love or a thought of self-interest.

Dr. Leared.—You laud the Turkish character. How, then, do you account for it that the Turkish bath, even in Turkey, has become so altered and so enfeebled?

Mr. Urquhart.—I was not speaking of the modern Turks.

Dr. Rogers.—I think it would be useful to know the specific faults in the bath that exist.

Mr. Urquhart.—They cannot be mended, they must be swept away. An edifice such as those in Constantinople is about to be constructed in London. The impulse on which the money was subscribed was the announcement that Dr. Barter was about to invade England with his "improved" Turkish bath. Let us but get a proper one and so establish the practice; and then the door will be open to the introduction throughout the land of a practice that will improve the condition of the whole people. In the first bath at St. Anne's I gave them the three essentials: 1st, the building; 2nd, the heat; 3rd, the shampooing. I gave them also the distinction between the "clean" and the "dirty:" also the method, the style, and some sense of the dignity of the procedure. These are now lost or vulgarized. The temperature, I understand, of the Dublin bath is only

H

10° above* that of the tent with double canvas roof used by our officers in the plains of India, and to which they have to retire for protection against the sun. As warm rooms for washing in, with an abundant supply of hot and cold water, they are most commendable; and in as far as the run of sickness goes, their habitual use would be of more service than the contents of all the apothecaries' shops in the Three Kingdoms. But this is not the bath. In addressing lately an audience largely composed of medical men and students, with a medical man in the chair, in a town where the whole faculty have adopted the bath, and where it has been introduced into the infirmary by Sir John Fife, the man of highest professional reputation out of the capital, I thus entered my protest against the whole of the speculations known under the name of " Turkish Baths" :—

" The only apprehension I have is, that, remaining satisfied with the first attempt, and content with empirical innovations, you stop short of the perfect thing; and instead of recovering the luxury, pride, enjoyment, and strength of the most luxurious and philosophic, learned and military of the races of the earth, this endeavour shall pass away as a troubled dream. It is thus I am driven to address you, not only by the desire to introduce for my countrymen a benefit of which I know and experience daily the value in my own person, but also by the necessity of preventing this experiment

---

* An attendant in the bath at Dublin being attacked with typhus, and not being able to give him a higher heat than 130°, they had to send him to the hospital!

from lapsing, by reason of self-love and speculation, into a disastrous and shameful abortion." *

Mr. Urquhart.—Now, then, let me give you a "fact" of injury from the bath. It will be neither anonymous nor supposititious. It has been already the subject of a letter from me to the *Medical Society.* It has been examined by Mr. Erasmus Wilson, who reported on it, in the first stage, in writing. His letter is here, if you wish to refer to it. The patient is a woman between forty and fifty ; her name is Stocker ; she is housekeeper to Mr. Rolland, and the incident occurred in his bath. She was suffering from a complication of maladies, some of old standing. She was wasting away; there was only before her to take to her bed and die. Observing the effect of the bath on others, she had the idea, without consulting any one, of taking it herself. She went in at a heat of 170° to 180°. She experienced unpleasant sensations, but she persevered. She went on, I believe, for a couple of hours, and was brought out at last with her body swollen, and in something described as convulsion. However, satisfied that the bath was her only chance of life, she repeated the experiment three times, and always with the like results. When Mr. Rolland became acquainted with what had happened, he did not know what to think or what to do. It never occurred to him to consult me. So he sent her to Mr. E. Wilson, who sent her back, saying that nothing could be done for her. His words were, "It is one of the non-perspiring cases." There the matter would have rested, had I not by the

* *Newcastle Daily Journal,* January 22, 1861.

merest accident met her,—I think it was just as she had returned from Mr. Wilson. I was passing, in haste, and just heard these words,—" She was taken ill in the bath, and cannot perspire." I called out from the cab I had got into, " Send her down to Riverside, and she will return next day all right."

She did return all right the next day. From that time she took the bath at Mr. Rolland's regularly, and in a few weeks recovered her health. You may suppose this as an extreme if not unparalleled case, and to have given me much trouble. Not the slightest. Nor was it till days or weeks afterwards that I learnt the antecedent circumstances which I have related. On arriving, I sent for the housekeeper, and said to her, " Mr. Rolland's housekeeper is coming down to-morrow to take the bath, as she cannot perspire. Go in with her yourself, to-morrow evening and the morning afterwards ; and see that she perspires." This is my ' fact ' of injury from the bath.

· *Dr. Rogers.*—How was she made to perspire? Is Mr. Rolland's not a good bath ?

Mr. Urquhart.—She could have perspired just as well in Mr. Rolland's as in mine ; only it requires to know how. It is simply gradual heat that is wanted. She was probably kept a couple of hours at 130°, perhaps she had alternate ablutions of hot and cold water— perhaps she was well soaped and scrubbed—perhaps she was sponged with vinegar—perhaps she had a pint of lime-juice to drink. My housekeeper having orders to make her perspire, would employ the necessary means to that end.

Dr. Rogers.—What is the case that occurred at Mr. Witt's. Is Mr. Witt's not a good bath ?

Mr. Urquhart.—Oh, Sir James Clark! I am glad you mentioned it, as these two cases furnish the whole list of incidents against which precautions have to be taken. True, they are both of rarest occurrence ; yet I myself was once affected in the same way as Sir James Clark, and I owe to it my having my attention originally fixed on the bath, as furnishing physiological lights unknown to modern science. I made this statement on the last occasion on which I was subjected to scientific examination.* The affection itself was at that time unknown and unnamed. It is Dr. Simpson's discovery of *anæsthesia.* Mr. Witt's bath was no more in fault in this case than Mr. Rolland's had been in the other ; only, neither Sir James Clark nor Mr. Witt knew how to deal with a case which any Turkish shampooer would have relieved in an instant—if, indeed, they knew what it was. But on this subject I must refer you to Dr. Thudichum, who mentioned it to me. Had Sir James Clark taken the bath here, nothing of the sort would have happened. I repeat to you, I never had any case of injury whatever. I never heard of one in the East ; I never heard of one in Ireland : I cannot so much as imagine such a case. It is, however, as dangerous to go into a bath as into a boat, unless you know that you have to step on the thwarts, and not on the gunwale.

Dr. Leared.—I am desirous of knowing if you have

* See First Dialogue, p. 3.

turned your attention to the operation of the bath on the digestive functions; how it conduces to appetite, and what its effect is in cases of dyspepsia?

Mr. Urquhart.—As to appetite and digestion, I have nothing to say; they belong to the healthy state; and you cannot improve upon health. As to indigestion or dyspepsia, the bath, by calling the blood to the surface, affords relief to the stomach. There must be inflammation when there is difficulty of digestion. That inflammation must impair the force of the digestive juices, and disqualify the stomach for dealing with food, so that it lies there a source of increased irritation, as any other foreign matter might be. Those present, not medical men, and who have never handled a human stomach, may apprehend the difference between a healthy and a dyspeptic one by taking the first to resemble this sheet of writing-paper, and the second to resemble this sheet of blotting-paper. The one is to the other as inflamed to uninflamed skin on the arm or the leg. The inflamed leg has to remain quiet and get well; but the inflamed stomach has to go daily on with its task. Seated in this dark interior which cannot be reached, the malady presents insuperable obstacles to such treatment as medical men would employ if it appeared on the surface. They would apply poultices and emollients in one stage, lotions and astringents in another. The process of digestion calls to the stomach, and all the organs immediately connected therewith, a mass of blood inconceivable to those who have not followed the cruel operations upon animals by which we have, so

to say, inspected with the eye the internal operations
of the body. Now, disease in the stomach permanently
produces the effect of disturbing the equilibrium by
congesting the blood within. You can, therefore, judge
of the relief afforded by determining the blood to the
surface, even if it be for a very limited space of time in
the course of the four-and-twenty hours. The stomach
also will be relieved in another way. Oxygen being
more available, the assimilation takes place more rapidly
and more completely. Thus, less food sufficing, there
will be less digesting to be got through. There is also
less detritus from the body, and therefore less waste to
be made good. Whilst the patient is exposed to a
high heat, there is during that period a reduced demand for animal heat, for the production of which so
much of our food is required. I am satisfied that the
constant use of the bath diminishes by one third the
amount of food required. My servants have given up
one of their three meals a day.

I would also refer, if in but a single word, to a
consideration of the highest importance, and equally
ignored by medical men—the *temperature of the diseased
stomach.* Against the chance of perceiving this point,
which alone to perceive placed larger therapeutic means
in their hands than the whole Pharmacopœia affords,
they have carefully bandaged their eyes by the proposition that the temperature of the body remains the
same in all zones, and whatever the external temperature may be. We have been experimenting here
latterly, and the results have been given in Dr.
Thudichum's paper at the Medical Society. I may add,

that I have since been repeating the experiments, and have found, in addition, that the temperature within the body rises in the same degree as that of a thermometer cased in wet flannel.   Now, in case of fever, the heat is seeking to ascend, to attain to the purifying and perspiring power.   Not so that of the stomach.   By stimulants, by the superimposed heat of the surrounding viscera, and, above all, by the unnatural excitements of reiterated meals—that dreadful maxim, "Little and often,"—you maintain a decomposing heat. Often a single shock of cold water on the external body will brace it for a day.   Why not brace the afflicted stomach in like manner ?   Combine, then, the two processes: call the blood to the surface by external heat ; then supply internal cold ; but do not use the relief thus afforded to be expended on medicine, on stimulants, and on that iteration of meals which is the primary cause of all dyspepsia. It is not, however, going in for an hour once or twice a week that will effect anything.   It is a great effort that has to be made.   When a man is ill, it is his first duty to get well; and he must endure whatever has to be borne for that purpose.   He must be in two or three hours a day.   In that period of relief afforded from the internal pressure of blood and consequent heat, the vessels can regain their contractility against the inevitable recurrence of the labour of digestion. But this malady in its progress will involve all the other organs.   Now, that relief which is afforded to the stomach by directing the blood to the surface, is in like manner afforded to the other organs secondarily involved, whilst in several and separate ways the symptoms of disturbed functions are alle-viated.

Yet what avail the means I offer you of alleviating this disorder, if you only use the margin to fill it out? You have produced it first by indulgence, and then by theory. England originally had but two meals ; and they did not dabble with eating or drinking in the intervals. The old verse runs—

> "Up at five, dine at nine,
> Sup at five, bed at nine."

Having indulged themselves without reserve, they then convert their practice into maxim ; and no longer the weak man says to himself, but the physician to his patient, " You must eat little and often." I invite you to the examination of that most important of all con-siderations for the medical man who would do his duty by qualifying himself to understand the origin of those ailments which afflict in an extraordinary degree that species which is the most perfectly constituted, and amongst whom there should be no malady save old age. If he does so, then he will use the instrument I place in his hands, not to allow his patient a further latitude of self-indulgence, but to enable him to bear up against the consequences of a vicious habit which he is now resolved to rectify.

Digestion is a frightful operation, from its difficulty : repeat it not, then, oftener than is required. You must lose the capacity for taking food, or you must take more than is needed. Look, in the latter case, at the toil you impose on all the organs to get rid of it. It is not, then, the food that supports you—you have to support the food. I wish I could parade before you the array of persons that I myself have restored to health and comfort by persuading them to this abstinence. People have often said to me, "Why are you not a doctor?" My answer has been, " Were I a doctor, I would starve at least in England; for the apothecary here makes the physician, and the apothecary would not approve of the plan."

In ancient times, among Romans, Greeks, and Persians, the discipline for the young consisted in subjecting them to privations: they had to endure heat and cold, to endure hunger and thirst. Now it is "warm clothing," it is "plenty of food," and nothing is more dreaded than an "empty stomach." I have the—advantage, I was going to say,—but, at least, the occasion of studying this disease in myself.* A feature of dyspepsia is the craving for something to put into the stomach. This is a symptom not peculiar to dyspepsia, but it is also common to those disorders that are connected with the use of stimulants. The bath has the quality of allaying that craving, as it does even in extreme delirium tremens.

Dr. Thudichum.—Will the counterpart of this view hold? That is to say, suppose we have an external irritation analogous to the internal irritation, will the determining of the blood to the surface injure in that case, as it relieves in the other?

Mr. Urquhart.—In all cases of external inflammation, abrasion, bruise, sore, incision, suppuration, relief

* See note at the end, on "DYSPEPSIA TREATED BY ONE MEAL A DAY."

is immediate. The exposure of an abraded surface is supposed to be injurious, in consequence of the action of the air. You go into the bath with the part exposed : you suffer no inconvenience from the air ; you are relieved from the irritation of the ointment or plaster, and you get the benefit of the heat. In surgical cases the bath will be found to be a wonderful agent. I have as yet had but a single case. The operation was one of the most painful and precarious ; it was attended with long suffering. The patient, when capable of removal, was, with my friend Mr. W. Fergusson's concurrence, and by his advice, brought down here. The change in the aspect of the wound in four-and-twenty hours was wonderful.

Dr. Leared.—A recent French writer has advised dipping the patient into icy-cold water; and he says that they come out with an appetite to which they have been strangers before.

Mr. Urquhart.—Well, I give icy-cold water, as well as burning-hot air : that is a partial groping only. Without the heat, the application of cold is a very foolhardy experiment. Dr. Marshall Hall has used this means in cases of suspended animation. If he used the cold *only*, he would ensure death. The concomitant effect—the sending the blood backwards and forwards, from without to within—calls the whole frame into action. You have never seen men suffering from dyspepsia who are exposed to great stress on the system. Races exposed to precariousness of food acquire great powers of digestion.

Dr. Druitt.—As a matter of fact, I differ from you

there. Many cases of dyspepsia within my experience have been brought about by unusual abstinence.

Mr. Urquhart.—I said " races,"* not individuals. I said that races exposed to privation are not dyspeptic. A man brought up as you are will, of course, suffer from going without his luncheon.

Dr. Druitt.—The Laplanders suffer a great deal from dyspepsia.

Mr. Urquhart.—The Laplanders! Can you digest blubber and tallow ? Admitting that they are dyspeptic, you have to go to the Pole for an instance and then to a race subjected to more than privation. My object has been, in the experiment I have made, not to go to the limit of depression, but to find the limit of fortitude. I must hit the point where the power of expansion shall not be curtailed, where the power of endurance shall not be passed. You have before you a specimen of another race — a being brought up from infancy in another manner. He will be proof against dyspepsia at one hundred years, but then he will presently be on one meal a day.

Mr. Rolland.—The Red Indians are frequently exposed to privation for several days without food in their hunting excursions ; so are the Hottentots : yet they never suffer from dyspepsia, although they gorge themselves frequently afterwards. To establish this point, take any book of travels. Take Dr. Darwin's " Adventures of the Beagle ;" take Parkyns, take Atkinson, or any other traveller, it does not matter who. The less a man has

* See " MARSH'S GENERAL THERAPEUTICS," 1863.

studied the subject the better, because he gives you the result of observation.

Mr. Urquhart.—I have myself gone through all this. I have reduced myself to one meal a day in order to be able to go through with my work, which has for years prevented me from taking an hour's exercise or recreation : and so I have been able to work sixteen hours a day, and sometimes twenty ; and also to pass from the one extreme of inaction and fatigue to the other. Before I fell into this practice, which arose out of my observing the Mussulman fast of the Rhamazan, I was tortured with that form of dyspepsia called heartburn. It disappeared, not that I noted the change at the time, under that practice. Returning to Europe and relaxing into the ordinary meals,—I mean, two a day, with tea and coffee, or the like,—all returned in an aggravated form. Cicero tells somewhat the same story of himself. Ackbar did the same, as mentioned by Abul Fazel. Talleyrand, I was told the other day, also reduced himself to one meal. I hold that one meal in the twenty-four hours is the intention of nature, as made plain by the dimensions of the stomach and the *necessity of filling it to obtain perfect digestion.* I am, moreover, satisfied on historical grounds, that a race exceeding two meals a day can no more be permanent than an empire that sends its phosphates down its rivers.* The physical con-

* The earlier legislations took care to prevent this waste. They did so by enjoining, not discussing. They enjoined their professors not to pollute the elements. In this the moderns have only seen superstition. Pliny (Nat. Hist., L. xxx. c. 2) thus explains the objections of the envoy of Tiridates to go on board ship :—" Navigare noluerat, quoniam expuere in maria,

dition of permanency must be—1st, the restoration to
the soil of the elements of vegetation ; 2nd, the preservation of the stomach for the digestion of its food.   We
have a specimen in the Chinese as contrasted with the
Romans in former times, and the British to-day.   They
have seen the first rise, change from one meal to two,
and then to three and fall; and so will they the
second.

Before leaving dyspepsia, let me say that the influence
of the bath on this malady is comparatively small; the
command by it of the disordered stomach by no means
corresponds with its control over the disordered head,
heart, liver, or kidneys.   I want now to come to what to
me is the important part of our subject—perspiration.

Dr. Druitt.—What is your experience as to the
lowest temperature at which a man can be comfortable ?

Mr. Urquhart.—Comfortable is a very fanciful word.

Dr. Thudichum.—I can say there is no limit to the
time during which I can be naked in a cold room at
this temperature and not feel cold; but I begin to feel
cold as soon as I put on my clothes.

Dr. Druitt.—Now, we are anxious to hear what you
have to tell us about perspiration.

Mr. Urquhart.—It would be better brought out by
question and answer than by mere statement.

Dr. Druitt.—What amount do you believe a man

aliisque mortalium necessitatibus violare naturam cam, fas non
putant." They had for this season no cities on the coast.
The Chinese and Japanese take individual measures for saving
the matters requisite for the continuous fertility of the soil.
See Appendix to "Liebig's Natural Laws of Agriculture."

ought to lose from his skin daily, weight of solid matter —not of water?

Mr. Urquhart.—If you want mere chemistry, I must refer you to Dr. Thudichum.

Dr. Thudichum.—When you first stated to me the effect of the bath, the principal feature you described was perspiration. First, as to quantity; secondly, as to quality. Will you give us your opinion on the part played by perspiration in the human economy. But the first question I would ask is, respecting the relationship between perspiration and disease?

Mr. Urquhart.—Time will not admit of my doing more than putting it in general terms. I have found in acute general disorders, and in topical affections, whether acute or chronic, that disease and inability to perspire are coincident; consequently, force perspiration and you subjugate the disorder. It would seem, then, that nature works towards the discharge by the skin, or, as Hippocrates puts it, "purgation by the skin," or that *disease only manifests itself* when the effort falls short. You may experience the very condition, and then trace this action distinctly as with the eyes. I burn my finger: not the finger only, but the hand—not the hand only, but the arm refuses to perspire. On going into the bath, the faculty of perspiration is evidently suspended in the injured part, and in the surrounding parts. But heat in time forces it out. This is what the physician dimly looks for by means of diaphoretics, diuretics, sudorifics, purgatives, and blisters.

By what process the skin is thus locked up—

whether it be so locked up as a consequence of disease, whether disease is a consequence of the locking-up of the skin, is beyond me to inquire into. Nor do I care to inquire into it, since I am in possession of the remedy. This is true and certain, that coincident with disease, is the suspension, more or less, of the perspiring faculty; that that faculty is recoverable by the application of external heat. Then the disease is subdued. If physicians have not thought of external heat, at least they have sought after perspiration. They seek to obtain it by specifics administered internally. This only renders it the more marvellous, that during so many ages they should have neglected the first of the powers of nature, by means of which they operate in the laboratories, by which all culinary operations are carried on, by which all mechanical arts subsist, by which the earth gives her produce, and, in a word, the whole mechanism of the universe is put in motion.

Were there no physicians, the common sense of mankind would readily find its way back to the remedy. A letter on the table from Jamaica, from Mr. Percy Smith, mentions that, on explaining to them the bath, they immediately said, "Oh, that will stop the yellow fever, for a man is saved when he perspires." A man at Sheffield cured cholera by placing the patient before a hot fire, with blankets round him, and was in consequence shut up in a madhouse. Medical science has not only neglected heat, but has invariably put it down. In my experience, there has been no case of sufficient obstinacy not to yield to heat when raised sufficiently high, and continued sufficiently long.

Dr. Thudichum.—Now let us have, if you please, your answer with respect to the contents of perspiration.

Mr. Urquhart.—First as to perspiration itself. I am lost in the magnitude of the subject. It is in reference to our bodies what free will is in reference to our minds. In all other emunctions we are not free agents; in this one we are free agents. Our neglect will not absolutely destroy us; but on our due culture of ourselves depends our perfected health. What comes forth by the lungs is under the control of involuntary muscles; it neither depends on the circumstances of your life, nor on the exercise of your judgment. In the same way, what passes from the kidneys, and what passes from the bowels, these are operations which nature performs for herself, and in which you are compelled and constrained to do your part. But what passes from you in the way of sweat, depends upon the habits of your class or the operations of your mind. Thus, if you allow that a given quantity of the poisons that have to make their escape has to pass through the skin, that portion not being subject to fixed rules belonging to your frame, there can be no ratio established between that portion so escaping and the other portions otherwise escaping. For these nature provides; for this you yourself are left to provide. Supposing the emunction by three or four processes all equally necessary, your perfect condition of health depends upon what you yourself do with reference to the skin.

Dr. Thudichum.—I had that beautifully expressed in one of your letters :—" While the other functions are

I

withdrawn from our interference, the function of the skin is committed to our care."

Dr. Druitt.—Is that the fact with the skin more than the other organs? Are not they all by various means more or less under the control of the will?

Mr. Urquhart.—The subject is physical; the distinction is metaphysical.

Dr. Thudichum.—You will find that you can remove as much from the skin in one hour in the bath as can be removed by any other organ in twenty-four hours. That is a point which no scientific man has hitherto observed. It is a point of the greatest importance, which we must make up our minds to study and look at in every direction.

Dr. ———.—What amount of perspiration can be got rid of in a given time, say in an hour?

Mr. Urquhart.—With the skin in a good condition, and with the means of passing from one temperature to another, so as to be able to continue the operation with comfort—say with one temperature at 130°, and another at 180° or 190°,—you would discharge from a pound to a pound and a half an hour, and twice as much at higher temperatures.*

Dr. ———.—What will that amount to, as regards the whole blood of the body?

Mr. Urquhart.—If the general supposition of thirty pounds of blood were correct, it would thus at the lower rate take about twenty hours to refresh the blood. But

---

* For further experience on the amount of perspiration, see *postea*, "CONSTRUCTION OF A RADIATING CHAMBER."

as this estimate is erroneous by one half, and as the vital portions of the blood will in either hypothesis remain the same, I reckon that seven or eight hours in the one case, and four or five in the other, will suffice for exchanging dirty for clean blood, supposing that the operation could be endured without drinking.

Dr. ——.—So, then, it becomes a long operation.

Mr. Urquhart.—That is as it may be considered. If you, as a medical man, proposed to purify entirely the blood of a man in a corrupted state, and if you attempted to do so by means of medicine, you would probably claim merit for expedition, as well as success, if you effected your purpose in weeks, or even months.

(After a pause.)

If there are no more questions, I should wish to conclude by one further consideration. I become thirsty in consequence of perspiration. Water is at once available. It has not to be digested ; it is so managed that it passes almost instantaneously into the blood. We suppose that the cravings come from the stomach ; but that is not the case. Here the cravings come direct from the blood. Give a man salt water, and he will not be a bit the less thirsty, but more so. Let him fill his stomach with salt water, and he will be more thirsty than he was before, because of that power of salt in regulating the distribution of fluid between the stomach and the circulation. In my first gropings in the dark, I looked at perspiration as local and circumscribed. For instance, in point of cleansing, I imagined that if I perspired, I had a clean skin. I was then in total darkness as to the whole history before us. Now I know that the source of perspiration is the blood itself, and the whole blood, *minus* the serum and the globules. Perspiration is not like the produce of the kidneys; it is not a secretion, it is *simple condensation.* When, the other day, the discussion between Mr. Erasmus Wilson and Dr. Thudichum was going on, I made no remark. They were speaking of the amount of the perspiratory vessels being equal in amount to two-thirds of the kidneys. I was anxious not to interrupt, for fear of losing anything. I now say, that no ratio can be established between the one and the other, because the kidneys are a secreting organ; by which I mean that a chemical change is effected. At the time, I interposed the word " sponge;" and I would convey the difference by that word. The perspiratory organs are only recipients; they catch the water dropped by the blood under the increased action of the heart, whether accompanying or produced by the action of the muscles, or merely as the result of extraneous heat applied to the body, at the moment of the transfusion of the blood from the extreme vessels of the arterial system into the extremities of the venous system. At that moment when it is set free from its organs, down drops into these spongy vessels the watery portions, and the remainder passes on. The peculiarity is this, that all extraneous matter accompanies the outgoing part. That extraneous matter consists of chemical products. These products are the causes of disorder, unless discharged. All escape with the watery portion ; it charges these sponges, and thence issues forth by the spiracles to the surface. The source being then the whole blood ;

the purification takes place not only in so far as the
skin is cleansed, but also in so far as the whole body is
cleansed. Each particle of blood is, so to say, wasted.
That purification has not been effected until you
have removed the whole of the watery portion. This
cannot be done at once: circulation could not go on;
you require to replenish it by taking liquids into the
stomach; and in proportion as you do so, you soil the
newly-injected liquid, so that the operation must be prolonged far beyond the time that would be required
for a simple extraction. That is the ground of my
discovery of heat as a mode of cure. I put it
into this shape that you may treat it as a specific
proposition to be accepted or confuted. Wherever there
is disease, there is impure blood: you cannot pretend to
say you can cure that disease unless you remove this,
its cause. You can remove it in one way—you can
remove it by washing the blood; you cannot remove it
without washing the blood. Therefore, when I get a
case of acute disorder, I am certain of cure; for I put the
patient into the bath, and keep him there till he has
discharged the whole of the impurities in his blood.
But you get in such disorder a change in the nature of
the vital portion of the blood itself: what are you to do
then? The evil is not limited to the presence of the
foreign matters, but extends to their effects. Instead
of making use of these millions of vessels placed at your
disposal by nature, you go and tap the human body.
But you say, " We reduce inflammation thereby—the
blood that is drawn exhibits at once its corrupted state;
its very appearance shows the necessity of getting rid

of it." I take out the impurities floating in the blood, and by the self-same process I restore the vital portion of the blood to its healthy state. The discharge called perspiration effects the first, and the heat which evokes it effects the second. The one takes away the disease, the other removes the symptoms. I have used the latter word, not in your sense, but in my sense. For that to which I apply the word "disease," you have no analogous term; that is, the unremoved poisons, products of the phenomena of life. My word "symptom," is your word "disease;" *i. e.* the inflammation, the fever, the gout, scrofula, consumption.* The difference of appreciation shows itself in the two practices. I handle the blood, change its contents, renovate it, restore it, carefully preserving every particle. You take this fluid life out of the man and put it into bowls; these bowls you confide to the care of a nurse, to inspect next day. If the patient survives, you say, "How lucky for him, he called me in in time!" Or, you apply a blister, and rob the man of a portion of his *serum.* The other night, at the Medical Society, it was admitted that heat changes the corpuscles; one of the speakers said, "We know very well that heat will change the colour from venous to arterial."

Dr. Thudichum.—I believe that was based on a fallacious experiment.

Mr. Urquhart.—Whether the experiment was fallacious or not, the conclusion is true. I need only refer to Watson's late work.

---

* See *postea,* "GOUT A SYMPTOM NOT A DISEASE."

Dr. Thudichum.—There is one point upon which I may, perhaps, make a remark. It is this: whereas, on the one hand, the digestive organs are only enabled to take up the nutritive material which has a certain degree of dilution, and whereas, on the other hand, the blood has the power to nourish the body most effectually when it possesses the lightest specific gravity, and whereas those two extreme conditions are opposed, it is clear that perspiration, by removing from the blood the watery particles, and thereby increasing the specific gravity, must put the blood into the most favourable condition for producing muscle.

Mr. Urquhart.—This valuable reflection comes appropriately to close the subject. I have now been answering questions seven or eight hours. I trust we will drop the bath at dinner, and not renew it afterwards. Permit me, therefore, a final observation. If any material specific were announced as added to the Pharmacopœia for the cure of one disorder, and for which remedies are already possessed, it would be a subject of interest to science. Here is a mere habit, which operates for the removal of all disease. I, least of mankind, can be under any illusion as to the difficulties in the way of the acceptance of such a means by the faculty. Doubtless, it does open to the individual medical men who are the first to accept it a large field of professional distinction. There can be no question that being able to cure is one element of medical success. This career is, however, only open to those who are possessed of an ingenuous mind ; for it can only be entered upon after the sacrifice of professional self-love. The medical man is called upon for the highest effort of abnegation that it is possible for him to conceive—the suffering of his patient to stand on the same level as himself.*

The faculty has not made the discovery ; it is an issue which is forced upon them.   I have done my best, and shall continue to do my best, to render it impossible for them to avoid either accepting or rejecting it.   My object is neither scientific nor professional ; it is the good of my fellow-creatures.   In the first case, it is in their power, or in that of any eminent individual belonging to their body, to make this discovery promptly available.   I desire to obtain the help of medical men.   If I do not obtain such help, then it will be by their own act that I shall be forced into striving to make each man his own physician.

* About this time a fierce war was waged against the Bath by the medical journals.   In replying to one of these, Dr. Thudichum wrote as follows :—

" The public in this matter is far in advance of the medical profes-sion.   Our duty, as doctors of the healing art, simply is, to make our-selves acquainted with the use of this therapeutic instrument."

The following is the description of the bath taken by the members of the Medical Society then present :—

The Bath of Riverside.

FROM MR. ERASMUS WILSON'S "TURKISH BATH."

LET me endeavour to draw a sketch of Mr. Urquhart's bath—a bath dear to the memory of all early bathers— the bath at Riverside. We arrive at the door of the Frigidarium; we loosen the latchets of our shoes, and

we leave them behind the lintel; the portal opens, and
we enter. The apartment is small, but it is sunny and
bright; through the glass doors we see a balcony
festooned with the tendrils of the rose, now leafless and
out of bloom, for it is early winter; beyond the parapet
of the balcony are terraces of which the rose is still the
favoured ornament; further on, the rippled surface of a
boisterous, noisy stream; then meadows with grazing
herds and flocks, and the faithful horse; beyond, the
wooded hill, arching like an eyebrow around the bright
spot in which, as the apple of the eye, sparkles the
bath. At our side is a dureta, over-against us a
reclining chair, and along the sides of the apartment
a soft-cushioned divan; in mid space, a *sofra* supporting
a nargillé; while around are books, some Turkish orna-
ments and chibouques. We tread on the carpet of Persia,
and the clean, fresh matting of India. Opposite the
glass doors is an immense sheet of plate glass; through
it we see marble steps, and in the depths to which these
steps descend there is the reflection of the sun. Shades
of Mæcenas and Pliny, will ye not smile? Shade of
Seneca, look not austere at the luxury of this Briton of
ancient descent, who courts the rays of Phœbus, smiling
through festoons of roses, to visit the deepest pool of his
bath. Here he can swim, while the sun glistens in the
crystal drops that linger on his skin, or makes mimic
rainbows in the spray that he dashes before him in his
plunging revel.

A door opens by the side of the immense barrier of
glass; we enter; the door closes behind us. Then a
second door; we pass through that, and we are greeted

with a delightful atmosphere; experience tells us that
no place of terrestrial existence can yield that soft,
balmy, warm æther but one;—that one, the bath. We
descend two steps, and reach a platform, all of whitest
marble ; we become sensible of an increase of warmth
to the soles of our feet as we descend, and we are glad
to find soft napkins spread on the lower steps to catch
our footfall. Two steps more, and then another platform : the apartment expands at this point into a large
square lofty hall, and the marble platform stretches
from side to side the whole breadth of the hall. We
are sensible, as we stand on this platform, that we have
reached the tropical line of the bath, and that at no
great depth beneath our feet must be the Hypocaust.
To our right is a small square tent, surrounded with
scarlet hangings ; this is the *hottest of hots*, the Spartan
Laconicum ; it is placed immediately over the furnace.
We glance within the parting curtains of the entrance;
we see a cushioned divan of tempting softness. At a
later stage of our bath, we pass ten minutes in that fiery
tent ; its customary temperature is 240° or 250°.

On the left of our present station is another divan,
not enclosed by curtains like the other, but admitting
of being so if required. On this divan, at a later stage
of the bath, I spent many minutes of genuine enjoyment;
being farther from the furnace, but still over the meridian of the Hypocaust, it was less hot than the enclosed
tent : its common temperature is 170°. " If you would
like a breath of fresh air," said my host, " draw out
that plug." I saw a plug just above my head, just near
enough to reach by stretching out my hand. I with-

drew it, not because I wanted air, but in a spirit of obedience, or, if you will, of lazy indolence. What a reward! what a delicious gush of ambrosial air! Heavens! what Sybaritic contrivance is here? I looked round for the shade of old Pliny, expecting to see him peering over my shoulder; but he was not there; the modest Roman shade was abashed, was vanquished by the modern Mæcenas: the perfume was that of mignonette! Although the last of the season, enough remained to enable my fancy to judge how delicious that air must have been a month or two earlier. This was one of the ventilating-holes of the bath, and my host had brought the air that was to cool his bath from the perfumed atmosphere of a bed of mignonette. How I longed at that moment for one half-hour of summer, that I might test the other spiracles, that I might perchance inhale the breath of roses here, and violets or lilies there!

And now comes a deeper descent (four steps), and behold, I am on the floor of the bath. Still costly marble greets my tread. In the corner opposite the fiery tent is another divan; here, far removed from the torrid meridian, the temperature is still lower (about 150°), but the atmosphere is everywhere fresh: it is clear that ventilation is perfect, and there are no vapoury mists, no fleeting gauze of ghost-like moisture.

I am permitted to gaze about me for a while, when my host leads me to a small recess on the side corresponding with the couch of perfume. A curtain is withdrawn, and I perceive that the bottom of this recess is below the level of the floor, and that a marble step placed at one end breaks the descent to the bottom. The bottom, also, is peculiar : the marble slab slopes downwards to an opening, through which water finds its way into the drain. I am aware that this is the Lavaterina or Latrina—that here the novitiate is made to pass through the first ordeal of the bath. Before he entered the sacred precincts ·of the Apodyterium, he undid the latchets of his shoes : he left his shoes beyond the door ; he brought with him none of the dust of the external world into the portals of the bath. In the Frigidarium, or rather in the Apodyterium, he left behind him his vestments, and assumed the simple garb of the inner bath. Now, and before he can claim to select his place on the divans, he pays a further tribute to the god of purity : the outer layers of his scarf-skin must be peeled away—he must yield up his skin to the ordeal of the glove, the *gazul*, or the soap ; and then, semi-purified, he may range at will the apartment—he may explore at leisure the mysteries of the bath.

We seat ourselves on the clean marble at the edge of the Lavaterina ; our host plays the soft pad of *gazul* over the head, the back, the sides ; we complete the operation on the limbs and feet ourselves. Basin after basin of warm water rinses the *gazul* and the loosened epidermis from the surface, and we rise from the Lavaterina to recommence our observations.

Immediately in front of the flight of steps already described, and occupying the centre of the remaining wall of the hall, is a square pool, between four and five feet in depth, and reached by several steps. In this pool are two feet of water, perfectly cold, with a tap

from which as much may be obtained as may be
required. This water is pumped up from the river, and
filtered before it is admitted into the bath : it, like the
bather, is made to leave its dusty shoes outside the door,
and is thoroughly cleansed before it is permitted to
invade the sanctuary. In this pool, this *piscina*, the
bather refreshes himself with a plunge in cold water—
in the summer cooled down with ice—when he issues
heated from the " hottest of hots," or when he completes
the bath ; and here he may take his dip or his plunge,
his douche or his swim, with the sun shining in upon
his polished skin.

Having received my freedom of the bath in the
Lavaterina, I commenced a series of visits to all the
soft, the warm, the perfumed, the hot, the cool, the cold
nooks, that I could find. I rolled in enjoyment on the
divan by the side of the *piscina*, watching my " com-
panions of the bath," and especially a little Antinous,
or rather an infant Hercules, of five years of age, who
one while crept into the fiery tent, and another while
disported himself like a young sea-god, with evident
delight, in the cold *piscina*. I then took my place in
the higher temperature of the torrid zone, on the divan
that was breathed over by the sweet expirations of the
mignonette ; and anon crept into the tent with the
scarlet curtains serving as a door, and wondered that I
could breathe an atmosphere heated to 240° without
inconvenience.

It was now approaching the hour of breakfast, and
however disinclined I might be to leave the warm
world in which I had spent more than an hour, I was

ready to acknowledge certain material warnings of the charms of breakfast. Before, however, I could quit the bath, it was necessary that the pores, which had been all this while filtering the waste fluids of the body through their numberless apertures, should be made to close; and with this intent I descended into the pool, to experience and enjoy a new sensation. I crouched under the tap, while a cold torrent poured over me, the little Hercules catching greedily on his head any waste jets that glanced aside, and then shaking his flaxen ringlets over his face and shoulders with a joyous laugh. But my last experience was to come. At the word " Hold firm ! " a full pail of hot water rushed upon me like an avalanche, and was instantly followed by the same quantity of cold: this was repeated in quick succession a number of times, and then, when my host's arms seemed tired of the further repetition, I arose from the pool, and shook my soused frame on the platform above, with a feeling of freshness and vigour that I shall long remember—*remember when the bath and all its vagaries shall have become too familiar to suggest a note of their early impressions.*

I was soon warm enough to quit the region of water, and ascend into that of air—to quit the region of fire, and mount into that of the sun, then smiling beamingly in at the window. My host gave my head a good rub with a warm, soft Turkish napkin, and threw a warm mantle over my shoulders; and it was with a feeling of "divided duty," the bath on one side and the breakfast on the other, that I ascended to the Frigidarium. Throwing myself on a softly-cushioned dureta, a half-hour was spent in suggestive and instructive conversation, and then " to breakfast with what appetite we may." Shade of immortal Shakspeare! Speaking for myself, I should say, with the appetite of a man. Need I say more? This is my memory of the delicious bath at Riverside.

My host placed before me a dish, or rather a basket, of that wonderful Moorish food, the *kuscoussoo*, and our conversation naturally drifted away to the mode of preparing food pursued by different nations, and particularly to the mode of its preparation in the countries where each particular food is indigenous. I was struck with my host's remark, that while we draw food from other countries, we fail to learn the native manner of preparing that food; and that from our ignorance on this point we frequently deteriorate, and often destroy its properties altogether.

It is to be regretted that the very highest branch of the science of chemistry—that which has for its object the *preparation of the food* which God in His goodness has bestowed upon us for the sustenance and preservation of His greatest work, man himself—should be so miserably neglected. How much happier man's state would be if this department of chemistry were more cultivated and better understood!—how greatly would the nutritive power of food be developed, how much would be economized in its use! How much might even the life of man be prolonged! Of the many that die daily in their beds, surrounded by warm coverings, costly hangings, and sorrowing friends, there are many who die of absolute starvation—starved, because the modern science of culinary chemistry has no better nourishment to offer than abominable beef-tea, wretched mutton broth, miserable arrowroot or sago, or detestable gruel. Tell me, ye sick who have so narrowly escaped death, whether what I am saying is not perfectly true ; and that between nauseating physic on the one hand, and equally nauseating diet on the other, have you not " run the gauntlet " of destruction, from which your escape is indeed miraculous ?

Subjoined are the Regulations of this Bath.

Regulations.

The two baths at Riverside are open for the use of persons suffering from disease, only on the following conditions :—

The bath being the practice of a cleanly and a polite people, the habits of cleanliness and politeness must be observed. Visitors, therefore, must seek to learn from the attendants how to conduct themselves.

They must learn the distinction between the clean and the dirty. The clean is the part, whether of the apartment, furniture, or dress, which has not been exposed to pollution, or which, having been polluted, has undergone purification. Everything is polluted which has been in contact with filth. That is clean which, after having been washed clean, has had pure water poured over it. Shoes and boots which have

K

touched the dirt of the streets, can never touch the
" clean,"—that is, the floor of the apartment, whether
matting, marble, tiles, or boards, on which the clean
persons sit or walk.

In the East, the foot being always clean, the distinction of dirty and clean is marked by the shoe or the
bare foot. Until the same result is obtained here, it is
necessary to assume that the foot is clean, although it
be not so.

If any person, through heedless habits of Europeans,
steps with his boot or shoe on the clean part, it will not
do to say " Oh ! " and pull it back ; but he has himself
to announce to one of the attendants what he has done,
or he has, himself, to wash clean the part which he has
polluted : otherwise he will be practising deceit.

When a vessel of water is placed beside a European,
and he is told by means of it to wash a limb clean, he
will immediately take the filthy limb and pollute the
clean water, by putting the limb into the vessel, instead
of taking some of the water out of the vessel to wash
the limb. The habits of politeness and cleanliness enjoin
the contrary.

The European, not being accustomed to feet, but to
boots and shoes, when reduced to the use of feet by
entering the bath, is liable to accidents, by not knowing
how to manage his feet on polished marble: it is, therefore enjoined upon him to be very observant in the
manner of planting his feet.

In like manner, he must be very observant in order
to learn how to sit down, how to rise up, how to walk,
and how to move, and, above all things, to take care not

to sit on and crush cushions, which are intended for his support and comfort after he has seated himself.

Bathing is a process : that process is an elaborate one ; it comes without thought to those accustomed to it, and no form of words can convey it to those who are not. It can be acquired only by observation ; but no one can observe without desire and acuteness ; and herein lies the difficulty, because Europeans think that they know everything, sneer at what they do not know, and, not being polite, cannot be observant.* This is the cause why, during so many centuries, the bath has not been introduced ; and, the bath being introduced, this is the danger of its falling into desuetude. To make the people cleanly, it becomes necessary to make them also polite.

[The subject of Pollution and Purification has been treated of in the First Dialogue.]

* "The Japanese find it hard to forgive Europeans for walking in their boots over the matting which they only tread in their stocking feet. It is in their eyes as great an outrage as it would be in ours if a guest were to walk about on the table-cloth at our dinner, leaving his mark at every step. Yet there is no help for it ; and this the shop-keepers have begun to discover, for they frequently lay strips of cotton over their mats to preserve them from the foreigner's foot."—Niphon and Peehili, 6, E.B., Fonblanque, p. 20.

The Bath of the Finns.

(*See page* 83.)

FROM "TRAVELS OF ACERBI IN 1798-9," p. 296.

ANOTHER particular that appeared very singular among the customs of the Finns, was their baths and manner of bathing. Almost all the Finnish peasants have a small house built on purpose for a bath. It consists of only one small chamber, in the innermost part of which are placed a number of stones, which are heated by fire till they become red. On these stones, thus heated, water is thrown, until the company within be involved in a thick cloud of vapour. In this innermost part, the chamber is formed into two stories for the accommodation of a greater number of persons within that small compass ; and, it being the nature of heat and vapour to ascend, the second story is, of course, the hottest. Men and women use the bath promiscuously, without any concealment of dress, or being in the least influenced by any emotions of attachment. If, however, a stranger open the door and come on the bathers by surprise, the women are not a little startled at his appearance ; for, besides his person, he introduces along with him, by opening the door, a great quantity of light, which discovers at once to the view their situation, as well as forms. Without such an accident they

Bath of the Fins in 1807.

remain, if not in total darkness, yet in great obscurity, as there is no other window besides a small hole, nor any light but what enters in from some chink in the roof of the house or the crevices between the pieces of wood of which it is constructed.

I often amused myself with surprising the bathers in this manner, and I once or twice tried to go in and join the assembly; but the heat was so excessive that I could not breathe, and in the space of a minute at most, I verily believe must have been suffocated. I sometimes stepped in for a moment, just to leave my thermometer in some proper place, and immediately went out again, where I would remain for a quarter of an hour, or ten minutes, and then enter again, and fetch the instrument to ascertain the degree of heat. My astonishment was so great that I could scarcely believe my senses, when I found that those people remain together, and amuse themselves for the space of half an hour, in the same chamber, heated to the 70th or 75th degree of Celsius. The thermometer, in contact with those vapours, became sometimes so hot that I could scarcely hold it in my hands.

The Finlanders, all the while they are in this hot bath, continue to rub themselves, and lash every part of their bodies with switches formed of twigs of the birch-tree. In ten minutes they become as red as raw flesh, and have altogether a very frightful appearance. In the winter season they frequently go out of the bath, naked as they are, to roll themselves in the snow, when the cold is at 20, and even 30 degrees below zero.*

* I speak always of the thermometer of a hundred degrees, by Celsius.

They will sometimes come out, still naked, and converse together, or with any one near them, in the open air. If travellers happen to pass by while the peasants of any hamlet or little village are in the bath, and their assistance is needed, they will leave the bath, and assist in yoking or unyoking, and fetching provender for the horses; or in anything else, without any sort of covering whatever, while the passenger sits shivering with cold, though wrapped up in a good sound wolf's skin.

There is nothing more wonderful than the extremities which man is capable of enduring, through the power of habit.

The Finnish peasants pass thus instantaneously from an atmosphere of 70 degrees of heat, to one of 30 degrees of cold—a transition of a hundred degrees, which is the same thing as going out of boiling into freezing water! and what is more astonishing, without the least inconvenience, while other people are very sensibly affected by a variation of but five degrees, and in danger of being afflicted with rheumatism by the most trifling wind that blows. Those peasants assure you that without the hot vapour baths they could not sustain as they do, during the whole day, their various labours. By the bath, they tell you, their strength is recruited as much as by rest and sleep. The heat of the vapour mollifies to such a degree their skin that the men easily shave themselves with wretched razors, and without soap.

Waste of Fuel in England.

Note to page 64.

THE prodigality of nature in endowing England, as she has done, with a supply of fuel, has engendered among us a recklessness and wantonness in respect to it, which have entailed costliness to ourselves in the expense together with the destruction of the material itself.

Nor is it costliness alone that has ensued from wastefulness, but disease also. The very element by which we might attain to health when afflicted by disease, has been converted into a means of generating disease in the healthy body.

Warmth, especially with draughts, is the hot-bed of disease—*heat* is its cure. The open fire-place which destroys 23 parts out of 24 of the fuel, creates this warmth and prevents the idea of heat from arising as to curative means.

I had fixed on the proportion of 23 parts loss in 24 by experiments made long ago. I built two apartments, one with the ordinary open fire-place, the other flued, and found the difference as above stated.

I have since found this estimate too low. Taking the Hammam in Jermyn-street, and comparing it with so many London apartments of equal dimensions, multiplying them by 3 for the difference of temperature, and again by 2 for the continuity of heat during the night as well as the day, I find the difference of cost between what is charged in an hotel, or in lodgings, and the expenditure at the Hammam to stand as 39 to 40. The given apartments would cost for fires 120 shillings a day; the charge for the Hammam is three shillings !*

Were one of the Tartars, whose flued habitations are described by Atkinson, to visit London and to be asked on his return what he had seen as most remarkable in that capital, might he not be supposed to answer ?—

"I have seen a people to whom God has given much wood under ground. Some of them busy themselves in digging it up. Others spend the day in consuming it in open fire-places, and sending it to heat the clouds through straight chimneys."

We have hitherto indulged in the belief that the supply was inexhaustible. That likewise is now rudely brushed away. Buckland some years ago uttered the ominous words, " *The Extinction of Coal!*" Recently, Sir William Armstrong made this matter the feature of his address at Newcastle to the *British Association*. He said :—

"The question is not how long our coal will endure

---

* Since the period referred to there has been an increase of price of one shilling; this will be repaid by the improved working of the furnaces.

before absolute exhaustion is effected, but how long will these particular coal mines last which yield coal of a quantity and at a price to enable this country to maintain her present supremacy in manufacturing industry? So far as this particular district is concerned, it is generally admitted that 200 years will be sufficient to exhaust the principal seams, even at the present rate of working. If the production should continue to increase as it is now doing, the duration of those seams will not reach half that period.

"In an ordinary furnace employed to fuse or soften any solid substance, it is the excess of the heat of combustion over that of the body heated which alone is rendered available for the purpose intended. The rest of the heat, which in many instances constitutes by far the greater proportion of the whole, is allowed to escape uselessly into the chimney. The combustion also in common furnaces is so imperfect, that clouds of powdered carbon, in the form of smoke, envelope our manufacturing towns ; and gases, which ought to be completely oxygenized in the fire, pass into the air with two-thirds of their heating power undeveloped.

"Not less wasteful and extravagant is our mode of employing coal for domestic purposes. It is computed that the consumption of coal in dwelling-houses amounts in this country to a ton per head per annum of the entire population ; so that upwards of twenty-nine millions of tons are annually expended in Great Britian alone for domestic use. If any one will consider that one pound of coal applied to a well constructed steam-engine boiler evaporates ten pounds, or one gallon of water; and if he will compare this effect with the insignificant quantity of water which can be boiled off in steam by a pound of coal consumed in an ordinary kitchen fire, he will be able to appreciate the enormous waste which takes place by the common method of burning coal for culinary purposes.

" The simplest arrangements to confine the heat, and concentrate it upon the operation to be performed, would suffice to obviate this reprehensible waste. So also in warming houses, we consume in our open fires about five times as much coal as will produce the same heating effect when burnt in a close and properly constructed stove. Without sacrificing the luxury of a visible fire, it would be easy, by attending to the principles of radiation and convection, to render available the greater part of the heat which is now so improvidently discharged into the chimney. These are homely considerations— too much so, perhaps, for an assembly like this ; but, I trust, that an abuse involving a useless expenditure, exceeding in amount our income-tax, and capable of being rectified by attention to scientific principles, may not be deemed unworthy of the notice of some of those whom I have the honour of addressing."

Clothing not Requisite in our Climate.

(See p. 88.)

Cork Examiner, January 1857.

THE subject of the costume of the ancient Britons has often been discussed; it has been asserted that they were naked. Those who opposed that view adduced as reasons the coldness and variable nature of the climate. The question has been set at rest by an experiment which has recently been made on a child at St. Anne's, Blarney, near Cork. The child is fourteen months old, and is the son of Mr. ——, who determined to ascertain what the human frame would bear. The child is perfectly naked night and day; he sleeps without any covering, in a room with the thermometer at 38 degrees; from this he goes into a bath at 118 degrees; he sometimes goes to sleep in the bath; he is perfectly indifferent to heat or cold; is lively, active, cheerful, and intelligent; his appearance constantly reminds the observer of the best efforts of our best painters and sculptors. Therein is the "beau ideal;" he is the reality. His simple, graceful, natural, easy, and ever-varying postures are charming. He arrests the attention and commands the admiration of all who see him. The peculiar character of his skin is very striking; it is exquisitely healthy and beautiful. It may be compared to the rays of the sun streaming through a painted window.

During the progress of the experiment, he has cut three teeth without manifesting any of the disagreeable symptoms usual to children in that condition. He appears to be quite insensible to pain. Occasionally he has an ugly fall, but not a sound escapes from his lips. His manners, demeanour, and general behaviour are equally striking. His mode of saluting a person is to take the hand in a graceful manner and kiss it. He is under the complete control of his father, and is perfectly quiet during meals, and also whenever he is told to be so. He goes about all day, amusing and occupying himself in a quiet way. No one accustomed to children would know there was a child in the house. So incredible are these results, that some of the residents at St. Anne's regard the whole matter with mingled feelings of horror, amazement, and wonder. Those who have made a careful observation for themselves, and prefer the evidence of their eyes rather than their ears, see nothing but to admire and respect. No doubt, some of them would even go so far as to repeat the experiment on their own children, were it not for the fear of that terrible question, "what will Mrs. Grundy say?"

Dyspepsia Treated by One Meal a Day.

(See page 106.)

SINCE the period when this answer was given I have had further experience, which I desire to record, on two grounds. First, as the first case in which I found the bath of no value directly; and secondly, because relief, and I may now say cure, was obtained by a treatment based on the general grounds relating to dyspepsia laid down in my answer of February, 1861.

The species of dyspepsia was that manifested by pain in the regions of the stomach, that is at the entrance under the left ribs, after the operation of digestion had been gone through ; never appearing whilst there was food in the stomach, not evincing itself merely at the end of digestion, but continuing long afterwards, sometimes extending to ten hours. It was momentarily allayed by food, but then it involved inability to receive food, as evinced by loss of appetite and repugnance for food. The term dyspepsia, meaning difficulty of digestion, is not in this case properly applied, since the digestion was excellent, but only the appetite failed. Whatever I could eat I could digest, the difficulty was to find out a species of food that I could swallow. Every kind of food was tried without the slightest difference as regards the pain.

When the pain first manifested itself it was relieved by a small dose of alkali. But as each day went by and it returned with unerring regularity, the dose of alkali had to be increased. Likewise the effect was only temporary. In an hour, or half an hour, or a quarter of an hour, the pain returned in full vigour. At night this became exceedingly distressing : just as I dropped off to sleep I was awakened by the pain, and after I had taken a certain amount of alkali there was no more sleep for me until morning dawned.

The disorder having gone on increasing in violence and intractibility, had reached in November last the point at which there seemed to be no longer any hope. Sleep deserted me, strength was gone, neither sofa nor bed afforded me any rest; the extremities were hot and cold by turns, at times cramp possessed itself of the limbs ; all mental exercise was impossible, and life became a burden. When, by change of place or weather, I recovered a little, five minutes of mental application, or even a passing, if a painful thought, would at once reproduce the pain and the prostration. My only relief was in the alkalies, which I took to the amount of an ounce and a half in one night.

I continued the use of the alkali despite the objection of my medical advisers, as I was resolved, if possible, not to allow the substance of the stomach itself to be injured.

· The malady had grown upon me whilst I was taking
the bath, and despite of it. I therefore gave it up for
considerable periods, but without the least benefit. It
did, however, afford me alleviation of the pain for the
moment ; and to it I must attribute the power of throwing off the large amount of alkali, and subsisting on the
very small amount of food I was able to take. During
this time I tried all kinds of diet—at one time meat,
at another vegetables, at another fish ; the least objectionable I found to be turtle soup : total abstinence
from wine and other stimulants for weeks together.

I submitted myself to medical treatment, and in
every case aggravation of the symptoms followed the
administration of the remedies. There were severally
prescribed for me, arsenic, quinine, opium, belladonna,
strychnine, carbon, bismuth with hydrocyanic acid, and
colchicum. That is to say, I was treated for sub-acute
inflammation of the stomach, ague, flying gout, &c. So
that to the bodily suffering was superadded utter hopelessness by the uncertainty attached to every reasoning,
and the failure of every system.

Thus it was that at the end of the month of September, being thrown entirely on my own resources, I made
up my mind that the malady from which I suffered
could be nothing save an undue discharge of gastric
juice. On this diagnosis I immediately proceeded to
act, in the first instance by ice taken internally ; and
subsequently by reducing myself to one meal a day. I
swallowed the ice crushed and in large quantities, the
extremest limit being 1½lb. in a quarter of an hour.
The effect was instantaneous. I was on the first occa-

sion for forty-eight hours without a trace of pain; unfortunately I again yielded to the representations of a medical friend, diminished the dose of ice and took some belladonna and opium. The pain returned again. For two months I continued the ice, but not to such an extent as at first; I abstained from everything hot, and from taking anything between my two meals. During this time there were intervals of days during which I was quite free from pain. Still it was evident that I had not overcome the morbid state, as the least mental exertion or anxiety brought it back again.

In the month of November I had recourse to the further expedient of putting myself upon one meal a day. My medical friends looked upon this step with as much alarm as they had done upon the use of the ice. There was, however, one of them who had previously treated me on the theory of "tender patch" with bismuth and hydrocyanic acid; who, on my stating to him the conclusion I had come to, and the treatment I had consequently proposed to adopt, used these words:

"That is pathology and logic combined. It is a treatment that deserves to succeed. As appetite grows you may have a struggle to maintain your resolve. Do not give in through a feeling of faintness: yield only to positive hunger."

On the 3rd of February I wrote to a medical friend, who has laid me under heavy obligation for the anxiety he has expended on the treatment of my case.

"Red House, Feb. 3d, 1864.

"I am now in the fourth day of *absolute freedom* from pain; after this long loathing of food, an enormous appetite. Also the

symptom I wrote to you about has disappeared. As the result
has not been arrived at, as at the beginning of the experiment,
under a total cessation of mental occupation, and as the progress has been gradual and the period of time extended, and as
moreover, the weather is at this moment anything but favourable for me, I think I may consider it now as conclusively
obtained. It is now above four months since I resorted to the
ice, and above two months since I adopted the one meal a day.
"In further confirmation I have to add that, following Dr.
Bryce's suggestion, not to give in from a feeling of faintness,
and only to yield under the pressure of positive hunger, I have
during the last few days been taking almost two meals a day.
I am, in fact, now living again instead of dragging on a miserable
and hopeless existence.
"I have mentioned this as it will be satisfactory to you, not
only on my account, but I hope also as establishing the proposition in respect to the treatment of dyspepsia, that the way to
ruin a human stomach is to eat little and often. In this, as in
the other points which I have worked out bearing on bad
habits, a medical man is debarred from accepting it and employing it save on the condition of recantation. This can be dared
only by a pure and upright as well as a strong and courageous
mind. This is a natural and necessary consequence of ceasing
to administer drugs and commencing to rectify evil habits.
"I beseech you do not run off on there being cases when an
invalid cannot endure food and must have it administered in
infinitesimal doses : I refer to 'little and often' as *applied to
the treatment of dyspepsia*. It is against that persuasion that I
say, dyspepsia is the production of 'little and often.' In
other words, where 'much and seldom' prevails, dyspepsia is
unknown. But of course patients are impatient. They will
swallow anything, but abstain from nothing.
"I have further to say that if I had to deplore the obstinacy
with which my ailments refused to adapt themselves to your
theory of interchangeable maladies, I now have to rejoice
thereat. For if gout, herpes, and dyspepsia would invade me
simultaneously, they have now simultaneously taken their flight,
as foul harpies driven from their meal."

L

The last sentence suggests the " one meal a day" as the treatment for other maladies, beside those of the stomach. Here were two concomitant maladies; these have wholly disappeared, together with the alleviation of the stomach disorder. Had I had recourse to the one meal a day for the herpes and for the gout, and either had been removed, a strong case would have been offered in favour of this treatment for either. I have already stated as a proposition, that all constitutional derangements (blood poisons) proceed from the stomach, and that the disturbance of the stomach proceeds from indulgence, not in regard to the nature of the aliments, but in regard to the repetition of the meals.

With regard to appetite, the return of it was the first effect of the one meal a day; so that after the first twenty-four hours of abstinence I was able to eat more in the one meal than I had formerly done in the two. I must observe that I had suffered from an exceedingly bad appetite for some months before the pain showed itself.

Shortly after the date of this letter the pain returned. I consequently returned to the one meal a day, and again after ten days subdued the pain. I have gradually proceeded in this fashion, until I have now got back to the two meals without recurrence of suffering.

A tumbler of milk gave rest for one hour and a quarter exactly; my greatest sufferings have resulted from the attempt to allay the pain by these repeated draughts of milk. This expedient I had recourse to whilst still looking to medical conclusions, and yielding to my medical man's anxiety that I should " *give the stomach something to do.*"

I have found that brandy and water (sugar and lemon included) produces no evil effects. So also in Beaumont's experiments on St. Martin, brandy did not excite the flow of the gastric juice.

During this experiment I made an incidental discovery which may prove hereafter a great alleviation for human suffering. I can best describe it as "MOTION AS A MODE OF CURE."

I had been several days at Cowes, on shore, and suffering very severely. I was then several days afloat, but at anchor immediately opposite the window of the Gloucester Hotel where I had endured so much pain, but there days and night enjoying complete immunity. Had I gone to sea I should have of course attributed the change to the vague words—now at least felt to be vague and unmeaning—"at sea." I at once suspected that it was the motion that had wrought the change. However, to leave no doubt on the point, a corroboration was afforded me day by day, during a fortnight, in a friend troubled with insomnia, who slept soundly every night that I was free from pain, and who was unable to sleep on two or three nights during that fortnight, when also my pains returned; that is, on nights when being under canvas or at anchor there was absolutely no motion.

The rationale being evident for medical men in the connexion of the stomach and the brain, and in the effect of motion on the latter, I will not dwell on.

The motion of the waves (for very little sufficed) being easily imitated by a swinging cot, caused to vibrate, it follows that by means of the assiduity of a single donkey, during the night a hundred patients might enjoy invigorating sleep, who now seek that solace in vain from morphia.

This motion is not exercise, it is motion applied externally. It is well known that the nausea of sea sickness is counteracted by exercise.

I should, therefore, wish to add something to my answer on the 25th of February, 1861.

" The caustic juices required in the part of the operation performed in the stomach itself, would, if emitted without the presence of food, waste and corrode it. The emission of the gastric juice is therefore an electrical and most delicate operation. It may be compared to a hair trigger. A person eating frequently is like a boy taking a pistol with a hair trigger and snapping it, until at length it flies off at half-cock. No medicine will reach it. The medical man may, indeed, reach it, if at once a physiologist and a logician. The bath will be of service to him, however, by allaying the craving or false appetite, so that less mental effort will in abstaining from food more than once a day be required."

The bath can no more reach this malady than it could an arrow-head lodged in the leg. The malady is in the strength of the secretion, the bath does not tend to dilute secretions. I have thus discovered a disease in which the bath will act but a subordinate part.

The discoverer of a cape is considered entitled to give to it a name. Diseases are not so easily or so often discovered as promontories. We have the rare example of Dr. Bright who discovered the malady, but not the cure, and died of the malady that bears his name. Had I been afflicted with his disease I should not have been able to define it, but I should have had the remedy. Having discovered this species of Dyspepsia, I have the right of giving it a name; that name shall be PEPTO-RHÆA, or *flow of gastric juice,* implying undue discharge, as the due discharge would not be a disease.

This malady is not correctly defined by the word, though included in dyspepsia. In dyspepsia, food is not digested because the solvents are feeble; in Pepto-rhæa the stomach is disordered and ultimately destroyed, because they are strong.

The treatment, however, is the same, because in both alike irritation has to be allayed.

It may be said that there is no novelty in the symptoms here described. Symptoms in some respects analogous, no doubt, are common. There is pain after digestion has been completed, and pain relieved by alkali. This is mentioned by Dr. Watson as one species of dyspepsia, and he ascribes it to an undue quantity of acid remaining in the stomach as a result of digestion, but whether derived from the gastric juice or the food, he is uncertain. If this were all, however, how is it that the pain returned after having been removed by alkali, although no food had been taken in the meantime? It is evident that if the malady in my case began in this common form, it afterwards transformed itself into another, and that form one to which Dr. Watson's theory does not apply. I think I may then conclude that this disease is fortunately as rare as it is extreme. It seems to be contingent on a peculiar condition of cerebral super-excitation, into which there enters at once continuous effort and unceasing anxiety.

I cannot end without subjoining some extracts from the standard work of Dr. Watson, because the observations he makes are suggestive of the conclusion I have arrived at; and would, I apprehend, have led him to the same, but for the habit of connecting the exhibition of some particular drug with every morbid condition of the body.

DR. WATSON ON THE GASTRIC JUICE.

"Dr. Budd believes the secretion of the gastric juice to be a reflex process; which he assimilates to, and illustrates by, the secretion of tears. Tears may be presently made to flow by direct mechanical irritation of the conjunctiva, or indirectly, by pungent vapours acting upon the nostrils, or by certain feelings of the mind. In like manner the secretion of the gastric juice may, he conceives, be excited, not only by some stimulus applied immediately to the mucous surface of the stomach, but also under certain diseased conditions, or injuries of distant organs (as the brain and lungs), and even by *mental emotion.* In this way he would explain the occurrence of perforation or softening, after death, by blows on the head, when no food had been recently introduced into the stomach, and after death by pulmonary consumption. That more or less digestion of the tissues of the stomach after death is exceedingly *common*, is a fact which was well known to John Hunter, but which has been lost sight of by the majority of more recent observers."

He then refers to Dr. Budd as pointing out circumstances that interfere to prevent this effect of the gastric juice, one of which is the presence of ammonia and alcohol in the stomach, which have been given in some medicinal form. Because "the solvent property of the fluid is arrested whenever its acidity is neutralized by the admixture of an *alkali.* This has been fully proved by Spallanzani, and others. The same is true of *alcohol.*"
—*Watson's Principles and Practice of Physic*, p. 412, 413.

Medical Treatment of Rheumatism.

(See page 94.)

IN perusing the following description of the means to which medical science has recourse in the hope of affording a precarious relief, the reader must bear in mind that the malady is one which immediately yields under a change of climate—the Turkish bath is no more. The case of rheumatism is not peculiar, it is only given as an example.

" Most persons who have been for any considerable time in practice have their own favourite method of conducting the disorder to its termination. While many employ free blood-letting, and other antiphlogistic remedies, some, on the contrary, even in the present day, put their trust in bark. Some give large doses of calomel in the outset of the disease, such as half a scruple or a scruple, without or with a grain of opium ; and they repeat the dose daily, or oftener, with purgatives perhaps intervening, till the urgent symptoms give way ; and in this manner I have seen the disease apparently cut short. But I have also known many instances in which the disease was painful and protracted, and obstinate, although this practice was adopted early, and fairly prosecuted. Some physicians give smaller and more frequent doses of calomel and opium ; and some think opium alone to be as useful as this combination. Others believe or depend mainly upon colchicum ; others, upon large and repeated doses of conium; and some attempt the cure of acute rheumatism by sweating the patient by means of guaiacum, and similar stimulant medicines, and a profusion of bed clothes."

" We may by leeches, or cupping, or cold applications, be able perhaps to subdue the inflammation in a knee or an elbow ; but from the *migratory character of the disorder*, we incur the risk by such topical measures of *repelling the poison into the circulating blood*, and of thus giving it a new and more serious location."

" I believe few persons now adopt the plan of forced perspiration for the cure of acute rheumatism. Formerly it was the fashion to give sudorifics, Dover's powder, or antimony in large doses, and the patient was ' accintus ad sudorum ;' covered up in bed between thick blankets, with a hot bottle or brick at his feet. But in the severe unequivocal fibrous form of rheumatism the perspiration is profuse without any artificial means being used to excite it, and it is not accompanied by the smallest alleviation of the pain : nay, sometimes the patients will tell you that they are worse, in that respect, while the sweating continues."

" Colchicum is very apt to produce deadly nausea and vomiting, griping and diarrhœa; and when these consequences ensue from its use, the inflammation of the joints often subsides entirely. At any rate if the rheumatism does not give way when the stomach and bowels become thus affected, you may be certain that to push the colchicum further would be useless."

" There are some cases which yield readily to calomel and opium; and in the fibrous disease, I think that calomel and opium are the remedies to which, after sufficient bleeding, you will do well to trust. For it is under this character that the extension of the disease to the membranes of the heart is so liable to happen; and if anything can protect the patient against this fearful complication of a malady, which previously attended by no danger, becomes by this addition, almost necessarily fatal, it is in my opinion *mercury*."

" Dr. Latham has given a masterly analysis of the purpose, and the effects of the main remedies for acute rheumatism, both in their separate use and in their varied combinations. He shows how, in one case, venæsection may suffice, by subduing vascular action and febrile heat; how, in another, opium may solve the disease by allaying nervous disquietude and pain; how calomel and purgatives, in a third, may cleanse the liver and bowels, and the whole system of a *colluvies of morbid secretions, and so set the sufferer free;* and finally, how, in most instances, these three remedial remedies may together, or with occasional interjection of colchicum, achieve the desired end more certainly, and with less of distress, and of expenditure of vital power, than could either of them singly."

" In the form of chronic rheumatism, what some call passive, the remedies that answer best are of a different kind. The pain is alleviated by friction of the joint, and the patients are most comfortable when they are warm in bed, and especially when moderate perspiration is present. *They are singularly benefited by summer weather.* Persons who are much troubled by this wearing complaint, and who can afford to live where they please, would do well to take up their residence in a warm climate. Wheresoever they may be, such patients should be protected against atmospheric *vicissitudes by warm clothing :* they should *be cased in flannel from the neck downwards.*"*

The effect of " summer weather," which ought to have taught everything, is lost, being converted into " warm clothing," which is exactly the reverse in its action on the morbid human body of " summer weather."

Rheumatism is no more a disease than gout, scrofula, consumption, cancer, or St. Vitus's dance ; it is merely a symptom of that general disease—an inert skin.

* Watson's Principles and Practice of Physic, vol. ii., pp. 677-683.

One Meal a Day—Milk Diet.

(See.p. 93.)

No expositions on this subject have descended to us from antiquity, but indications are not wanting* which confirm the existing records of ancient practice in the subsisting habits of races of unchangeable character.

To me it seems an impossibility that the earth should have ever been peopled, had man either required or indulged in, three or even two meals a day. I hold, also, that the important historic periods of the human race have been the passage, 1st. From the one meal to the two; 2nd. From the two to the three; and 3rd. From the three to a still greater number. The first epoch seems to extend downwards to that great disturbance of pre-existing things by general conquests,

---

* In that interesting portion of the correspondence of Cicero with Atticus which refers to his government of Cilicia, we are incidentally informed that the old military practice of the Republic was, to eat once a day. Cicero, relieved the provincials from the charge of feeding his troops. His lieutenant disobeyed him under the authority of an edict of the Senate. Still, as Cicero remarks, it was but *once a day*, conformably to the old rule, that this exaction was made.

such as were carried on by the Macedonians and the Romans.*

The second epoch for the Western world may include the period since the Roman conquest to our days. The continent of Europe knew no third meal to the close of the great wars. It is since then that the English breakfast has invaded the European races, though only as yet partially.

The third epoch has commenced in England only within a couple of generations, but it has advanced among the English colonists of the new world, where already the most alarming symptoms of decay reveal themselves in the organs. The dentists, aurists, oculists, and druggists of the United States surpass in proportion those of England, as much as those of England do those of the Continent.

Having met the most pertinacious and bitter scepticism in physiologists and medical men, whenever I have narrated what I myself have witnessed among primitive tribes, and among those which subsist exclusively on milk—being constantly told that it is impossible for a man to do his work on a single meal, or to subsist at all on a single meal, if consisting only of milk, I subjoin a couple of notes giving incidental testimony on both points.

15, St. George's-terrace, South Kensington,
March 9th, 1864.

DEAR SIR,—About three months ago I had the privilege of some conversation with you, when you mentioned that you had derived benefit from taking only one meal a day. This

* See De Quincey on " The (no) Breakfast of the Romans."

reminded me of the custom of working men in Chili. A short time afterwards I asked a gentleman whom I had known in Valparaiso if I was correct. He could not speak with certainty on the subject as regarded Chili, but he had travelled on horseback in Mexico and the country about Buenos Ayres, and there, he said, the invariable custom amongst the travelling servants was, to take a cup of chocolate before starting, and take one full meal on arriving at the end of the day's journey.

It was not until yesterday that I had an opportunity of asking another gentleman, from whom I hoped to obtain more definite information.

He told me that the Copiapo miners, who are amongst the strongest in the world, and do very hard work, dine in the middle of the day on red beans (frijoles); but they do take a light supper.

The workmen in Uruguay take only one meal a day, which consists of beef and maize.

　　　　I am, &c.,　　　　Andrew John Robertson.

————

　　　　　　　　33, Westbourne Villas,
　　　　　　　　Blomfield Road, Paddington, W.
　　　　　　　　30th December, 1863.

My Dear Sir,—There are Hindu hermits or penitents called Tapasees, who live in the depths of forests and mountains, in almost every part of India, from Cashmere and Nepaul to Cape Comorin. Their food is exclusively the milk of the cow. They generally boil it in order to be certain that it is pure and unadulterated. Our gymnosophists are now fast disappearing; there are, however, a few instances here and there. At Cashmere, for instance, there is one now living, whose only food is milk. As to people generally, in domestic life, they live upon milk and fruit only on fasting days. As regards the question of one meal per day, there is a class of Brahmins called Sarāvugēe, who follow that custom; these men are employed as soldiers in the British army in the present day, and it is a custom extended even to their families. I may also mention that many persons, from a religious motive, restrict themselves to one meal a day, and are, on that account, greatly esteemed.

Believe me, &c.,   C. Pooroshottum.

Veneration in any part of the East can be obtained by no one save on this condition. As to India, the record of early usages is preserved alike in the Brahminical rule of eating but once of a meal, in which fire and water are required, and in the observance of widows who are allowed but one meal.

The periods of meals, like all these phenomena in connexion with the use of various degrees of temperature, may be understood some 500 years hence, should in the interval a man of head arise. That it is possible that such an idea should penetrate into a modern and even a scientific mind I have proof of in a note from Dr. Brereton before his departure for Sydney, in which he expresses his regret at not being able to pay me a parting visit, in order that we might discuss "that most important of all propositions, as affecting the permanent condition of man—the periods of his meals."

It is a mere indication that can·here be given, to treat the subject properly would require a volume.

On the Art of Constructing a Turkish Bath ;

ITS ECONOMY AS A MEANS OF CLEANLINESS.

Read at the Society of Arts, February, 1862.

THE subject to which I have the privilege of inviting your attention this evening, is neither a construction of art, nor a principle of nature ; it is neither a social institution, nor a pathological operation ; it is neither a domestic convenience, nor a religious observance ; it is neither a means of sobriety, nor an economy of food ; it is neither a psychological adaptation to relieve the over-strained brain, nor a gymnastic device to strengthen the body. It is none of these as exclusive of the others, for it combines them all—a habit.

A habit is only spoken of when unknown : it is, therefore, a habit to be introduced. This habit, by rendering us more cleanly, will give us greater strength of muscle, greater power of digestion, greater immunity from disease, greater facilities in recovering health, a longer term of life, a greater contentment in life, more

DIAGONAL ANGLES

MAG

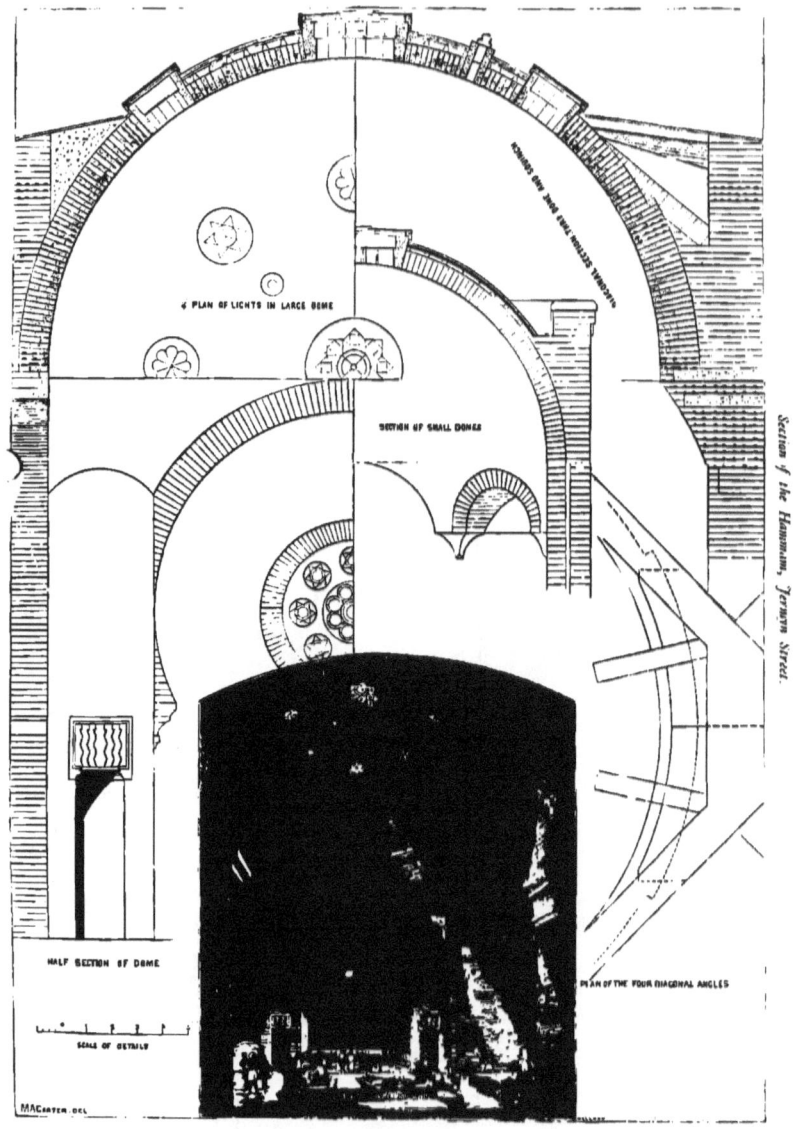

PLAN OF LIGHTS IN LARGE DOME

SECTION OF SMALL DOMES

HALF SECTION OF DOME

SCALE OF DETAILS

PLAN OF THE FOUR DIAGONAL ANGLES

MACARTER. DEL

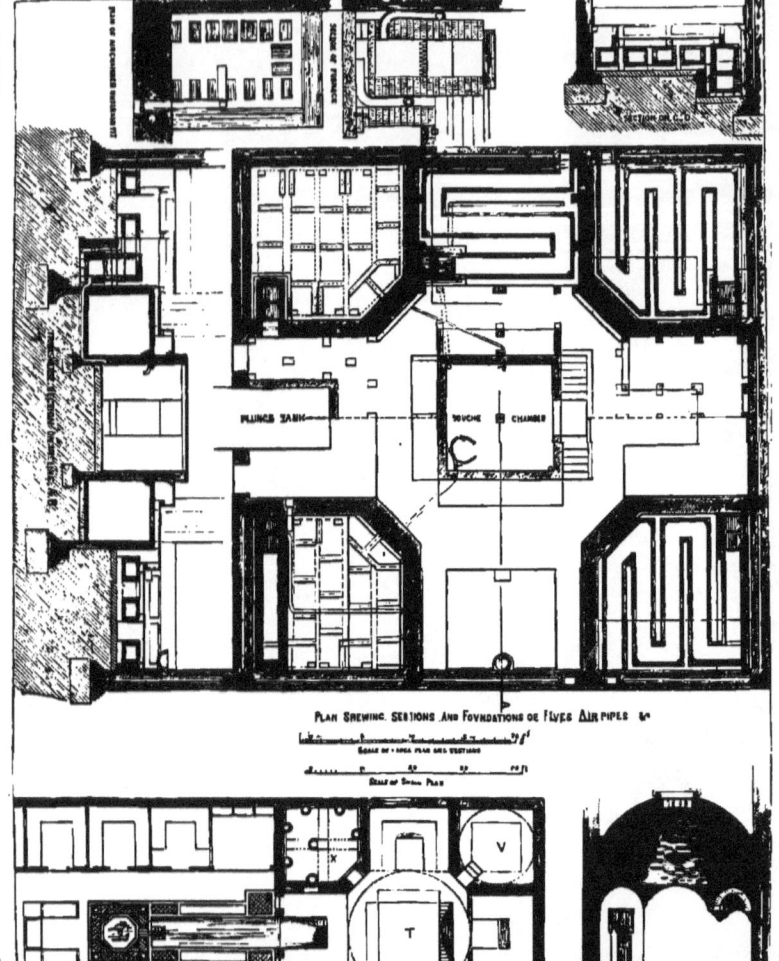

PLAN SHEWING. SECTIONS. AND FOUNDATIONS OF FLUES AIR PIPES &c

PLAN OF BATH AND PORTION OF COLD ROOM

equanimity of mind, less desire for foreign stimulants, whether physical or mental, which will bring with it a larger share of self-respect, and diminish those causes of disrespect to which we may be exposed from others.

This habit is no invention. It is as old as the human race. . It has ruled in all climes ; it has belonged to every grade of human culture, or human destitution. It has prevailed long ago in these very islands, to whose inhabïtants it has now to be presented as something claiming their study and deserving their adoption. I do not, however, disguise from myself the arduous nature of the enterprise I have undertaken. The introduction of a habit, judged of by human experience, must be far more difficult than the conquest of an empire. Religions may be introduced, constitutions implanted ; but the engrafting of the familiar practices of one people on the stock of another, by the rarity of its occurrence in the history of man, must evidently be attended by next to insurmountable difficulties.

We have arrived at a stage peculiarly adapted for calm and fruitful investigation ; the subject is neither strange as new, nor uninteresting as familiar. It is but the first uncertain steps of experiment, that have doubtingly as yet been made. There is enough to show that it may command public adoption, and yet enough to show that it is exposed to public reprobation. We are no longer at the point when, speaking as in the air, it has to be said, such and such is a Turkish bath. The obstacle and danger now proceed from the impressions derived from false experience. Persons go to the so-called baths spread over the country, and, with only rare exceptions, come away thinking they understand, and saying they have been to, a Turkish bath. The experiment would have been profitably made only, if they said, "I now know what a Turkish bath is not." At least, it can now be said to them, "It is neither a cellar with a furnace, nor a row of hospital beds. Do not imagine that in entering and passing through rooms strangely fitted up, in London and provincial dwelling-houses, you any more experience the sensation of a Roman or a Turk, than you behold the majestic Thermæ of the one people, or the Hammam of the other."

Time must be invested in every enterprise which he is destined to consecrate. Time, if put to profit, is experiment, and experiment that is profitable means failure. Failure has ever signalised the strides towards perfection. You have commenced your experiments; they are excessively encouraging in this sense. It now depends on the public temperament alone whether this shall pass off as an ephemeral delusion, or remain as an increase of the good things that fortune showers down, and a diminution of the pains and penalties attached to the larger number of our fellow-creatures, too lowly for her smiles to reach.

This nation at this moment presents the spectacle either of a prey furnished to unscrupulous empirics, or of a public judgment adapting itself to admit a great conviction. But it is by the effort to discard the spurious imitation that the public judgment will have disciplined and qualified itself to admit and to accept the new conception.

When on other occasions you have met or may meet

in this place, the inducement is the acquisition of knowledge. The order in which the spheres revolve, the processes by which the various arts of life are carried on, how some man has added an additional dose of sand to bricks, or extended the limits of the chamber in which combustion is effected. This evening that to which you will listen concerns yourselves. The knowledge to be acquired is, how a man may do for himself in reference to matters concerning him in the most vital manner, and which he has absolutely hitherto committed to others. Each has, therefore, not something to learn in regard to what others have done, but something to acquire as a possession for himself—a possession which, from my own experience, I can state, and in this I am confirmed by many, that if it were to be calculated in money, I would not exchange for any sum that could be set down, if considered as entering into the superfluities of existence.

Nor is it only what a man may do for himself, but, if so minded, the well-being of others becomes a part of his own by his desire to promote it, and here is an opportunity of effecting much at little cost. The effect upon the domestic condition of the working classes of the habit which prevails among the similar order of the Turkish population, would require, as a parallel in relief, that some ten millions were remitted in the yearly taxes, or an equivalent subscribed by individual charity. I do not mean to say that the benefit to be derived from this habit would be of no more value to them than that number of millions a year, but that, by promoting this habit among the working classes, each may contribute more to the public well-being, and therefore to the public fortune, than any amount of

M

private sacrifice for other objects would effect. The first public address I ever delivered on this subject was in 1847, to a body of working-men in the borough I then represented in Parliament. When I had concluded, a medical man, who was in the chair, said, " You are poor men, and every penny is to you of value. Yet I will tell you, without the slightest hesitation, that had a fifty pound note been put in each of your pockets, the value to you and to your families would not be equal to what you have received to-night, if you only have sense enough to put it to profit."

Among remarkable things, perhaps there is none more so than the losing of discoveries. We have had in this island of ours, 2,000 years ago, the enjoyment of this benefit and luxury. You are now assembled to learn something in regard to this matter, which has neither been heard of nor dreamt of during these long years. In the meantime, in those lands, where the Romans equally had sway, those happy habits of social and domestic life have been preserved by men destitute of philosophic tendencies. Turkey, which offers to you the bath to-day, will have it no longer in two generations. I myself have seen, in one country, the extinction of it. My first acquaintance with it was in Greece. Greece knows it no longer. That polished Greece—that accumulation of small and fervid existencies—where the imagination of man burnt most brightly, when engaged in its struggle with the Turks, and, under the imitation of the West, dropped their bath. To-day, at Constantinople, the young Turks, imitating Europe, abstain from going to the bath; and the last time I

visited that capital the only bath in which I found the
old usages maintained was in a small nook of the
Dardanelles. What we are doing now in England may
prevent its loss in the East. A series of articles in the
Medical Gazette of Constantinople, wherein, for the first
time, type has been used in reference to the bath, has
been prompted by what we have been doing in England.
If the thing itself be of any value, it is worth having,
not only because of its worth, but because otherwise it
will be lost to future generations. We have had the
ruins of the Romans—we have had the classical literature of our universities; that has not sufficed to convey
the thing to us. Dead knowledge will not give you the
living thing. You cannot prepare a dinner out of the
organic remains of extinct breeds of cattle; no more
can you get the habits which belonged to institutions,
and the practices which are dependent upon those
habits, by mere ink and paper. Even in familiar
conversation familiar things find no part; it is the
exceptional which alone claims attention. To a far
greater degree the rule holds in formal composition.
Notwithstanding the habits of literary description
among us, a future age would find it impossible to
arrive at any exact perception of our mode of carrying
through the most ordinary of the occupations of life.
How much, then, is the difficulty increased of ascer-
taining, by written records, what the practices are and
were of those nations who have or had the bath, being
or having been, all of them, the reverse of loquacious?
We are, to this day, unable positively to say, what were
the taxes in Rome. It is not, therefore, surprising that

we should be absolutely destitute of data as to the origin among them of the bath, and nearly in the same condition as to the original process, and the modifications in successive ages of the operation itself. It is, therefore, utterly impossible that any remains of Rome can enable us to-day to construct the thermæ of Rome for the use of our people. And this is the reason why I make it a point that this shall be called the "Turkish bath." That word irritates no doubt our self-love. Each man says, "Am I to be taught by barbarians?" A man better than others is distinguished by the moderation of his self-esteem. But how can you constrain a man, when falsely confident in himself, to adopt a new thing unless you conquer his pride? The Turks have preserved the bath from ancient times; they have also the habits and manners belonging to it; and, therefore, when you say "Turkish bath," you confess that you have to go to the Turks for it.

We have, indeed, the living practice of the Turks, but were the bath to disappear from amongst them, what record would remain to a future age? Scarcely more than a wholly undidactic incident in the Arabian Nights. Nor have our travellers, with all the desire to find pictures to transfer to their volumes, served us better. When my attention was first turned to the subject, and I commenced immediately to investigate, I took up successively every work on the East, and the disappointment which followed set me on noting and recording the operation. With that description I will now begin. I will then proceed to the edifice, so as to connect the operations with the structure. I will then lay before you the steps which, under the influence of trifling incidents, I made towards the investigation of the action of heat, whence has arisen the present application of the bath to the cure of diseases, and then I shall indicate the new field opened in regard to science, both chemically and pathologically, in the distinction between transmitted and radiating caloric. The application of the whole will consist in showing that this best method of cleanliness is also the cheapest, and may easily be realised for the whole body of the people, either gratuitously or at a trifling cost.

The bath, when first seen by the Turks, was a practice of their enemies, religious and political; they were themselves the filthiest of mortals ; they had even instituted filth by laws and consecrated it by maxims. No sooner did they see the bath than they adopted it ; made it a rule of their society, a necessary adjunct to every settlement. Princes and Sultans endowed such institutions for the honour of their reign.

In adopting they purified it from immorality and excess, carrying the art of cleanliness to perfection; they made themselves the most sober-minded of the nations of the earth. This arose from the simplicity of their character and the poverty of their tongue. They had no fallacious term into which to convert it, and no preconceived ideas by which to explain it. Knowing they were dirty, they became clean ; having common sense, they did not rush on a new device, or set up either a " water cure," or a joint-stock washing company, but carefully considered and prudently adopted what the experience of former ages presented to their hands.

The operation consists first of the seasoning of the body; second, of the manipulation of the muscles; third, of the peeling of the epidermis; fourth, of the soaping. There are three essential apartments: the great hall, or *mustaby*, open to the outer air; the middle chamber, where the heat is moderate; the inner hall, which is properly the *thermæ*. The first scene is acted in the middle chamber; the next three in the inner chamber; and the last in the outer hall. The time occupied is two hours; the operation is repeated once a week.

On raising the curtain over the entrance to the street, you find yourself in a hall, circular, octagonal, or square, covered with a dome open in the centre: it may be one hundred feet in height. The Pantheon of Rome, relic of the baths of Agrippa, may be taken as the type—

" Simple, erect, severe, austere, sublime."

This is the *apodyterium, conclave*, or *spoliatorium* of the Romans. In the middle stands a basin, the " sea " of the Jews, the *piscinum* of the Romans; a fountain plays in the centre. Plants are trained over or around the fountain, and by it is placed the stall to supply coffee, pipes, or nargilles. All round there is a platform raised about three feet. You are conducted to an unoccupied couch to undress; your clothes are folded, and deposited in a napkin, and tied up; you are arrayed in the bathing costume, three towels, two yards by one, soft and rough, with broad borders in blue or red of raw silk. This costume has an air of society, not of the laundry or washhouse. One is wrapped with an easy fold round the head, so as to form a high and peculiar turban ; the second is bound round the loins ; this is the ordinary costume of the attendants, and known in antiquity as περὶ ζῶμα, *præcinctorium* and *subligaculum,* which have been of difficult interpretation, as implying at once a belt and a clothing. The third is thrown over the shoulder. They are called *peshtimal;* the proper name is *futa,* a word borrowed, as the stuff is, from Morocco. While you change your linen, two attendants hold a cloth before you. The strictest decency is observed, though the apartment is not cut up into boxes. There is nothing which more shocks an Eastern than our want of decorum, and I have known instances of servants assigning this as a reason for refusing to remain in Europe, or to come to it.

Thus attired, you step down from the platform into wooden pattens (*nal* in Turkish, *cob cob* in Arabic), to keep you off the hot floors, and the dirty water running off by the entrances and passages ; two attendants take you, one by each arm above the elbow, walking behind and holding you. The slamming doors are pushed open, and you enter the region of steam.

Each person is preceded by a mattress and a cushion, which are removed the moment he has done with them, that they may not get damp. The apartment he now enters is low and small ; very little light is admitted ; sometimes, indeed, the day is excluded, and the small flicker of a lamp enables you to perceive indistinctly its form and occupants. The temperature is moderate, the moisture slight, the marble floor on both sides is raised about eighteen inches, the lower and centre part being the passage between the two halls. This is the "cold chamber" of the Turks, the Roman *tepidarium*. Against the wall your mattress and cushion are placed, the rest of the chamber being similarly occupied; the attendants now bring coffee and serve pipes. The object sought in this apartment is a natural and gentle flow of perspiration ; to this are adapted the subdued temperature and moisture; for this the clothing is required and the coffee and pipe ; and, in addition, a delicate manipulation is undergone, which does not amount to shampooing ; the sombre air of the apartment calms the senses, and shuts out the external world.*

During the subsequent part of the operation, you are either too busy or too abstracted for society; the bath is essentially sociable, and this is a portion of it so appropriated—this is the time and place where a stranger makes acquaintance with a town or village. Whilst so engaged, a boy kneels at your feet and chafes

---

* One of the luxuries of the Roman baths consisted in their brightness, the command of the prospect around, and in various strange contrivances. By one of these, the bather, while swimming in warm water, could see the sea; by another, the bathers within were seen magnified without. "They were not content unless they were coloured as well as washed," says Seneca, *Epist.* 87.

Multus ubique dies radiis ubi culmina totis,
        Perforat, atque alio sol improbus uritur æstu.—Stat. l. i.

This excess of light in a bath savours of indecency. See Suéton., *Apoll.* lib. ii., epist. 2. It was not the early practice of Rome, nor certainly of those from whom the Romans took the bath. "Our ancestors," says Seneca, "did not believe a bath to be warm unless it was obscure." "Redde Lupi nobis tenebrosaque balnea Grilli."—Mart. i. 60.

them, or behind your cushion, at times touching or tapping you on the neck, arm, or shoulder, in a manner which causes the perspiration to start.

2nd Act.—You now take your turn for entering the inner chamber: there is in this point no respect for persons,* the bathman (the *tellack* of the Turks, the *nekaës* of the Arabs, the *tractator* of the Romans) has passed his hand under your bathing linen, and is satisfied that your skin is in a proper state. He then takes you by the arm as before, your feet are again pushed into the pattens, the slamming door of the inner region is pulled back, and you are ushered into the *adytum*,—a space such as the centre dome of a cathedral, filled—not with dull and heavy steam—but with gauzy and mottled vapour, through which the spectre-like inhabitants appear, by the light of tinted rays, which, from stars of stained glass in the vault, struggle to reach the pavement through the curling mists. The song, the not unfrequent shout, the clapping (not of hands, but sides),† the splashing of water and clank of brazen bowls, reveal the humour and occupation of the inmates, who, here divested of all covering save the scarf round the loins, with no distinction between bathers and attendants, and with heads as bare as bodies and legs, are seen passing to and fro through the mist, or squatted or stretched out on the slabs, exhibiting the wildest contortions, or bending over one another, and

---

* The Roman expression, *quasi locus in balneis*, was equivalent to "first come, first served."

† The bathing men give signals for what they want by striking with the hand on the hollow of the side.

appearing to inflict and to endure torture. A stranger might be in doubt whether he beheld a foundry or Tartarus; whether the Athenian gymnasia were restored, or he had entered some undetected vault of the Inquisition. That is the *sudatorium*. The steam is raised by throwing water on the floor,* and its clearness comes from the high and equal temperature of the air and walls.

Under the dome there is an extensive platform of marble slabs : on this you get up; the clothes are taken from your head and shoulders; one is spread for you to lie on, the other is rolled for your head ; you lie down on your back; the *tellack* (two, if the operation is properly performed) kneels at your side, and bending over, gripes and presses your chest, arms, and legs, passing from part to part, like a bird shifting its place on a perch. He brings his whole weight on you with a jerk, follows the line of muscle with anatomical thumb,† draws the open hand strongly over the surface, particularly round the shoulder, turning you half up in so doing ; stands with his feet on the thighs and on the chest, and slips down the ribs ; then up again three times ; and lastly, doubling your arms one after the

---

* "Let the air of all the rooms be neither particularly hot nor cold, but of a proper temperature, and middling moist ; which will be effected by plentifully pouring temperate water from the cistern, so that it may flow through every room."—Galen, "Therap. Meth." l. x.

† "Percurrit agili corpus arte tractatrix,
   Manumque doctum spargit omnibus membris."
                                        Mart. iii. 82.

other on the chest, pushes with both hands down,
beginning at the elbow, and then, putting an arm under
the back and applying his chest to your crossed elbows,
rolls on you across till you crack. You are now turned
on your face, and, in addition to the operation above
described, he works his elbow round the edges of your
shoulder-blade, and with the heel plies hard the angle
of the neck ; he concludes by hauling the body half up
by each arm successively, while he stands with one foot
on the opposite thigh.* You are then raised for a
moment to a sitting posture, and a contortion given to
the small of the back with the knee, and a jerk to the
neck by the two hands holding the temples.

3rd Act.—Round the sides there are cocks for hot
and cold water over marble basins, a couple of feet in
diameter, where you mix to the temperature you wish.
You are now seated on a board on the floor at one of
these fountains, with a copper cup† to throw water over
you when wanted. The *tellack* puts on the glove—it is
of camel's hair, not the horrid things recently brought
forth in England. He stands over you ; you bend
down to him, and he commences from the nape of the
neck in long sweeps down the back till he has started
the skin ; he coaxes it into rolls, keeping them in and
up till within his hand they gather volume and length ;
he then successively strikes and brushes them away,
and they fall right and left as if split from a dish of

---

* "Et summum dominæ femur exclamare coegit."
                                        Juvenal, Sat. vi. v. 422.
† These basins are the *pelves* of the Romans.

macaroni. The dead matter which will accumulate in a week forms, when dry, a ball of the size of the fist. I once collected it, and had it dried—it is like a ball of chalk : this was the purpose for which the *strigil* was used. In our ignorance we have imagined it to be a horse-scraper to clear off the perspiration, or for other purposes equally absurd.*

4th Act.—Hitherto soap has not touched the skin. By it, however strange it may appear to us,† the operation would be spoiled. The alkali of the soap combining with the oily matter, the epidermis loses the consistency it must have to be detached by rolling. A large wooden bowl is now brought; in it is a lump of soap, with a sort of powder-puff of *liff*,‡ for lathering. Beginning by the head, the body is copiously soaped and washed twice, and part of the contents of the bowl

---

* " The *strigil* was used after bathing, to *remove the perspiration*. The hollow part was to hold oil to soften the skin, or to allow the scraped grease to run off."—Dennis, vol. ii. p. 426.

† Whenever our writers touch on these matters, they fall into inevitable confusion, *e. g.* :—" In the baths of the East, the bodies are cleansed by small bags of camel's hair woven rough, or with a handful of the fine fibres of the Mekha palm-tree combed soft, and filled with fragrant saponaceous earths, which are rubbed on the skin, till the whole body is covered with froth. Similar means were employed in the baths of Greece, and the whole was afterwards cleansed off the skin by gold or silver *strigils*." — *Manners and Customs of Ancient Greece*, J. A. St. John, vol. ii. p. 89.

‡ Nut of the palm, and consequently hard and not fit to use on the person. The Moors, though they do not use soap in the bath, always use their soft *liff* with their soft soap, which practice the Turks have imperfectly followed.

is left for you to complete the operation yourself. Then approaches an acolyte with a pile of hot folded *futas* on his head, he holding a dry cloth spread out in front. You rise, having detached the cloth from your waist, and holding it before you; at that moment another attendant dashes on you a bowl of hot water. You drop your wet cloth ; the dry one is passed round your waist, another over your shoulders; each arm is seized ; you are led to the middle chamber, and seated; the shoulder cloth is taken off, another put on, the first over it; another folded round the head; your feet are already in the wooden pattens. You are wished health : you return the salute, rise, and are conducted by both arms to the outer hall.

The platform round the hall is divided by low balustrades into little compartments, where the couches of repose are arranged, so that while having the uninterrupted view of all around, parties or families may be by themselves. This is the time and place for meals. The bather having reached this apartment is conducted to the edge of the platform, to which there is only one high step. You drop the wooden patten, and on the matting a towel is spread anticipating your foot-fall. The couch is in the form of a letter M* spread out; it takes less space than a chair. As you rest on it the weight is everywhere directly supported—every tendon,

---

* The *duretum* introduced by Augustus at Rome. " On trouve alors des lits délicieux ; on s'y repose avec volupté, on y éprouve un calme et un bien-être difficiles à exprimer. C'est une sorte de régénération, dont le charme est encore augmenté par des boissons restaurantes, et surtout par un café exquis."— D'Ohsson, t. vii. p. 63.

every muscle is relaxed ; the mattress, fitting, as it were, to the skeleton ; there is a total inaction, and the body appears to be suspended. The attendants then re-appear, and, gliding like noiseless shadows, stand in a row before you. The coffee is poured out and presented, the pipe follows ; or, if so disposed, you may have sherbet or fruit ; the sweet or water melons are pre-ferred, and they come in piles of lumps large enough for a mouthful ; or you may send and get kebobs on a skewer, and if inclined to make a positive meal at the bath, this is the time.

The hall is open to the heavens, but nevertheless a boy with a fan of feathers, or napkin, drives the cool air upon you. The Turks have given up the cold immersion of the Romans, yet so much as this they have retained of it, and which realises the end the Romans had in view to prevent the breaking out of the perspiration ; but it is still a practice with the Turks to have cold water thrown upon the feet. The nails of the hands and feet are dexterously pared with a sort of oblique chisel ; any callosities that remain on the feet are rubbed down ; during this time the linen is twice changed.* These operations do not interrupt the chafing of the soles,† and the gentle patting on the

---

* Galen ("Method. Therap." l. x. c. 10,) says, "Let then one of the servants throw over him a towel, and being placed upon a couch, let him be wiped with sponges, and then with soft napkins." How completely this is the Turkish plan, one familiar with the bath only will understand. Explanation would be tedious.

† If you desire to be awakened at a certain hour, you are not lugged by the shoulder or shouted at in the ear ; the soles

outside of the folds of linen which I have mentioned in the first stage. The body has come forth shining like alabaster, fragrant as the cistus, sleek as satin, and soft as velvet. The touch of the skin is ·electric. Buffon has a wonderful description of Adam's surprise and delight at the first touch of himself. It is the description of the human sense when the body is brought back to its purity. The body thus renewed, the spirit wanders abroad, and, reviewing its tenement, rejoices to find it clean and tranquil. There is an intoxication or dream that lifts you out of the flesh, and yet a sense of life and consciousness that spreads through every member. Each breastful of air seems to pass, not to the heart, but to the brain, and to quench, not the pulsations of the one, but the fancies of the other. That exaltation which requires the slumber of the senses—that vividness of sense which drowns the visions of the spirit—are simultaneously engaged in calm and unspeakable luxury; you condense the pleasures of many scenes, and enjoy in an hour the existence of years.

But "this too will pass."* The visions fade, the

of your feet are chafed, and you wake up gently, and with an agreeable sensation. This luxury is not confined to those who have attendants, few or many; the street-porter is so awakened by his wife, or child, or brother, and he in turn renders the same service. The soles of the feet are exposed to a severity of service which no other muscles have to perform, and they require indulgent treatment, but with us they receive none.

* Motto of the Vizir of Haroun el Raschid, when required by his master to find one which should apply at once to happiness or adversity.

speed of the blood thickens, the breath of the pores is checked, the crispness of the skin returns, the fountains of strength are opened; you seek again the world and its toils; and those who experience these effects and vicissitudes for the first time exclaim, "I feel as if I could leap over the moon." Paying your pence according to the tariff of your deserts, you walk forth a king.

A writer in the "Library of Travel" says:— "Strange as it may appear, the Orientals, both men and women, are passionately fond of indulging in this formidable luxury; and almost every European who has tried it speaks with much satisfaction of the result. When all is done, a soft and luxurious feeling spreads itself over your body; every limb is light and free as air; the marble-like smoothness of the skin is delightful; and after all this pommelling, scrubbing, racking, parboiling, and perspiring, you feel more enjoyment than ever you felt before."

This chief of luxuries is common, in a barbarous land and under a despotism, to every man, woman, and child; to the poorest as to the richest, and to the richest no otherwise than to the poorest.* But how is it paid for?

* Volney once entered a Turkish bath, and, in horror and dismay, rushed out, and could never be induced to enter one again. Lord Londonderry was more submissive, and endured its tortures to the end; but rejected the coffee, and pipes, and civilities then proffered. He has given us a detail of his sufferings, which appear to have been national. Sir G. Wilkinson, in his work on Thebes, cites them at length, and this is all that he deems it requisite to tell the strangers who arrive in Egypt on this subject.

How can it be within the reach of the poor? They pay according to their means. What each person gives is put into a common stock; the box is opened once a week, and the distribution of the contents is made according to a scale; the master of the bath comes in for his share just like the rest. A person of distinction will give a pound or more; the common price that, at Constantinople, a tradesman would pay, was from ten-pence to a shilling; workmen, from twopence to threepence. In a village near Constantinople, where I spent some months, the charge for men was a halfpenny,* for women three farthings. A poor person will lay down a few parahs to show that he has not more to give, and where the poor man is so treated he will give as much as he can. He will not, like the poor Roman, have access alone, but his cup of coffee, and a portion of the service like the rest.† Such habits are not to be established, though they may be destroyed, by laws.

This I have observed, that wherever the bath is used it is not confined to any class of the community, as if it was felt to be too good a thing to be denied to any.

---

* The charge at Rome was a quadrant, or farthing; children paid nothing. " Nec pueri credunt, nisi qui nondum ære lavantur." —Juvenal, Sat. ii. v. 152. In some baths it would appear that even grown persons were admitted gratis. " Balneum, quo usus fuisset, sine mercede exhibuit."—Jul. Capit.

† A poor man will go to the shambles, and cut off a bit of the meat that is hanging there, and the butcher will take no notice of it. If he goes to have a cup of coffee, and has not five parahs (one farthing), he will lay his two or three on the counter, instead of dropping them into the slit; the next customer will lay down ten, and sweep them in together.

N

. All these practices vary among the Moors. First, there is no bath linen. They go in naked. Then there is but one room, under which there is an oven, and a pot, open into the bath, is boiling on the fire below.* There are no pattens—the floor burning hot—so boards are used. At once the operation of shampooing commences. There is a dish of gazule, for the shampooer to rub his hands in. You are seated on the board, with the legs straight out ; the shampooer seats himself on the same board behind you, stretching out his legs. He then makes you close your fingers upon the toes of his feet, by which he gets a purchase, and, rubbing his hands in the gazule, commences upon the middle of the back with a sharp motion up and down, between beating and rubbing, his hands working in opposite directions. After rubbing in this way the back, he pulls the arms through his own and through each other, twisting you about in the most extraordinary manner, and drawing his fingers across the region of the diaphragm, so as to make even a practised bather shriek. After rubbing in this way the skin, and stretching at the same time the joints of the upper body, he places himself at your feet, dealing with the legs in the like manner. Then thrice taking each leg and lifting it up, he places his head under the calf, and raising himself, scrapes the leg with a rough brush, for his shaved head has the grain downwards. The operation concludes by his biting your heel.

* An incident, at Athens, in the time of Demetrius Poliorcetes shows a similar cauldron, with a lid in the Greek Thermai.

A great deal of learning has been expended upon the baths of the ancients, and a melancholy exhibition it is —so much acuteness and research, and so little or rather no profit. The details of these wonderful structures, the evidences of their usefulness, have prompted no prince, no people of Europe to imitate them, and so acquire honour for the one, health for the other. The writers, indeed, present not living practices, but cold and ill-assorted details, as men must do who profess to describe what they themselves do not comprehend. From what I have said, the identity of the Turkish bath with that of the Romans will be at once perceived, and the apparent discrepancies and differences explained. The *apodyterium* is the *mustaby*, or entrance hall; after this comes the sweating apartment, subdivided by the difference of degrees. There two operations are performed, shampooing, and the clearing off of the epidermis. The Romans had in the *tepidarium* and the *sudatorium* distinct attendants for the two operations, the first shampooer receiving the appropriate name of *tractator;* the others, who used the strigil, which was equivalent to the glove, being called *suppetones.* The appearance of the strigil in no way alters the character of the operation. They used sponges also for rubbing down, like the Moorish gazule. They used no soap; neither do the Moors; the Turks use it after the operation is concluded. The *laconicum* I understood when I saw the Moorish bath, with the pot of water heated from the fire below, boiling up into the bath. I then recollected that there is in the Turkish baths an opening, by which the steam from the boilers can be let in, although not frequently so used, nor equally placed within observation. Many of the Turkish baths have, doubtless, been originally Greek. The change in respect to the use of cold water is compensated for* by the cold air of the outer room, into which the Turks come, and is preserved in the partial use of cold water for the feet. The hot-water reservoirs, the *labrum* and *solium*, are still to be seen in the private baths; they are in those of the Alhambra. When used, the character of running water, an essential point among the Turks, is given to them by a hole being left below, which is unplugged, and a stream kept running in from a cock. It would appear that the Romans followed the same method. The *piscinum* of the Romans is found in the Moorish gardens. In the use of the depilatories, or the shaving off the hair, the practice of the Turks is exactly that of the Romans; the parts of the bath appropriated to that purpose being the same. The *olearea* are alone wanting. The Mussulmans would consider the smearing of the body with oil or ointments not as a part of the bath, but a defilement, for which the purification of the bath was requisite.

The Romans took the bath daily; the Turks have restricted its use to once a week. The Romans entered

---

* "On entering, they remain in the hot air, after which they immerse themselves in hot water, then they go into cold water, and then wipe off the sweat. Those who do not go from the *sudatory* at once into cold water burst out, on returning to the dressing room, into a second sweat, which at first is immoderate, and then ceases, and leaves them chilly."—Galen, "Method. Med." l. x. c. 2.

the bath naked; the Turks have introduced a bathing costume; the Romans allowed the two sexes to enter promiscuously—the Turks have wholly separated them. Preserving the good, they have purified it from excesses, which, to a people of less discrimination, might have appeared to constitute its essential character, or to be entailed as its necessary consequences. Our studies and learning have furnished us with no such results. These very excesses have been assigned as a reason for the disuse of the bath by the early Christians. If the explanation were true, the difference between the Christians and the Mussulman would amount to this, that the first could see and reject the evil, the second perceive and select the good.

There is one point connected with the bath on which I must say a few words, especially as in this case our usages do not present any obstacle to the adoption of a good habit, and I have repeatedly had the gratification of finding that the suggestions which follow were of use.

Those who wash the rest of their body often, except the head; the practice of smearing it with oil almost universally prevails. The Easterns do the reverse—they shave it. A greater comfort there cannot be than a bald pate. Washing the head is in no case prejudicial. Unless you wash the head, the washing of the body is neither complete nor satisfactory. The refreshment of washing the head may often be procured when it is impossible to wash the body. Soap and water are injurious, not to the hair, but to the hair-dressers. The men of the East have no hair to show, but if soap and water

injure the hair, whence comes the luxuriant abundance
of that of the women? The hair of the head, like the
fur of animals, is made to bear rain and wind, and to
be a protection against them. You cover it up. The
fur of animals thickens and strengthens when exposed
to air and wet. Your hair falls off, and you oil it. If
it grows weak, change its habits. If it is not washed,
and if it is oiled, begin to wash it, and leave off oiling it.

Every week an Eastern lady has her hair thoroughly
washed at the bath. It is first well soaped and rubbed.
They are very particular about soap, and use none but
that made of olive oil. The Castile Soap, which in this
country is sold at the apothecary's, is the soap the least
injurious to the skin. This is twice repeated. After
the soap, they apply a paste of Armenian bole and rose
leaves. This is rubbed into the roots of the hair, and
left to imbibe all the grease of the head; it is then, like
the soap, washed off with bowls of hot water, and leaves
the locks perfectly clean and silken. From time to
time they dye it. On these occasions an attendant
mixes up a handful of henna-dust in hot water, and
thoroughly smears with it the hair, which is then turned
up into a ball, and bound tightly with a napkin. In
this state they go through the bath. When the napkin
is removed, and the henna-paste washed out, the hair,
if before black, will have become of a bronze auburn,
and if grey, red. The bath occupies from three to four
hours, with the smoking, chatting, music, and dancing
which accompany it, in an atmosphere which excludes
every unpleasant sensation. The women are not, like
the men, contented with the bathing linen and apparatus

which they find there; but are followed by female
slaves, who bear bundles of towels, in silk and satin
wrappers, boxwood pattens, incrusted with mother of
pearl, silver basins and bowls, or sometimes enamelled
ones, and aloe-wood and ambergris to perfume both the
apartment and their coffee. This finery is less than
what they indulge in in their private baths.

The Romans and Greeks, in like manner, were accompanied by their slaves, and did not trust to the
service of the *thermæ.* Each person brought his strigil
and his anointing vase (strigilis et ampulla, λήκυθος καὶ
ξύστρα)* or sent them by his slave. The practice
furnishes the familiar metaphors which express the
different conditions.† The strigil was the sign of
comfort, and also of sobriety and industry. It was,
according to Cicero, necessary to the happiness of the

---

* The two instruments were slung together. The *guttus*
was round, and from its round flat orifice the oil distilled.
"*Guttatim tenticulari forma, terite ambitu, pressula rotunditate.*"
—Apuleius. On coins, vases, and bas-reliefs, it has been mistaken for the pomegranate, for a bulbous root, or a lustral vase.
A curious Greek papyrus, in which a reward is offered for a
runaway slave, or Lechythophoros, has cleared this matter
from all ambiguity. Mr. Letronne has restored and translated
the papyrus. It is also to be seen in the Lycian tomb, of
which a cast is in the British Museum, and one of the groups
is given in colours in Fellows's "Lycia."

† Αὐτολήκυθος, signifies a poor man. 'Εμαυτόν Βαλανεύσω,
was equivalent to "I am my own butler." "Have you dreamt
of Lechyth, or Xystra? that is the sign of a woman that attends
to her household (οἰκούριον) or of a faithful handmaid."—Artemid,
"Oneiroc." i. 64.

Roman citizen; it had to do with the fortunes of the
Roman state.   Rome was indebted to her strigil no less
than her sword for the conquest of the world.

Mr. Chadwick has asked me some questions which
I wish to answer :—"Is not the strigil a substitute
for the shampooer, or may it not be referred to as the
poor man's substitute; ought it not to be tried ?   How
were shampooers to be got in sufficient number for the
crowded baths of the poor ?   One of the shampooers
told me that twelve hours a day exhausted him.   At
that rate, would not 6d. per person be about the charge
for the labour ?   This would be an obstacle to the very
poorest, and I apprehend turn the scale of the warm
water bath.   Does not the use of the strigil meet such
cases ? "

My answer is as follows : — As to your question
respecting the strigil, I have to reply that it is the
instrument of the shampooer, and cannot be a substitute for him.   But the shampooer is not only the
professional man, he is also every man.   It was after
a month that I visited the experimental bath in Jermyn-
street, where the patients from the Consumptive Hospital
had been taking it, and I found them all dependant
upon the regular shampooers.   When I expressed my
astonishment at such a sight, they on their side expressed themselves much delighted with the idea of
shampooing one another.   It is one of the desirable
results to be obtained from this new method, to break
down that sense of menial service attached to the assistance that man has to render to man, and which belongs
to the coarseness and vulgarity of our manners, and

which so pervades us that we read ourselves only in the picture of the most opposite character held up to us by the East to-day, or by antiquity.

I have more than once quoted the expression, σεαυτον Βαλνευθεις, or "a man bathing himself," as the designation of all that was wretched, mean, and sordid. But Englishmen, reading the word, and finding it even accompanied with my explanation of it, can only see in it "independence."

I once went to the bath with Ahmed Pasha, then High Admiral, and the first man in the empire. Six Pashas accompanied us. They performed the service. The Captain Pasha himself insisted on shampooing me, and further took the charge of Chiboukji. You can have no idea of the difference it makes to life, when on the one hand there is dignity and etiquette, and on the other a readiness and a love to perform every service by which one man can render himself agreeable to another. As politeness is of all things that which it is desirable for the people of this country to learn, so of all means does the bath present in its operations the readiest for inculcating it and practising it.

Therefore you will see that there will be no increase of expense in connexion with shampooing. Nor do I think it will be desirable to introduce the strigil, because the rubbing off the skin by means of the glove is a far more efficacious as well as agreeable process, than scraping it off with the strigil.

This constant washing occasions, it may be supposed, an enormous waste of water. A Turk uses less water than an English gentleman. It is true every Turk, high and low, uses the same quantity, and washes in the same manner; but the utensils and conveniences are differently adapted.   There are no wash-hand basins and ewers in bedrooms, no foot-pans, hip-baths, shower-baths, &c.   They do not dabble in dirty water, defiling a great quantity.   They wash under a stream of water running from a fountain, urn, or ewer.   A handful serves to moisten the soap and to rub with it, and a couple more rinse it completely off.   The fountains are placed in the passages, staircases, &c.   By the mosques, and in the streets, they are so arranged that, by sitting on the step you can wash the feet and the head.   When you wash in a room, one attendant brings the basin, *laen*, with its pierced cover, and kneels before you; another the ewer, *ibrik*, with its long, narrow neck to pour the water.*   In the bath, steam and perspiration cleanse, and two or three large saucerfuls suffice for rinsing;—fifty persons may be bathed with the same water that serves to fill our trough for washing one.

What a difference it makes in domestic comfort to be certain that every person around you, and everything you touch and eat, are absolutely clean!   After this manner of life, the habits of Europe are most painful;

* I find the most convenient substitute, a vase holding about two gallons of water, with a spout like that of a tea urn, only three times the length, placed on a stand about four feet high, with a tub below; hot or cold water can be used; the water may be very hot, as the stream that flows is small.   It runs for a quarter of an hour, or twenty minutes.   The Castilian soap should be used in preference to the made-up soaps of England. Of English soaps, the common yellow washing soap is the best. N.B.—A clean sheet on the dressing-room floor, and no slippers.

you are constantly oppressed with the touch, or sight, or knowledge of things which, by the European, are not considered unclean, or are submitted to as unavoidable. It would but faintly describe my impressions to say, that I felt as if passing from a refined to a rude condition of society. Neither do we know how to cultivate or handle the body. One of the first thoughts was, "What shall I do in sickness?" All Europe's seductions and luxuries put together will not make up for this one.

The European is clean, in so far as he is so, for appearance; he has clothes and shoe-brushes, blacking, starch, smoothing irons, &c.; in these consists his neatness.* The clean shirt is put upon the dirty body; the hands and face, being alone open to the air and sun and the eyes of the neighbours, are washed. Nothing is filthy that is unseen.† The Eastern has no brush or blacking; no care is expended or expense incurred for neatness. He has his religious ablutions for prayer.‡

---

* *Neat* and *proper*, are two words which we have changed from their original sense to cleanliness.

† Granting that the English are tolerably clean in the matter of their faces and hands, their houses and clothes, it must be confessed that they do not seem sufficiently impressed with the importance of keeping their whole bodies clean. Suppose the English were the cleanest people in the world, it would be fearful to think, when we know what they are, how dirty the rest of the world must be.—"Family Economist," p. 40.

‡ The *abdest* of the Mussulman consists in washing hands to the elbow, feet, face, and neck, five times a day in cold water, without soap. The *wadhan* of the Jew is only three times, and does not extend to the feet. The priests washed feet and hands.

He will not tell you that he washes for his comfort or his health, but because it would be a sin not to do so.

Our intercourse with the lower orders is broken off by there being no settled occasion on which we are in contact with them, and by the want of cleanliness in their persons. Here both classes are constantly brought into the presence of each other. Contempt and distaste are removed on one side, degradation and irritation on the other; they know one another; the intercourse of various ranks requires and sustains a style and demeanour which strikes all Europeans, who are astonished that the bearing of the peasant is as courtly as that of the Pasha,—he is as clean as the Pasha. What must Easterns think of us where the difference of condition can be traced in speech, manner, and washing? The bath is of as great value to society as to the individual. A political economist, glorifying his age, exclaims—"Augustus in all his splendour had neither glass for his window nor a shirt to his back." The slave and the beggar in Rome were daily in the enjoyment of luxuries which no European monarch knows.

There is an impression that the bath is weakening. We can test this in three ways: its effects on those debilitated by disease, on those exhausted by fatigue, and on those who are long exposed to it.

1. In affection of the lungs and intermittent fever the bath is used. The effect is to subdue, by a healthy perspiration in a waking state, the unhealthy one in sleep.

2. After long and severe fatigue—fatigue such as we never know—successive days and nights on horse-

back—the bath affords the most astonishing relief. Having performed long journeys on horseback, even to the extent of ninety-four hours, without taking rest, I know by experience its effects in the extremest cases.

A Tartar, having an hour to rest, prefers a bath to sleep. He enters as if drugged with opium, and leaves it, his senses cleared and his strength restored, as much as if he had slept for several hours. This is not to be attributed to the heat or moisture alone, but to the shampooing, which in such cases is of an extraordinary nature. The Tartar sits down and tumbles himself up; the shampooer (and he selects the most powerful man) then springs with his feet on his shoulders, cracking his vertebræ; with all his force and weight he pummels the whole back, and then turning him on his back and face, aided by a second shampooer, tramples on his body and limbs; the Tartar then lays himself down for half an hour, and, perhaps, though it is not necessary, sleeps. Well can I recall the *hammâm* doors which I have entered, scarcely able to drag one limb after the other, and from which I have sprung into my saddle again, elastic as a sinew, and light as a feather.

You will see a *hammal* (porter), a man living only on rice, go out of one of those baths, where he has been pouring with that perspiration which we think must prostrate and weaken, and take up his load of five hundred-weight, placing it unaided on his back.

3. The shampooers spend eight hours daily in the steam; they undergo great labour there, shampooing, perhaps, a dozen persons, and are remarkably healthy.

They enter the bath at eight years of age ; the duties of the younger portion are light, and chiefly outside in the hall, to which the bathers retire after the bath ; still, there they are from that tender age exposed to the steam and heat, so as to have their strength broken, if the bath were debilitating. The best shampooer under whose hands I have ever been, was a man whose age was given to me as ninety, and who, from eight years of age, had been daily eight hours in the bath. This was at the natural baths of Sophia. I might adduce, in like manner, the sugar-bakers in London, who, in a temperature not less than that of a bath, undergo great fatigue, and are also remarkably healthy.

The Romans furnish another example. Unlike the Arabs, who restrict its use to once a week, they went into it daily. The temperature was gradually raised, until, in the time of Nero, it became excessive. Their habits, in other respects, were not such as to be conducive to health, and must have disqualified them for using the bath, if it did debilitate ; it served, therefore, as an antidote to their manner of life, and relieved the excess of the patrician, as it does to-day the fatigue of the Tartar.

Life is chemical and galvanic, but both these agencies result in, and depend upon, motion ; the vessels are constructed for conveying fluids—the muscles for gene-rating power. Thus, shampooing exerts over the human body a power analogous to that of drugs administered by the mouth. A blow which kills, a posture which benumbs, pressure which in long disease becomes a chief obstacle to recovery, exercise which gives health and strength—are all evidences of the influence of motion over our system.

Who has not experienced in headaches and other pains, relief from the most unartful rubbing? You receive a blow, and involuntarily rub the part. Cold will kill; the remedy is brandy and friction. The resources of this process surely deserve to be developed with as much care as that which has been bestowed upon the Materia Medica. Where practised, human suffering is relieved, obstructions are removed, indigestion is cured, paralysis and diseases of the spine, &c., arising from the loss of muscular power, are within its reach, while they are not under the control of our medicines. Here is a new method to add to the old. Wherever it can be employed, how much is it to be preferred to nauseating substances taken into the stomach; how much must the common practice of it tend to preserve the vitality of the whole frame! Even if disregarded as an enjoyment of health, it offers a solace which ought to be invaluable in the eye of a medical man, as of course it must be of the patient. We have all to play that part.

Where the practice is familiar, it is used not merely in the bath, but upon all occasions. It is to be found without the bath, as among the Hindoos, some Tartar tribes, the Chinese, and the Sandwich islanders—the latter present one of the most remarkable phenomena. The different ranks are of different stature. The chiefs are sunk in sloth and immorality; and yet it is not they who, like the grandees of Spain, are the dimin-

utive and decrepid race—they are shampooed.* A
practice which our epicures and our stoics, our patients
and our doctors, would alike despise—counteracts the
consequences of gluttony, intoxication, debauchery, and
sloth, and supplies the place of exercise and temperance ;
and a people which can boast no school of philosophy,
whose nostrils have never been regaled by compounds
of Beauvilliers, and whose pulse has never been
stretched out to a Halden, is able to combine the
health of the Brahmin with the indulgence of the
Sybarite.

The human body is formed for labour, and requires it,
and this labour is accompanied by perspiration. It is
the safety-valve for the heart—the sewer of the secretions — the scavenger for the skin. Those who are

---

* " The chiefs of either sex are, with very few exceptions,
remarkably tall and corpulent. For this striking peculiarity
various reasons may be suggested. * * * But in addition
to any or all of these possibilities, one thing is certain—that
the easy luxurious life of a chief has had very considerable
influence in the matter ; he or she, as the case may be, fares
sumptuously every day, or rather every hour, and takes little
or no exercise, while the constant habit of being shampooed
after every regular meal, and oftener, if desired or expedient,
promotes circulation and digestion, without superinducing
either exhaustion or fatigue. Whatever may be the cause or
causes of the magnitude of the patricians, the effect itself so
seldom fails to be produced, that, beyond all doubt, bulk and
rank are almost indissolubly connected together in the public
mind—the great in person being, without the help of a play
upon the words, great also in power."—SIR GEORGE SIMPSON'S
" Voyage Round the World," vol. ii., p. 51.

thrown repeatedly into perspiration possess, however seldom washed, many advantages over those who have not to undergo severe bodily toil, however often they may use soap and water to the surface.

The bath substitutes an artificial and easy perspiration, and this explains how the people who use it do not require exercise for health, and can pass from the extreme of indolence to that of toil.

The functions for carrying on life are of the nature of a steam-engine and chemical apparatus; lethal gases are given forth as from a furnace; poisons are produced by every organ; from every function there is residuum, and the body, while soiled by labour, is rusted by repose.

The extremities of the vessels become charged with unctuous matter; the deadened cellules of the epidermis are covered with a varnish, which is partly insoluble in water, and this internal accumulation and external coating prevent the skin from performing its functions, which are not confined · to those of shielding the body, but are essential to the chemical processes within. The skin has analogous duties to those of the lungs, supplying oxygen to the blood at the extremity of its course, and when most completely in need of it. It has to aid at the same time the action of the heart. In its health is their health, and its health is cleanliness. Unlike the two other organs, it is placed within man's reach, and confided to his care; and curiously interspersed through it are glands secreting peculiar odours, that the touch and sight shall not alone warn, but a third sense be enlisted in the guardianship, crying aloud on every

o

remissness, and charging and reciprocating every neglect.*

The Russians come out at a steam at 160° to roll themselves in the snow. This is explained by the fervour of the circulation, which enables them to withstand the shock. If so, the strong and healthy might bear it—not the weak and suffering, the octogenarian and the child. The sudden passage from a Russian bath† to a glacial atmosphere is attended by neither shock nor danger; and far from the oppression that would result from the absorption of vital action in the efforts of the heart to overcome the violent contraction of the circulation by the cold, there is a sense of ineffable relief. You seem to take in and throw forth your breath in mere playfulness, no longer dependent upon it momentarily for life. In fact, the lungs and heart are discharged in part from the toil of that unceasing labour which, beginning with the cradle, ends with the grave. Of what service must it not be to aid a machine, the efforts of which, in the most delicate girl, are equal to a steam-engine of fourteen horse-power?‡

* "Rectè olet ubi nihili olet."—PLAUTUS.
† In the Russian bath the heat is obtained, as in that of the Mexicans, by stones heated in a furnace, and on which water is thrown. They have seats at different heights, and, by ascending, increase the temperature (the *concamerata sudatio,* as painted in the baths of Titus). They have a cold douche, which descends from the top of the chamber, and is repeated twice during the bathing. They do not shampoo, but with a bunch of birch, with the leaves on, thrash the body all over, laying it along, first on the back then on the face.
‡ The vessels running through the skin would extend in a

" The bath has the effect of several classes of medi-cines; that is to say, it removes the symptoms for which they are administered; thus, it is a cathartic, a diuretic, a tonic, a detersive, a narcotic; but the effect is produced only when there is cause. It will bring sleep to the patient suffering from insomnia, but will not, like opium, make the healthy man drowsy; and relieve constipation without bringing on the healthy—as aloes would—diarrhœa; it is thus a drug, which administers itself according to the need, and brings on no after consequences.

" This is not a drug in a shop, to be exhibited by prescription after a visit to a patient. It would be something to obtain a new simple, or an improved plan of administering a known remedy in any one disorder. It would be much by such a suggestion to diminish, in a few cases, the pains of sciatica or of rheumatism, the tortures of gout or stone. This is a habit; one which shall become, when adopted, that of the whole people.

" To reason out the subject, I should require to be a profound physiologist and physician; but my deficiencies in this respect, and the appearance of presumption in speaking confidently on a medical subject, will not deter me from declaring that with full knowledge of the uses of different degrees of tem-perature, you have an entire command over those acute disorders which constitute nine-tenths of our maladies.

straight line twenty-five miles; the respiratories coming to the surface of the body, and opening through the epidermis, amount to seven millions.

All inflammation, local and general, can be subdued. Gout, rheumatism, sciatica, will equally yield. I am inclined to say the same in reference to the plague. I am certain of it with reference to the cholera.* As to consumption, that scourge of England, which sits by every tenth domestic hearth among the higher orders, its ravages may be arrested with certainty, I had almost said with ease, if taken in time."

These preceding paragraphs are not the result of experience, but the anticipation of it. It was written four-and-twenty years ago for a work I was then about to publish, and suppressed at the entreaty of a friend, as being too offensive to the British public. It was, however, printed in a subsequent work fourteen years ago. I now adduce it as having an historical value, and I do so at the suggestion of a friend, whose discrimination and long administrative habits, combine to constitute a profitable adviser.

Your curiosity may be awakened as to the effect of such a statement on the medical world, and my answer will be itself a curiosity. It produced no effect at all. The proposition, " Heat is the simplest, the easiest, and the most effective of remedial agencies, and it has the peculiar merit of never having been so much as noticed in any work of medicine," passed by as if no words whatever had been used. I utterly failed in my

---

* In Cork the men employed in cleaning out the brewers' vats, and who have thus been in a Turkish bath, were, during the prevalence of the cholera, free from that disorder. The other workmen in these establishments, at the time, petitioned to be put to that work.

attempt to secure so much as the attention of one medical man, when it was by means of forms of speech that I addressed myself to their understanding. I then adopted the other process. I built. Then medical men, by the processes of persuasion and reproach, being induced to enter, the road to the brain was opened through the skin. The first bath built was that of Dr. Barter, of Cork. When engaged on it, a friend, residing in Northumberland, came over with an architect, and the consequence was the first private bath in England. Sir John Fife was induced to enter it and as *a patient* experienced its effects. The result was the introduction of the Turkish bath into the Great Infirmary of the North. This has been the most successful operation for several years ; but no other infirmary or hospital has followed the example. Sir John Fife says to me in a letter :—" I state as the result of my experience, that in diseases of the skin, joints, liver, and kidney, the action of the Turkish bath is immediate and *direct*. When it is remembered that in most diseases the important viscera above mentioned are deranged in their action, we see at once in how vast a number of diseases the Turkish bath, by correcting the morbid action of these viscera, must inevitably exercise an influence beneficial and powerful, though *indirect*."

The report of this Infirmary says :—

" The class of cases first submitted to its influence were of a rheumatic character, both *acute* and *chronic*, *lumbago, neuralgia, sciatica* and *gout ;* and with such beneficial results, that in the course of a few weeks the bath had become most popular, and rheumatic cripples were being brought from all quarters; some with their joints much swollen, and suffering a martyrdom, were conveyed helpless down into the bath, into a species of elysium, where ache and pain vanished as if by magic. One of the worst cases of rheumatic gout that I have seen was admitted into the hospital, in October, 1860; he was a baker, aged 46; since 1855 he had suffered from the affection in his joints, and had been under treatment here and in another hospital, without gaining any relief; his elbows, wrists, fingers, knees, and ankles were much enlarged and stiffened, so as to cripple his every action. I quote his own words:—'For the last two years I had been getting much worse; during the whole of this period I had very little refreshing sleep, and had continued gnawing and acute pains in all my affected parts. I have experienced much benefit from every bath which I have taken, and can, at the present time (February, 1861), use my hands and arms with much freedom; previously I could not stand alone, now I am able to walk without any assistance.' Equally satisfactory results have followed in cases of *dropsy*, the profuse perspirations affording marked relief.

"In *catarrh*, *influenza*, and many affections of the throat and air passages, *diarrhœa*, and *dysentery*, the genial atmosphere of the bath, at a temperature of 130° Fahr., exerts an influence far surpassing the benefit to be obtained by medicine. As a simple illustration, I may mention the case of a gentleman who had travelled from the south, a journey of many hours; he was labouring under a severe cold, and had almost lost his voice; he was easily persuaded to enter the bath, and, in the space of a single hour, had completely recovered his vocal powers, and was enabled to attend a ball the same evening.

"The power the bath unquestionably exercises in equalizing the circulation, renders it peculiarly useful in all cases of *congestion* or *stagnation* of the blood, and obstructions of the viscera; hence the averting of the ague fit which I have frequently witnessed, the dispersion of hæmorrhoidal and varicose conditions, the neutral (tonic) cure of hernia, and the relief of stomach and liver affections.

"In *scrofula* affecting the *integuments, glands*, and *joints, incipient phthisis*, and other conditions attended by wasting, the *tonic* influence of the bath is speedily evinced by an increase of appetite, flesh, and general condition; while, at the same time, the patient himself voluntarily casts off the damp flannel that has chilled his breast for many a day.

"In regard to the treatment of disorders peculiar to females much might be said, and, under medical super vision and direction, much effected by the use of the bath.

"The hypochondriac, the man of no leisure, the book and desk-worm, to whom the bare crossing of the street proves an effort, will have reason to rejoice in what will assuredly relieve him of bile, vapours, and malaise."

I do not consider the bath in the Newcastle Infirmary as a test by which medical men can arrive at a due estimate of what can be effected by heat. They are only making use of perspiration. They are there as yet but in a state of transition, and in that respect, perhaps, their experience is the more valuable, as it smooths the way for others to enter by degrees on a path so perfectly at variance with the present practice, and to the admission of maxims which cannot be otherwise than repulsive and offensive to the body of science who have instituted a code of cure to the exclusion of the most powerful of the agencies which nature had placed at their disposal. Such an avowal will never be made save by men remarkable, and therefore rare; and even in the case of men of high moral worth and intellectual power, a great amount of logical constraint must be brought into play before they will even attend, far less capitulate.

Sir John Fife, in his enumeration of internal organs, has omitted the lungs. This is of necessity, there being no such patients there; while the heat employed, and the extent in time of its employment, are not calculated in the Newcastle Infirmary bath for more than alleviation. In my experience, however, the lungs figure as the organ over which the largest control is afforded by the use of heat. In the incipient stages it is as easy to stop the disorder as to wash the face. In the further stages, it can be arrested so long as there remains undisorganized substance sufficient for the functions of life. What is perhaps more remarkable is, that the substance of the lung already exhibiting signs of decay, can be brought back to the healthy condition. Some patients from the London Consumptive Hospital have been admitted recently to use a small experimental bath, on the premises of the Turkish Bath Company in Jermyn-street. One of the physicians of the hospital, Dr. Leared, writes as follows :—

" Three patients affected with consumption have been for some time subjected to the Turkish bath treatment. They were all in an advanced stage of disease, as the tubercular deposit in the lungs was not only considerable, but had become softened or ulcerated. The general symptoms of all are greatly improved, but the most remarkable circumstance is, that in one case the signs indicating softened tubercle have disappeared, the lung becoming, comparatively, dry and solid."

These patients were simply admitted to the hot chamber for an hour every second day, that is to say, for three hours every week, the temperature not exceeding 140 degrees, as marked by the thermometer. This I should consider as nothing at all, and as not to be rated as a means of action against a morbid state, and yet such were the benefits resulting from these trifling means. The word "bath" is utterly unmeaning. So soon as the operation comes to be regularly performed the word must be dropped, and the annotation, as the case will be, " so many degrees of heat radiating or transmitted, and so many hours of exposure to it."

I could fill a volume with interesting extracts and confirmatory evidence from letters of medical men. Those I have given will suffice to show that the practical commencement has now been made, and that medical science will now have to adjust itself on a new basis, and one not the result of its own discrimination or experiment, but fortuituously presented.

I must here observe that in the East, though the bath serves to secure health, and affords immunity from many of our diseases, it is not there employed as a remedial agent. For that a very different degree of temperature is required. Here the starting point was a stroke of the sun, which I received when without the reach of medical aid, when the idea occurred to me that if I could perspire I should be saved. In consequence of this, I had an ordinary Turkish bath raised to an inordinate degree of temperature, which of course expelled the moisture. I remained in it for six hours, that is, until the constriction of the skin was relaxed, and the perspiration flowed. Out of the incident came subsequently the entire system of hot air as applied to disease.

The next step was at the interval of many years, and occurred to me two years ago, when a difference of effect from the manner of the impinging of the heat, suggested to me the existence of a difference between transmitted and radiating caloric. It was to test thoroughly this difference that the experimental bath in Jermyn-street has . recently been constructed, and it was in that bath that the results were obtained as regards the consumptive patients, which I have above quoted.

Before leaving the medical aspect of the subject, I have to observe that with mere medicine the physician treats his patients, but here the patient treats himself. He must himself take in and understand what has to be done, and do for himself. He must know that while an agreeable temperature is very sufficient for a habit in health, the force requisite for counteracting disease has to be generated by a high, and the highest endurable degrees of heat. The terms *Hammâm, Sejac,* and *Thermæ* all mean heat, and if that word were employed by us instead of the inapplicable, the false, and the perverting one of bath, one branch of the lamentable quackery, at present to be listened to, would be excluded. I can assert, in regard to my own experience, that, though patients constantly come to me in desperate circumstances, and given over by medical men, I have never had a death. I can recall no case in which, if a cure has not been effected, alleviation has not been obtained, and a suspension of the progress of disease so long as the means were persevered in. Every man may thus become his own physician, so that what I have to propose is the bath, as a substitute for the hospital.

We have now to glance at a distinct but most important branch—private baths. The public bath is at best but an expedient. The real thing is the private one. In it alone are the luxuries and enjoyments fully presented, and there is the service to be rendered of stopping malady, or treating it. I have mentioned that of Mr. Crawshay, of Northumberland, as the first so constructed in England. Several years, however, before, one had been built by the Duke of Northumberland, but it fell into disuse owing to the difficulty of procuring the requisite attendance. This is the account of it which I have received from the Duke himself :—

"It is true that I established a Turkish bath in York-shire some years ago. In every respect it answered its purpose. But, in England, a proper attendance cannot be supplied for want of suitable instruction.

"Whether the Turkish bath is as efficacious in maladies as you suppose or not, I must leave others to decide; but it is most agreeable; it relieves fatigued limbs most miraculously; and it is not weakening. I never took one except in robust health, and I never felt or heard of any bad effects from it."

The drawing on the wall will show how an apartment in the centre of a house can be adapted for a private bath. It is that in my own country residence. It is so constructed that no pattens are required, and you enjoy the luxury of walking on the marble slabs with the bare foot, the hot air being let in. Here, in the same apartment, you obtain every variety of temperature, from 80 to 220. This chamber contains 3,200 cubic feet. The furnace consumes the same amount of fuel as two ordinary fires. By means of this one fire, independently of heating the baths, five fireplaces are dispensed with. Two bedrooms in the superior story are entirely heated by the hot air passing from the bath, and four public rooms adjoining to it, on the same floor, are either partially or entirely heated from it. Instead, therefore, of a private bath being an expense, it is a very great economy. At Constantinople, there are 300 public baths and 2,000 private ones.

Here is the description of the private bath of an Eastern. Some interest may also attach to it, as the name of the personage who built it has, unfortunately for him and for ourselves, become but too well known in this country—it is, Said Jumbellat Druze Sheik of the Lebanon. I read it from my work on "The Lebanon" :—

"Emin Effendi and the Caimacan being gone, Izzet Pasha busy with his census, and Sheik Said with his guests,—I betook myself to the bath. I had not visited this part of the building before. I did not look for the splendour of Ibtedeen, but I was surprised when led through an ante-room that held a wide sofa, into a small cupola of fourteen feet square, with two recesses equally diminutive; one of them containing the *haous*, the plunge bath, or *piscinum* of the Romans. It was neat, however; laid in slabs of Carrara marble, with steps between of their own beautiful stone running through a gamut of shades, from white, or pale stone colour, to brick red, and of a consistency from the friable limestone to flint. Of all species of apartments the bath is the one requiring, and calculated for, the display of marbles and mosaic. That of Sheik Said was the only ornamental part of what remained to him of his palace, and just the thing I have fixed upon wishing to have, and hoping to live to see, attached to every cleanly gentleman's establishment of modest fortune in my own country. I found, on inquiry, that the bath belonging to the old Serai had been ruined with it, and that this one had been built by Sheik Said, at a cost of about £350. In England it might be built for the same, or less, and, with a better and larger ante-room, might accommodate fifty persons a day." It was on this type that my own was subsequently constructed.

The bath-going population of Constantinople—the

Turkish and Armenian—do not much exceed 300,000. At this rate, and this habit being naturalised among us, we would require for London and its suburbs, 3,000 public baths and 20,000 private ones. This would fall far short of the proportion of Ancient Rome or Alexandria, the Romans going to it daily. This daily practice is commencing in England, and further it is used by the sick. At the rate of Rome we would therefore have to multiply this number by seven. Such is the possible field that is opened to this new enterprise. But then the necessary conditions must be these :—1st, Cheapness; 2nd, the idea on the part of the wealthy of contributing from their superfluities to the well-being of their fellow-creatures.

The baths of Prusias (now Brussa) having fallen into dilapidation, Pliny appealed to the Emperer Hadrian in these terms :—" The dignity of the city and the splendour of your reign alike require their restoration."

In like manner I appeal to you to restore the balnea which the Romans constructed on your soil, for the good of your people and the honour of your name.

This appeal I make with a confidence I could not have felt even a year ago. Then it would have been a mere intellectual conclusion to which I would have pointed. I can now show you practical results. Nerved thereto by those spurious imitations, and not as a commercial speculation, several gentlemen have associated to furnish me with the opportunity of erecting in this metropolis an edifice on the scale of the structures of Constantinople. The drawings and models are there before you ; although in the building now far advanced

towards completion, there has been a considerable modification, yet these exhibit what a bath ought to be.
There have been of necessity changes required by the
fuel of this country, and also as to ventilation, the
merits or demerits of which it would be premature to
enter on. This is the building which I now can offer
you for a model, and I trust that this very evening—
and a more auspicious spot could not be selected than
this, the Society of Arts—will see a commencement made
and the resolution taken, to construct baths, if not for
the gratuitous use of the people, at least to be opened to
them at a rate not higher than that of ancient Rome,
or of the present Constantinople.

Quadrante lavatum rex ibis, says our schoolboy friend,
Horace. The slave, his compatriot, went forth a king,
having paid but one farthing for the bath that made
him feel as such. With all our philanthropy, with all
our mechanics, can we not attain to this? If I cannot
persuade you, at least suffer me to shame you, into
being at once thoroughly clean in yourselves, and really
charitable to your fellow subjects.

As to expense, a bath might be had for one quarter
of the price of a glass of gin; for we have water in
more abundance, and fuel at a cheaper rate, than at
Rome or Constantinople.

But if a new charge be incurred, we have on the
other side to look forward to the possibility of retrench-
ment in consequence of the altered habits of the people.
The one that first presents itself is the diminution of
maladies, doctors' and apothecaries' fees and drugs, loss
of time from sickness and attendance; and here, to say

nothing of the different value of life, the saving for London alone will have to be reckoned by millions. Next are temperance and sobriety. At first sight the connexion will not appear so immediate; it will, however, be unquestionable to those familiar with countries where the bath is in use. I know of no country, in ancient or modern times, where habits of drunkenness have co-existed with the bath. Misery and cold drive men to the gin shop; if they had the bath—not the washing-tub—to repair to, this, the great cause of drunkenness, would be removed; and if this habit of cleanliness were general, restraints would be imposed on such excesses by the feelings of self-respect engendered. Gibbon has indulged in speculations on the consequences for Europe that would have followed had Charles Martel been defeated on the plains of Tours. One of these effects would have been, that to-day in London there would be no gin-palaces, and there would be a thousand baths.

The poor of England have never had an opportunity of knowing the comfort which is derived on a cold day from the warmth imparted by such an atmosphere. How many of the wretched inhabitants of London go to their chilly homes in the winter months benumbed with cold, and with no means of recovering their animal warmth but by resorting to spirits and a public-house fire.

Consider the heat and steam throughout the manufactories of England, which the instinct of a Russian boor, or Laplander, or Red Indian, would apply for the benefit of the miserable population engaged in those works, and now allowed to run to sheer waste. The filthiest population exists, with the most extensive means of cleanliness. A nation that boasts of its steam, that is puffed up with its steam, that goes by steam, does not know how to use steam to wash its body, even when it may be had gratis.

The people that has not devised the bath cannot deserve the. character of refinement, and, having the opportunity, that does not adopt it—that of sense. Servility, however, we do possess, and any person of distinction has it in his power to introduce it. That which all despise, when only a thing of use, will be by all rushed after when it becomes a matter of fashion. The sight of a bath of a new fashion, and enjoyed by another people, has impelled me to make this endeavour to regain it for my own. Is Europe ever to remain on the map the black spot of filth? Can she owe the bath only to the Roman sword or Moorish spear? Must she now await the Cossack lance? After ridicule for warning, the day may come when I shall suffer reproach for deprecating the event, and it will be said to me, "These barbarians, who, Providence-like, have come to compose our trouble—Roman-like to teach us to be clean!"

In conclusion I will claim your indulgence for one egotistical remark. I have expended great labour in bringing this matter so far to bear. I have encountered endless disgusts alike from the pride of science and the self-love of ignorance. Over and over again I should have given up the attempt, if not in aversion at least in despair, had it not been for one consideration which

P

never forsook and always sustained me—it was this. Those who are so favoured by fortune as not to depend for their daily bread on their daily and precarious toil, are so very few in number as compared with the rest, that each man so situated has to consider himself, not only as remarkably fortunate, but as bound in a solemn bond to make use of the time so left to his disposal for the good of those who have no time that they can call their own.   Before my eyes were ever present the daily drudgery of the millions of my fellow men, known as poor, the severity of their toil—the precariousness of their existence—the paucity of their enjoyments.   And I have worked on in the hope of bringing within their reach some compensation for their hard lot, in a practice which relaxes the frame after the effort of labour, and composes the mind worn by the load of care.

The Duke of WELLINGTON, in opening the discussion, said :—

"I am certain that all who have heard this eloquent and interesting paper must have received a lively impression of what a Turkish bath is ; and I am certain also that no one will consider it unworthy of consideration and discussion, when it is recollected how largely both in modern times, and also in the ancient world, the bath was considered, not only as a domestic, but as an important political and social institution."

Why does Man Perspire?

A LECTURE.

(From the *Newcastle Journal*, Jan., 1861.)

The chair was taken by GEORGE ROBINSON, Esq.,
M.D., who said they would sympathise with him in the
announcement he had to make to them, that, in consequence of the death of a very near and dear relative,
their friend, Sir JOHN FIFE, was unable to take the
chair to-night. He might, as a medical man, be allowed
to bear his humble testimony to the great benefits the
Turkish bath was likely to confer upon the inhabitants
of this country, both medically and morally. The
functions of the skin, and the importance of those functions on the animal system, had not yet been ascertained
with the exactness which is desirable. But whatever
light physiology had yet cast upon this subject, fully
justified the opinion that the general use of this important agent, the Turkish bath, would greatly tend to
the preservation of health, to cut short many painful
diseases, and, in conjunction with sanitary measures, to
the prolongation of human life. (Applause.) This

climate was exceedingly unfavourable to health, and to
the discharge of the proper functions of the skin, by
the general prevalence of damp and cold. The bath
gave a warm and dry atmosphere—conditions peculiarly
favourable to the copious performance of perspiration,
and consequently to the discharge of the various noxious
principles which, if allowed to remain in the body,
would prove injurious to health.   Though they were
indebted to Mr. URQUHART for the re-introduction of
this bath into Britain, yet nearly two thousand years
ago it was very generally employed, even in this district,
by the Roman soldiers who conquered and civilized it.
In some of the most remote and wild parts of Northumberland, they could find, as described in the work of
Dr. BRUCE, and other antiquaries, at various stations
along the Roman wall, and at the various encampments
which the Romans formed in this district, evidences of
the very general and prevailing use of the bath. (Hear,
hear.)   They all knew how working men had to toil,
and that anything which could afford to them a cheap
and wholesome luxury was in the highest degree
desirable; and he believed the Turkish bath and its
accompaniments, when properly introduced, would afford
that cheap and wholesome luxury; and he was sure that
Mr. URQUHART would derive great gratification from
knowing that he had contributed materially to the
health and general benefit of so many of his industrious
fellow-countrymen.   (Applause.)   He would beg for
himself to solicit from him somewhat of a detailed
explanation of his own bath; it would be a practical
objection, at the first introduction of a new system such

as this for preserving health, if anything should be lost by inattention to details. (Applause.) His friend, Mr. CRAWSHAY, who had provided a very perfect bath at his residence in Tynemouth, had in his possession a very important letter, which he would take that opportunity of laying before them.

Mr. CRAWSHAY said it was now precisely four years since he went to Ireland, where Mr. URQUHART was at that time building the first Turkish bath, and under his advice he lost no time in erecting a bath at his own house in Tynemouth. That was the first built in England since the days of the Romans. Sir JOHN FIFE had thus had the opportunity of trying it; and being satisfied, by his own experience, of its great value, had brought it before the Pathological Society of Newcastle, and, with the aid of the Duke of Northumberland, it was introduced into the Newcastle Infirmary. (Applause.) Mr. URQUHART returned from Ireland, and built a bath in Lancashire, especially for the working classes; and the consequence was, that gradually the working classes began to erect baths of their own, which spread very rapidly through many towns in England. It was, in fact, one of that class by whom baths had been established in London. Four years ago, this was a matter confined to a few individuals. It had spread so rapidly since that time, that on all sides you heard of it. He himself was unable to attend to all the applications and letters he received asking for information. As it happened that the heating of air was a much cheaper process than the heating of water, baths of this description were found to be profitable; and the consequence was an existing and rapidly-increasing danger, that by this great agency of health and comfort being taken up as a speculation by persons who are seeking only to make money, it may be perverted from its original design ; and, above all, quacks and impostors pretend to inventions and improvements, and claim some peculiar discovery of their own as that by which the benefits of the bath are to be conferred upon the English people. He found that even the proprietor of the bath in Ireland, who derived what little he knew from Mr. URQUHART, had since put forth pretensions to have made improvements in the bath; and he saw by the *Medical Gazette* that Dr. BARTER had taken out a patent.   Now, we occasionally read in the papers about trials about patents; and if it could be shown that a thing had been done a month before the patent was taken out, it fell to the ground; but he thought that in the whole history of patenting such a thing was never heard of as that—a process which was known to have existed for 4,000 years, which, as the chairman had told them, was enjoyed by the Roman soldiers in this country 2,000 years ago, should be made the subject of a patent. (Hear, hear.) When he said that, he had said enough to show them the great danger that existed, that this great event in the history of the human race—for it was a great event the re-introduction into the West of an institution which had existed from the earliest times that are known, but which had been lost in the West, and had been preserved in the East; for the Turks did not invent the

bath : they found it, and had the good sense to preserve it—should pass away without producing beneficial
results, owing to the perversions of men, who were
thinking, not of benefiting their fellow-creatures, but
of filling their own pockets. (Applause.) Therefore,
those who are sensible of this danger, have considered
how to guard against it ; and the only way to guard
against it is to take means to have the matter
thoroughly understood; and in order that it may
be thoroughly understood, they must come to the
gentleman who was there that night. Great discoveries were always simple. Mr. URQUHART pretended
to no discovery. He had acted with that common sense
which was so rare : he had observed ; he had used his
eyes and his senses. He had enjoyed the bath in the
East; he had been familiar with it ; he had studied it;
and he had put to himself the question—" Why should
it not be in the West?" And he had not been like
every other traveller who for hundreds of years had
been to the East, and had tried the bath, and who, not
seeing it in the West, had imagined it could not be in
the West, forgetting that it had been in the West.
The matter was so simple, that when you come to consider it, it only excited reflections on the stupidity of
mankind. Distinguished persons were only distinguished from the rest because they were not stupid ;
and when they did anything, everybody saw it was so
simple, they wondered they had not done it themselves.
Mr. URQUHART was not going to take out a patent, but
wished to convey to his fellow-creatures some information for their benefit. Mr. CRAWSHAY then read the

following letter from Dr. MILLENGEN, physician to the Sultan :—

"Constantinople, Nov. 6th, 1860.

" Dear Sir,—I beg, in conformity with the wish you express in the letter you honoured me with, to send you the article I published on the Thermæ in the East; and also what I consider of much higher value to you—the two plates, with a bath, copied after nature, and the plan of a public and also of a private bath. With these two models before his eyes, it will be an easy matter for an intelligent architect to build baths of any dimensions, and far superior to those counterfeits, or imperfect copies that have hitherto, as far as I am aware, been made in England; and allow me to remark to you that neither the Arabs nor the Turks have introduced, in the construction of their baths, any innovation of their own.

" These buildings have been handed down from generation to generation in everything (dimensions and magnificence excepted) identically similar to what they were during the Greek, Roman, and Byzantine periods.

" The principles on which they are constructed are so perfect as to admit of neither addition nor subtraction, without ensuring complete failure.

" I shall do my best to answer the principal of the questions you have put to me on the subject, and begin by your query— as to the application of the bath in the prevention and cure of diseases. The working classes among the Turks, for such classes (though in England you appear to ignore it) do exist, and are as numerous and fully more hard-working than elsewhere, know of no other means of prevention, on feeling indisposed, but the bath. In the numerous cases arising from sudden changes in the temperature of the body, a copious perspiration, which a stay of more or less duration in the calidarium is sure to occasion, does, in the great majority of cases, restore the body to the equilibrium of health. After over-exertion, again, the bath is had recourse to. In short, it is looked upon so much in the light of a panacea by the lower orders, that they hardly ever dream of consulting a physician when taken unwell.

If the bath does fail to cure them, nothing else will do so. This prevailing conviction accounts, in a great measure, for the total absence of dispensaries and civil hospitals, not only in this large city, but throughout all the empire. Yet I apprehend from the tables of mortality monthly published, that the mortality is not greater than it is in countries blessed with those institutions. The higher classes, and women especially, do not, as with us, know much about regular exercise, so that I perfectly agree with you that, were it not for the ample compensation afforded by the bath, they would not enjoy the excellent health they generally possess.

"You speak of the temperance of the people as being pointed out as the principal cause of gout being hardly known in this country. If this is partly true, on the other hand I must remark that intemperance of late years is much on the increase ; and, moreover, that it is carried on to an extent which, if stated, might be looked upon as fabulous. Yet the gout is not more prevalent, nor delirium tremens either. This immunity I can attribute to nothing else but to the expulsion of the alcohol circulating in the system by the lungs and skin during the stay in the bath. You wish to know how long, on an average, does a person remain in the bath. If a Moslem enters the bath for the object of a legal ablution, half-an-hour is amply sufficient ; if, however, a person wishes to go through all the stages of a complete bath, an hour, or, at least, one hour and a half, is the usual time.

"Have, forsooth, the English no holidays ? Do they never find time for coffee houses, taverns, gin-palaces ? In this, as in most cases, I suspect, if there was a wish there would be a way.

" I shall not only be most happy, but consider it a duty, to supply you, to the best of my knowledge, with any further information you may subsequently stand in need of ; for I consider that you are engaged in an attempt, which, if successful, will confer in a hygienic point of view, a service on our countrymen, as eminent as the discovery that has immortalised the name of Jenner. I have yet one question to answer, and it relates to works on the subject of the bath. Of modern authors I know not one, and this is but natural, who would write on a

subject falling into oblivion. Celsus points out the diseases in
which the baths were employed as curative means. Ramazzini,
in his works on diseases, points out often most admirably how
many of these are due to the disuse of the Thermæ.

"Begging to be most kindly remembered to Mr. Urquhart,

"I am, dear sir, very faithfully yours,

"J. MILLENGEN.

"P.S.—We have not here the statistical returns indispensable
to ascertain whether the moyenne of human life is above or
below the average in other countries. Instances of extraordinary longevity are far from being uncommon. I have known
and know yet, several individuals among the natives more
than a hundred years old."

Mr. URQUHART said: There is indeed imminent danger
for this incipient design in this country, through interested motives and empirical innovations. But whilst
danger menaces the very inception of the scheme in the
West, it is exposed to that of extinction in the country
from which it proceeds, namely, in the East. Among
remarkable things, perhaps, there is none more so than
the losing of discoveries. We have had in this island
of ours, as your Chairman has remarked, 2,000 years
ago, the enjoyment of this benefit and luxury. You
are now assembled, in this town of Newcastle, to learn
something in regard to this matter, which has neither
been heard or dreamt of during these long years. In
the meantime, in those lands, where the Romans equally
had sway, those happy habits of social and domestic life
have been preserved by men destitute of words, and
philosophic tendencies. Now, then, that same obscu-
ration is arising by which you have been so long
shrouded. Turkey, which offers to you the bath to-day,
will have it no longer in two generations. I myself

have seen, in one country, the extinction of it. My first acquaintance with it was in Greece. Greece knows it no longer. That polished Greece—that accumulation of small and fervid existencies—where the imagination of men once burned most brightly, because engaged in struggles with the Turks, and under the imitation of the West, dropped their bath, and are now without it. To-day, at Constantinople, the young Turks, imitating Europe, abstain from going to the bath ; and, the last time I visited that capital, I was unable to obtain what I should call a bath. In 1850, the only bath I had was in a small nook of the Dardanelles, where the old usages were still maintained. It is true that what we are doing now in England may prevent its loss in the East. I may instance the very letter which has been read to you, from the author of a series of articles in the *Medical Gazette* of Constantinople, wherein, for the first time, type has been used in reference to the bath—the alleged reason of the disquisition being that which I have been doing in England. The subject is so vast, so difficult because of its intricate complexity, it bears upon so many collateral branches, carrying you back into history with its interpretations—carrying you onward to the sources of your own impressions, that in the short time allowed for such a discourse, I can do no more than indicate. I am here in the town where the bath has been redeemed from the hands of quackery. It is in Newcastle to the cure of disease and in the service of the destitute, that the first application of it has been made. It is to the directors of the Infirmary, who could not have had the facilities of personal experience, who must have trusted a great deal to a natural and intuitive instinct, that the merit is due of having broken through the habits of routine in order to give this advantage to their fellow creatures. (Applause.) It is above all, to the physicians of that institution that my gratitude is due, and I think I may extend the pronoun and say our gratitude is due—(applause)—for having ventured to face the obloquy, more terrible for a medical man than for any other, of proposing something new. It is therefore quite excusable, if not absolutely necessary, that on such an occasion I should leave the historical, the social, the mechanical, or the practical bearings of the subject aside, in order to direct your attention to the value of this institution in reference to the cure of disease. I have had hitherto to meet medical men as enemies. I have had to discuss the matter with them at the point of the lance, I have had the further disadvantage of seeing the first experiment made by men, medical indeed, but not professional. I refer to hydropathical establishments—which has deterred medical practitioners from even looking into it. Here, however, the case is altered, and I may open the matter by stating that the father of the profession, Hippocrates himself, claims to have been the first of men to apply the bath to the cure of disease. Perhaps the most responsible duty that belongs to any man to perform in the present condition of society is the selection of his medical adviser. Beside this, it is a small matter to make the selection of a general to command an army. There is no man who will not consider his medical adviser as a man as well as a physician. He will think of his character, his disposition, his qualities. He will place himself in these respects in the seat of judgment, and being there he will be anxious to acquire the means of correct judgment. Now this matter furnishes to every man an additional test as to his medical adviser. While the cure of disease is the aim and end of medicine, the prevention of disease is the extinction of practitioners— (applause) ; and if you announce a means by which any particular malady shall be stopped or extinguished, you will have on the part of medical gentlemen two exclamations. The really scientific man will exclaim, "Thank God !" the practitioner of the opposite quality will utter an exclamation of a different order. (Laughter and applause.) The true medical man sees in the means of preventing disease, a great instrument : the false medical man, a great enemy. And in this you will have the new test by which to judge of the character of the man whom you employ as your physician. To the young medical man, let me parenthetically say, that whilst in the next generation the number of medical men will be diminished, and the quantity of money expended on drugs will be infinitely reduced, whilst the general health of the community will require very little attending to, that nevertheless to the medical man, who is the first or amongst the first to make use of those means to obtain the ends for which medicine itself is instituted, there will be no diminution of favourable circumstances as regards his professional career. Those who will seize on them as their portion from the first will deservedly obtain for themselves the full benefit of their sense, science, and integrity.

Now, then, in what consists this new medical power.
I have constantly to do with disease. I have to do
so solely because I am successful. I began with
myself. I have been requested to relate to you to-night
how I came to the discovery. I said that Hippocrates
had made it, it had to be made a second time. But I
was not the discoverer, and I will tell you how first
the idea arose ; the same thing might have happened a
thousand times, without becoming a point of departure.
I was suffering from ague. I was on board a steam
yacht belonging to Lord Dundonald, whom England
has recently lost. He said to me, " Heat must beat
cold ;" and rolling me in a blanket, being a strong and
tall man, he took me under his arm, and carried me
down into the stoke-hole, and stopped the fit. This
incident was forgotten by me till the other day, but
doubtless it influenced me. After a stroke of the sun
in the island of Scio, I insisted on having myself carried
into the bath, and succeeded, though with great difficulty, in getting the heat raised during six hours to the
highest possible pitch. At last perspiration broke out,
and I was saved. (Applause.) The next occasion was
in London. I was, at the time, in the hands of Mr.
Erasmus Wilson, and as I find that he mentioned himself the incident to a gentleman now present, I may
relate it. I was given over. I heard him say these
words—" It's now a matter merely to allow him to die
with the least pain." I succeeded in getting them to
take me down to a bath that then existed. It was a
room filled with vapour, until the walls were thoroughly
hot, so that the air was rarified, and you obtained a very

decent bath. This was under the charge of a surgeon, Mr. Walker, in St. James's-place. I was carried there. Observe, I was given over. There were no medical means that could reach my case. I was there ten days, most part of the day and night in the bath, and then I left it well. When, the other day, I was speaking about it with Mr. Wilson, who has now come forward as the medical expounder of the bath, he said to me, "Do you know it is very curious, but I derived no instruction from that incident;" and he added, "You know I was *doctus*, and you were not: how could I be instructed by you? I was astonished; that was all. I thought there must be some peculiar idiosyncrasy, and there I left it." I said to him, "I have, during these ten years, always had the idea that you would come to me one day, because it was impossible for you to get rid of the certainty I expressed of my cure with these means being used." "Well," he said, "I ought to have thought so, but the fact was I did not. I did not think anything about it; and that was all." I am giving you particular cases, and those my own, because I am explaining to you how I have arrived at the conclusions, which make me work as I am doing. I can bring you to my state best by endeavouring to pass you through my own experience. What I am going to mention now is, I conceive, the most important case which has ever happened in reference to this matter; and unless it had happened, the discovery still would not have been made.

[The incident is omitted, as it will be found narrated in the "First Dialogue."]

Now here is the point: it is not the bath. Let us drop, if you please, the word "bath:" it is heat. Let us away with that absurdity of "hot air." It is the application of heat to the human body. As you require a certain degree of temperature to boil an egg, to obtain a particular tint in dyeing, to perform any chemical or any culinary operation, so you require a particular degree of heat to act upon the human frame. Why is fever heat 112°? Why is not 111°? Why not 113°? These were the questions I put to myself, and the answer came at last, doubtingly, of course, at first. "If it were 113°, it would be no longer fever." Nature was struggling to get at its remedy. When the remedy was got at, the malady was conquered. Long before I had the opportunity of erecting a building, I obtained much of the benefit by merely using water at the highest endurable degree, say 115° or 116°, enduring it as long as possible, and then getting out into the open air again. I do not mean to say that if you get 113° you stop fever; but what I mean to say is this—that the malady is working towards its own cure, and that its own cure is heat. Now I know what I was then guessing at; now I know it, and see it as distinctly as I see your faces. How comes it that, by means of a slight increase of heat, there should be a sudden power given to the body to discharge water? Where does that water come from? It comes from the blood. When a man sits on a chair in a heated room, and sees the little loch spreading on the floor around him, he himself being its fountain, and then feels a craving for water, and takes

up a jug and drinks, it is to be supposed that even if
the least curious of the human race, he will put questions to nature—that is, to himself—and say, " Why
am I to have at one and the same time water drained
out of me, and poured into me? Why should water
run out, whether I will it or no, because it is hot? and
why shall I be left no choice but than immediately to
pour it in? This is water—that is water. Why, then,
cannot I be allowed to keep my own? " Having put
these questions, and got no answer, perhaps he will
begin again, and say, "But is it the same water?
Though it looks the same, may there not be a difference? May it not be that the water going out is
soiled, whilst that coming in is clean?" And this
question will be the solution of that great problem,
though never yet stated—WHY DOES MAN PERSPIRE?
Man perspires, because perspiration being the watery
portion of the blood, it, when discharged, carries outwards with it all extraneous matters. (Applause.)
The blood flows with intense and wonderful rapidity
through every portion of your frame. In the course
of an hour or two the whole mass of it goes through
every part. The limits I give may, as to time, be
questioned, because the quantity of blood is supposed
to be much greater than it is; instead of thirty pounds
of blood in the body, there is not more than one-half,
according to the experiments of Bishoff, of Munich.
That blood has to carry away the effete matter which
results from each motion of the mind or of the body.
Whilst depositing fresh fibre, it has to remove old
poison. In fact, that blood, with its watery part, is

washing the whole internal man every instant of time,
or it is constantly repeating back upon him his own
pollution. Well, apply a certain increase of temperature to that body, and instantly comes into operation
that wonderful provision of nature through which
that blood relaxes its watery parts, and with it discharges the whole of those poisonous matters. (Applause.) When a man makes an effort, the immediate
consequence is perspiration. The effort is the purpose
for which the engine was created. You live and you
act; your life is in your action ; therefore the action
itself is the purpose and aim of life. That action
relaxes those fluid contents of the blood. The same
happens whenever you raise the temperature. Life is
a chemical operation; it is being performed every
minute, every minutest subdivision of time. Every
human being on the face of the earth is inventing,
second by second, life. His existence depends upon a
chemical operation which he carries on. That operation, like all others, is retro-active. It is in chemistry
as in dynamics. If you discharge a broadside of shot
into your enemy's vessel, there is an equal impingement
on your own, only you parry the blow. Whilst, then,
you are constantly producing the phenomena of life,
you are as constantly producing the elements of death.
Death is the reaction, poison is the recoil. You know
your own breath will kill; there is not a more deadly
poison : all that comes from you kills. The effete matter of your own body is poison. The pollution of man
is from himself—is from within. This is the primary
sense of the words of Christ, " It is that which cometh

forth out of a man which defileth him." (Applause.)
If you impede—that is to say, if you interfere with the
natural facilities of that organ by which that poison is
to be carried off as rapidly as it is created, you superin-
duce a morbid condition of the frame. It matters not
to me in what manner it shows itself—whether it is in
incomplete health or in positive disease. Inflammation
is one of those results. When it is produced, it is itself
a disease. The symptom becomes disease, and you die
of the inflammation. Little matter, then, will it avail
if we only can remove the causes of the disease after
those causes have produced the symptoms which are
themselves lethal. But observe this wonderful provision of nature. You know fermentation is an operation dependent entirely upon the degrees of caloric;
that with all the ingredients requisite, you cannot
obtain it under a certain degree of heat, and you stop
it above another point of the scale. You cannot obtain
it under 90°, and it will stop at 140°. Now we are in the
habit—science itself, which has not regarded hitherto
this most wonderful of the manifestations of nature—
science, which has not perceived this first of the elements of cure, has already given the name of fermentation to certain classes of inflammatory disorders.
The term zymotic, now in common use, brings me
back to that case at Berlin, where 140° failed to effect
a cure. This was my reasoning. I started upon the
fever heat of 112°, and then went on to the point where,
taking the analogy between fever and fermentation,
fermentation should cease, viz., 140°. I said, "If I can
get the blood subjected to a heat of 140°, I will take

the inflammation—that is to say, the fever out of it."
How subject the blood to 140°? The human frame
has such a wonderful capacity for wrestling with higher
and lower degrees of temperature, that it will conquer
cold and assimilate heat. But the surface of the body
may be affected by heat so as to be brought up to the
necessary point, as shown by its causing the flow of
perspiration. A certain portion of the blood passes to
the surfaces, the ends of the arterial circulation dwin-
dling to nothing; the blood makes a leap by another
mysterious process into the extremities of the other
vessels, which constitute the venous system. . It is at
this portion of the body that these minute sponges,
which communicate with the exterior, are found; and
it is at this moment of sudden and mysterious passage
that the water of the blood is dropped to become sweat.
At that point, if you have the surrounding temperature
at 170°, or at 200°, or at 250°, you will surely get a
portion of the blood subjected to a heat which destroys
fermentation; and as that portion is rechanged in every
new pulsation of the heart, in the course of time the
whole of the blood will have passed through that
purifying process. (Hear, hear, and applause.) That
point is 140°. You will not get 140° in the body,
but observe, living and dead chemistry are different
things. Fire in a grate and life in a breast are chemically the same—the same aliment, the same product,
the same residue. The temperature only differs, the one
operation requiring 1,200°, and the other 100°. This
was the reason upon which I acted when I sought, at my
supposed last moment, to obtain an increment of heat:

it is a consequence of this reflection that I am now alive.

The skin is what you live in ; it is your habitation. You may not have thought of it in that point of view precisely, but you know it is your habitation. But it is also that by which you live. There are various organs which are each of absolute necessity to your existence ; you cannot give precedence to any one over the other. Such are the heart, the lungs, the kidneys, the liver, and so forth. The skin is not generally reckoned as such ; but the skin is just as important in that sense as any of the others. But I will show you the skin from a point of view in which you will admit that it has an importance which belongs to no other organ. To know anything and everything about the heart would assist no one out of difficulty in regard to it ; and so of liver and kidneys, these things being buried in deep obscurity. No man has seen his heart or his liver ; and it will not be a lucky day for him when anybody sees them. You cannot pull them out and place them on the table, and clean them and put them back again. They are not remitted to your judgment, and they are entirely secluded from your curiosity. You never know anything of them but when they are in a deplorable plight, and then you only know you can do nothing for them. You may go to some professor of dark mysteries, and ask him to feel your pulse and look at your tongue: he may give you poison to agitate one organ that is sound, to get a little relief for the one that is suffering; and when you have not been extinguished in the operation, you call your-

self lucky and your doctor learned. (Laughter.) That
is a very unfortunate predicament for a man to be in,
in reference to his own belongings; but he is not in
that predicament in reference to his skin. He can see
his skin and handle his skin; he can manage it himself
when he knows how. It is confided to his own judgment; and if he exercises his judgment upon it—which
he can do when he understands its nature, which he
cannot do when he does not—then not only can he
keep that skin in order for itself, but by means of it
he can deal with all the other organs that he cannot
otherwise reach. (Applause.)

There is a great affinity between the organs. Your
lungs may be pierced and bored; as if that was not
enough, you immediately have your poor heart affected,
as they call it, sympathetically. Your heart is in a
lamentable plight, and then your lungs suffer; and so
with the stomach. We never hear of any sort of regard
or relationship between one organ and the other, except
it is when the one interferes to disturb the other. Now,
it is exactly the reverse with the skin. A man comes
to me with diseased liver. I say to him, " I can cure
you." If he is philosophical, he will put questions,
" How will you cure me ? You won't give me drugs;
you are not a medical man." I will answer, "I will
make use of one of your parts to affect the other. I
will make your skin cure your liver. I will use your
skin by making it hot." (Applause.)

Now, I will tell you another use of the skin, for
which you are not prepared. You are all at this
moment engaged, not only in listening to me, but also

in digesting your dinners. Who do you think is busy on the latter? Your stomach, you will say. I answer, "Not at all; it is your skin that is digesting your dinner; and I will prove it." First of all, the lining of the stomach is skin. It is the external covering turned in. That, however, is not my proof. What I mean to say is, that the preparation of those juices, which, passing through the lining of the stomach, are poured into that vessel to dissolve the food it has received, depends upon the action of the external skin of the body. These juices come direct from the blood; and their purity, and with their purity their efficacy, depends on the purity of the blood. Thus it is in the stomach that the food is digested; but it is by the blood that the food is digested; and the blood means the lungs and the skin, which again are one, as conjointly required to fuse the blood with air.

The skin is what is between you and the world. It is made very wonderfully to bear the wear and tear of the world. A man does not live the same all his life : he is undergoing constant changes. He changes the tissue of his body just as much as he changes that of his clothes, but he does not require a tailor. The old suit or the old skin is not thrown aside like that of a snake, and you do not come out under it. It is constantly in process of reparation; it repairs itself; and as every organ is made for its purposes so must the purposes be for the organ. If your skin is made to bear the wear and tear of the world, and you prevent that wear and tear, then the excellence of the construction comes to be a source of decay. I beg your attention

to this, as I adduce it to meet a common objection, which
is, that it is empiricism to say that one medicine can
cure two diseases.   I have this morning been engaged
for the first time in reading through something that
has been written on the bath—the lecture of Dr.
Brereton ; and in that lecture I find these words—" It
is not a question for me as to what diseases the bath
will cure : it is a question to me what disease it cannot
cure."   The reason why heat cures all diseases is that
disease itself is a result of your departure from natural
habits.   I assert—and who will contradict me ?—that
man is the most perfect of God's works ; and if the
inferior orders of creation suffer only from slight and
rare disturbances in the form of disease, and live out
the natural term of their lives, it follows that, wherever
there is habitual disease in the human frame, it is as a
penalty for having disturbed the natural course which
Providence has appointed, and misused the means which
nature has supplied. (Applause.)   The very first of
these neglects has reference to that condition of the
skin with which I am now dealing.   You have to bear
the wear and tear of the world—I mean friction.   The
skin is constituted so that, in repairing itself, it fortifies
itself against external friction.   What do you do ?   You
go and place cases upon that body.   You confine it, you
close it up, you cover it over, you condemn it to existence
in a dark dungeon, you shut out the breath of Heaven,
you shut out the light of the sun, you extinguish for it
the natural and fortifying alternations of temperature,
and protecting it from that friction which is necessary
to rub it down, you leave it unavailable for the admission

of life-giving air and the emission of death-dealing gases. This is the cause of that abnormal· condition which is to be found whenever the clothes are fitted to the person.

Wherever you are right, you are not right as regards one point only, but all points. Beauty is a fruit of nature no less than health. Enter a studio, observe how a painter or sculptor will prepare himself fitly to present the human frame ; you will find he is not engaged upon specimens from the tailor's or milliner's shop. You will find him travelling back to the Romans and the Greeks to borrow the pallium and the toga to robe his figure.

Thus there may be a single cure for many diseases. In the bath, the most essential operation is the removal of the dead skin. I have brought, with a view of presenting to your eyes, as a means of fixing attention upon the subject, some implements which are used for this purpose. From the moment that integumental clothing was inflicted on man the clearing away of the dead epidermis became the first necessity, and, until that is done, a man has no sense of what life in his own person is. Those only who have undergone this operation can say, " I know what it is to be clean." Here is a substance which I have found in antediluvian baths, amid ruins compared to which the pyramids of Egypt dwindle down to the products of a toy shop. When I tell you that single stones built into the wall are equal in extent to the length of this hall, and about a half of its width, and a third of its height—you may imagine what manner of men

were those who raised them. In the lower part of
those structures there remain ashes of a peculiar kind
—ashes that are produced in the bath mixed with
the remnants of that substance which lies upon the
table. Now, this substance is found only in Africa.
It contains equal parts of the three principal earths,
and it has the peculiar faculty of rubbing off the dead
epidermis—of polishing the body. We find traces of
it in ancient India. But at present it is confined as so
applied to Africa. The skin throws out, as I have
said, matter for its own protection. That not being
cleared away, there is added to it the products of
perspiration—that is to say, matter left when it has
evaporated, the two together forming a varnish that
covers the skin and impedes the performance of its
duty, which is to throw off one half of the poisonous
matters that are produced in obtaining life. To bring
the body, therefore, into a wholesome state you must
remove that varnish. If the varnish were complete,
you would have only a few hours to live : if the surface
of the skin be rendered impervious to air—if it no
longer can admit the oxygen necessary for life, and no
longer allow the carbonic acid gas to escape from it,—
then you die. You die by suffocation just as much as
if a handkerchief was tied over your mouth. You do
not die so quickly, for in one case you will die in
two or three minutes; in the other case you will
require about twice as many hours. The increase of
heat enables you to remove the covering matter; but
the heat itself will not remove it. Go into a bath at
any heat you like you will not be clean. Perspiration

may pour from you, but unless you have cleared off that horny matter you will not have allowed the free vent to those impurities which as they are constantly recurring require an equal facility of ventilation and escape. Therefore is it that in those early times when men were simple, when the perceptions were true, when they, wholly ignorant, anticipated the result of science, this matter was carefully attended to. The first plan, of course, would be rubbing by the mere hand, and that is the best way : there is nothing more perfect, nothing can approach to it ; but the labour is very great. It was with the ball of the hand that the horse was shampooed, not curried. Still, after that we come to the different methods adopted by different nations and tribes. In the announcement of my lecture it is said that I should give you an account of the bath as practised among the ancients. I am afraid I have done very little to realize that promise: what I am now going to say you may take as an instalment. I would be an impostor if I told you I knew anything about the baths of the Romans. I know nothing about the baths of the Romans, but what I know is of the baths of Turkey : when any man talks to you about the Roman bath you may be sure that he is an impostor. Minute points may be known as the one I am going to quote, and perhaps that is the only one of which we have any positive knowledge. The peculiarity of the Roman bath was the Strigil. That was a curved piece of metal with which the dead matter was scraped off. The bath did not belong to the Romans any more than to the Greeks or the Turks. We trace it through them back

to that antiquity in which all good things are lost.
No good things have been invented; they have always
been found,—if there be indeed a distinction between
inventing and finding. The Romans, the Greeks, and
the Turks had a wonderful faculty in common—it was
the faculty of selection. When men have nothing they
have no pretence, and they look about them : when
they see anything desirable they take it, and when
they have taken it they hold fast to it. The Romans
were a set of bandits. Who were the Greeks? ask
even where they came from; and what but echo can
answer? Who were the Turks ? ravagers even within
the limits of history ; and yet these three races were
great through transcendant judgment. When, therefore, we refer to anything Roman, we have commenced
and not concluded an inquiry. In reference to the
strigil of Rome and Greece, the first thing will be its
name. The ancients were not philologists. Yet one
of the later Romans did indulge a little in that branch,
and he tells us that the word came from Mauritania.
Nor were the ancients antiquarians. And it is, therefore, to an epigrammatist that we owe the information that the strigil came from Troy :—

> " Pergamus has misit, curvo distringere ferro,
>   Non tam sæpe teret lintea fullo tibi."

The Strigil and the oil-bottle for anointing may be
seen on the bas-relief of the most ancient tombs and
caves of Asia Minor. A large cast of one of these may
be examined in the British Museum. The Strigil,
therefore, which represents one of the methods of

cléansing the skin, descends to us through the Greeks and Romans, from those populations of Asia Minor from whom the Greeks derived their arts, sciences, and letters, and, indeed, everything which we know as Greek. But these populations of Asia Minor were themselves but the offshoots of the Medes, the Persians, and the Assyrians, who were again themselves but the successors of the great Mohabadian Empire, which traces up to Jemshid and Cayoumeres. As it is to the Bath of Darius that the Greeks owed the knowledge of the structure itself, and as the permanency of the habits of these people has passed even into a proverb, we have to infer not only that the bath, but that peculiar modification of it in which the Strigil was employed, belongs to that great and glorious race, the splendour of whose renown, though obscured, endures through five thousand years—the ARIANS.

The second process, the rubbing or polishing down the body with Gazul, I fell upon, to my great surprise, in Morocco. Of such a process I had never heard in the East. No indication of any thing of the sort had I ever discovered in a book of travel—men cannot see what they do not understand, nor describe what they do not see. When I saw it I at once accepted it as the most perfect method. I did not, however, take it as a new invention, for in Morocco whatever you see is old. Going there is just the same as if you lived back five thousand years. It is the receptacle of things lost elsewhere. Flying populations were here stopped by the Atlantic, and the deserts behind protected them. I have already told you that gazul was employed in Syria before Noah built the ark. The traveller who goes to the East, and who there enters the bath, will be subjected to another process. After he has been sufficiently sodden in the heat, and after he has been worked and shampooed in all his limbs, the shampooer will put a glove or bag upon his hand, and, commencing upon him, will roll the dead skin from off him, and as he looks around he will see lying what he may at first take for pipes of maccaroni. Should the operation on his body have reacted upon his mind, he will begin to perceive what a difficult thing it is to make the body clean, and he may say to himself " How is it possible that I have lived all my life in this condition of filth?" The next reflection will be or may be, " Certainly these people understand the philosophy of life better than we do." Here then are the three processes :—The strigil covering the whole of the fields of classic antiquity, and reaching back to the earliest periods of history; the gazul which extends over the western portion of the old world and is co-equal in its claims to antiquity with the other. The mass of human beings subject to these processes have been pre-eminent for the energy of their bodies and their minds, and distinguished for their performances at once on the fields of dominion and of literature. The third is the glove of the barbarous Turks.

If ever there was a subject to enlist the attention of men by its connexion with their own well-being, or to command their respect by the charm which purification throws over intercourse with others—if ever there was a subject which gave vent to benevolence, it is the one I have endeavoured to call your attention to to-night. If I have succeeded in awakening that attention it will not flag, because it will demonstrate its benefits and power in every act and circumstance of domestic life. The only apprehension I have is, that remaining satisfied with the first attempts and content with empirical inventions, you stop short of the perfect thing, and instead of recovering the luxury, pride, enjoyment, and strength of the most luxurious and philosophic, learned and military, of the races of the earth, this endeavour shall pass away as a troubled dream. Unless the edifices are constructed not only with due regard to that which is essential to their own purposes, but also under such control as shall prevent their being turned to improper usages, instead of gratification and satisfaction in having commenced the enterprise, there will be for those who have done so only obloquy and reproach. It is thus I am driven to address you, not only by the desire to introduce for my countrymen a benefit of which I know and experience daily the value in my own person, but also by the necessity of preventing this experiment from lapsing, by reason of self-love and speculation, into a disastrous and a shameful abortion. (Loud applause.)

The Chairman, in tendering to Mr. URQUHART the vote of thanks, stated on behalf of himself and the medical profession of this town, that they were quite prepared to accept the Turkish Bath as a great boon to humanity, and as an important auxiliary to the cure of disease.

Consumption produced by Habits, not Climate.

THE Brahmins hold that all disease (excepting old age and accident) is a disgrace and a sin, as it can arise only from criminal indulgence of the lusts, or an equally criminal misuse of the reason.

It is more than twenty years since I have known Consumption to be an artificial produce, and, consequently, that the land can be lustrated from this pollution.

From that moment I felt myself laden with a heavy duty,—namely, the spreading of that knowledge by which others should be brought to co-operate with me in effecting the changes in our habits requisite for the extirpation of the disease.

The proposition was stated by me eighteen years ago in these terms :—

" As to Consumption, that scourge of England—that pallid spectre which sits by every tenth domestic hearth among the higher orders,—it is not only unknown where the Bath is practised, but is curable by its means." *

* " Pillars of Hercules," vol. ii., ch. on Bath.

At the end of these eighteen years, I find myself writing an introduction to the report of a regular Physician "On the Successful Treatment of Consumption by the Bath," published in the leading Medical journal of Great Britain.

Had this been foretold to me at the former period as to happen within a century, I should have held it to be an encouraging prospect. I accept it now as a recompense for the toil I have undergone, and also for that persecution which all must endure who, proposing beneficial changes in common habits, offend the self-love of their contemporaries.

Consumption is a modern disease. It was no more known formerly in England than it is known to-day in countries whose habits resemble those of England formerly, even when there is no bath.

There can be, therefore, no greater error than to suppose that the lungs are wasted by climate,—nor consequently, that change of climate is a remedy for Consumption. After the disease has made progress, relief may be so afforded. It is a chance, an incident, and no more. Such relief is, however, within the reach of a fraction only of the sufferers. Those who are so favoured by fortune as to be able to change their abodes, are at the present moment only flying from effective means of restoration which are now to be found at home.

Concurrently with the idea that climate produces the disease, the perception exists of the symptoms of the as yet undeveloped malady. "He (or she) is of a consumptive habit," is no uncommon expression. The least observant can point to the thin and pearly teeth, the pink complexion, and the flattened chest, and say, "There walks a doomed man." It is in the structure of the individual that the seed lies, if at the same time his habits are conducive to its development.

The causes of Consumption are as plain as those of the breaking of a bank or the fall of a structure—the insufficiency of the lungs.

The condition requisite for its development consists in covering up the skin, and in the exclusion of the pure air and sun-light. Thus is impaired the activity of another organ which, conjointly with the lungs, is charged with the duty of supplying air to the blood. That organ is the skin. The skin, the lungs being small, is called upon for increased service, and would supply it if healthy,—that is, when exposed to the air, the light, and friction. But the skin inclosed in close-fitting and dark garments of cloth and leather, and protected against alternations of temperature, is not only unequal to this supererogatory duty, but is even incapacitated for its normal work.

Putting these points together—seeing the distinctive signs on the one hand, and the facilities of precaution on the other, neither being abstruse and scientific, but both being evident and plain—so plain that the blind only will not see,—it follows that no one using his senses suffers from Consumption except because he likes it. But the modern man—that is, the man of the historical periods, from Abraham and Lao-tsee downwards, does not use his senses; he puts in their place ill-assorted and uncertain memories, the rummaging amongst which he calls his reason.

I am describing the condition of every skin in modern Europe. In cases of insufficient lungs those lungs being unequal to their own work, and having, in addition, a part of the work of the skin to perform, the effort becomes overpowering; thence distintegration of the tissues, deposition of morbid secretions, topical inflammation, sweating fevers; in other words, that disease to which the significant names — Decline, Wasting—have been applied by our people.

For such a malady there is no remedy in the Pharmacopœia.

Far, however, from considering this deficiency as alarming, I should hold it to be propitious for any consumptive patient in whom I took an interest; because the medical man is disabled from objecting to the other means, not medical, which may commend themselves to the common sense of persons uninstructed in the science, but nevertheless able to understand this disease quite as well as any physician.*

Were the patient afflicted with gout, the medical man would say, " I have my colchicum." The Phar-

---

* "The public in this matter is far in advance of the medical profession. Our duty, as doctors of the healing art, simply is, to make ourselves acquainted with the uses of this therapeutic instrument."—*Dr. Thudichum.*

macopœia—the knife—the lancet—would lay insuperable barriers in the way of enlisting the skin against the disorders afflicting severally the organs, or pervading by their poison the whole system. In Consumption, fortunately, the field is clear ; and the medical man who must at some point of the malady utter the word or the doom " MADEIRA," cannot say to his patient, or to that patient's relatives and friends, " I forbid you, on pain of death, the Turkish Bath."

When you go to a legal man, you get from him *law*. When you go to a medical man, you do not from him get *health*. He has acquired no amount of that commodity with his diploma to dispense to those who seek his counsel. No medical man can cure, or profess to do so. All he can legitimately pretend to, is to advise or assist the sufferer's body, so as to call forth its own resources in its struggle with disease. Now, the means to this end, in the age and country in which we live, consist chiefly in heat,—as by it alone can the skin be recovered from its inertness. But medicine has taken no account of heat. The chief agency of nature has been disregarded by medical science.* Having disregarded it, they have constructed theories of therapeutics ; and these now stand in their way, and prevent them, except in rare instances, from admitting as a medical agent, that " purgation by the skin," which is the

---

* "We have hitherto known nothing of heat as a treatmen for disease. I do not know any work where it has been referred to in the most distant manner."—*Erasmus Wilson.*

very foundation of the curative art,—at least, as in its origin expounded by Hippocrates, the first as well as the last of physicians, being the only great man that medicine has produced.

In the case of Consumption, let us see what the patient would gain by spending some time daily in an apartment with an elevated temperature and electrically isolated.

1. Warm air admitted to the lungs.

2. Complete external purification.

3. The results of exercise which he cannot take.

4. The saving of electricity (life), otherwise dispersed.

5. The cleansing of the blood from all floating impurities.

6. The blood being reduced as to liquid, firmer muscle is deposited,•and the power of repairing diseased tissues increased.

7. The healthy perspiration supersedes the unhealthy night-sweats.

8. The power of sleep is increased.

9. The advantages of a warm climate are combined with those of a cold one, and *vice versâ*.

10. The exposure of the body to the sun's rays, by which alone the ravages of Consumption can be arrested.

11. The freeing of the body, for a certain number of hours in the day, from the exhausting encumbrance of clothes.

12. The dead skin is removed by shampooing; so that

the oxygenation of the blood is carried on all over the body, to the relief of the heart as well as of the lungs.

13. Other organs, such as the liver and the kidneys which may be indirectly involved, are equally relieved.

Those who desire to follow out these various branches have the means of doing so elsewhere : it is but an outline I give. I will take now two points out of these thirteen for illustration,—Shampooing and the Rays of the Sun.

Shampooing.

I shall dispose of this by a passage written at Baalbeck in 1850 :—

"A man is not born into the world with clothes ; nor are ready-made hatters, hosiers, and tailors, natural products. Man is born in his skin, and is, so to say, his own clothier: it is that skin that has to sustain the wear and tear of the world ; and being endowed with that faculty, it is needful to it to undergo that wear and tear. Man is his own clothier: instead of having to go to a shop for a new suit of skin, he from within is constantly repairing that which he has. But, if he puts a covering over that skin, the wear and tear no longer takes place ; and the impenetrable varnish so supplied by nature not being worn off, the body becomes suffocated, and the man is afflicted, just as a plant would be when taken out of the light and excluded from the air. Thus it is that, from the moment that the verdant and partial covering of Adam and Eve was replaced by textile and general clothing, the first necessity of man came to be the removal of his dead skin,

" For this purpose four processes have been adopted throughout the families of the human race. The first was, the rubbing down with the ball of the hand, as still used for currying horses of high breed. The three others are, scraping, rolling, and polishing. The scraping was with the strigil, which we know of from the Romans and Greeks, but which is figured on the tombs of Lycia. The rolling is by means of the goat-hair glove, as to-day practised by the Turks. The polishing is with the gazul, and practised by the Moors, to whom it is confined, and who alone possess the admirable substance which is used for it." *

Rays of the Sun.

As to the effect in the way of cure, of the mere exposure of the body to the rays of the sun, what I have to say was stated in a lecture I delivered at Brompton in 1860, as follows :—

"Before I had a Bath to use, before there was one in this country, I was at Wakefield giving a lecture upon the subject, and I took Consumption as illustrative. After the lecture, the gentleman who had been in the chair came to me, and said, ' You have been describing what I have seen before my eyes day by day for years. I have seen it in an elder sister, in a wife, in a daughter, in a son : they are gone. I now see it renewed in a second daughter. We have had a consultation of medical men, yesterday, and she is ordered to Madeira. I know what that means. Will you come and see her ?' I went and saw her, and finding her a sensible woman, I made her understand the hopelessness of cure by art, while I showed her that there were natural means by which she might be so far restored as to enjoy life, if she was willing to alter her habits so as to use them. That lady is now alive ; and the last time I heard of her, she was able to walk a mile daily. The means that I employed were, divesting her of tight and dark clothing, and making her lie in the sun during every hour that he shone ;

* "The Lebanon." vol. ii., p. 386.

thus obtaining relief from the pressure of clothes, admission of air and of the sun's rays to her skin. The skin has a right to the rays of the sun, to the breezes of the air. We shut out those rays, and deprive it of those breezes: we shut out from it the alternations of heat and cold, we deprive it of moisture, and finally shut it up in a case, in which it is darkened and confined until at last we render it no longer serviceable for the purposes for which it was intended. We rebel against the laws of our existence, and justly are we punished for doing so. The case which I have related is useful as showing how much we can obtain even without the Bath, by restoring the order of things which has been interrupted. I esteem as the first of all these means, the direct action upon the skin of the rays of the sun: not sunlight, observe, as generally diffused, but the sun's rays striking the surface of the body." *

As a matter of mere experimental science, *Actinism* (Ray-ism) has been attracting attention in the United States and in Germany, without the suspicion arising of its importance for man. A physician of New York has, however, fallen upon it accidentally, as would appear from the subjoined extract taken from " Public Opinion " of the 8th of August, 1863.†

* Lecture at the Brompton Literary Institute, " On the Effects of Light and Heat on the Human Body," February 7th, 1860.

† " *Beneficial Effects of Sunshine.*—Seclusion from sunshine is one of the misfortunes of our civilized life. The same cause which makes the potato-vines white and sickly when grown in the dark cellars, operates to produce the pale, sickly girls that are reared in our parlours. Expose either to the direct rays of the sun, and they begin to show colour, health, and strength One of the ablest lawyers in our country, a victim of long and hard brain-labour, came to me a year ago, suffering with partial paralysis. The right leg and hip were reduced in size, with

Reasons, however cogent, in favour of a method, are as nothing compared with the objections, however frivolous, that are or may be urged against it. The objection in this case is, "*the Bath (perspiration) is lowering.*"

Dr. Leared has given the reply of experience in this very malady. I may add, that one of these patients (Wright) is at present engaged as a shampooer in the Hammam in Jermyn-street, being unable to pursue his ordinary avocation (wood-cutting) away from the Bath.

The maladies in which the most immediate relief is afforded, are where the head, the heart, or the lungs are affected. In these maladies no one would recommend

constant pain in the loins. He was obliged, in coming up-stairs, to raise the left foot first, on every stair, dragging the right one after it. Pale, feeble, miserable, he told me he had been failing several years, and closed with, 'My work is done. At sixty, I find myself worn out.' I directed him to lie down under a large window, and allow the sun to fall upon every part of his body,—at first, ten minutes a day, increasing the time until he could expose himself to the direct rays of the sun a full hour. His habits were not essentially altered in any other particular. In six months he came running up-stairs like a vigorous man of forty, and declared, with sparkling eyes, 'I have twenty years more of work in me.' I have assisted many dyspeptic, neuralgic, rheumatic, and hypochondriacal people into health by the SUN-CURE. I have so many facts illustrating the wonderful power of the sun's direct rays in curing certain classes of invalids, that I have seriously thought of publishing a work to be denominated the 'Sun-Cure.'"— *Dr. Warren.*

to the patients to *undergo labour* in the Bath. Yet there are no less than three persons engaged in the Hammam (the superintendent and two shampooers), because, being consumptive, they are equal to do work in the Bath, and are not so elsewhere.

The shampooers, who are engaged in the Bath for fourteen hours daily, enjoy perfect health. On making inquiry as to the amount of charges on their sick-fund, I was answered, that no money had as yet been paid, as no case of sickness had arisen. This among from twenty to thirty men, during seventeen months.

The history of the subjoined experiments is as follows :—

In February, 1861, the Turkish Bath was brought to the cognizance of the medical body through a paper read before the Medical Society of London, in which its claims were asserted, not only as a medical agent, but as one so pre-eminent as to call for the revision of pre-existent therapeutic theories.*

A discussion ensued after the reading of this paper, and twelve medical men, not one of whom had ever

---

* " Mr. Urquhart wrote to me, towards the close of last year, ' If we are not to wait these 500 years before we know anything about the Bath, if we are to experience in our lifetime the value and to learn the nature of these results, it will be by the appearance of a man capable of standing by himself, who, dropping the clouts and the finery of preconceived notions,— making renunciation of the past, and starting with freedom on the new career of experiment—the Bacon of the human frame, —will accomplish the *opus magnum* of pathology. By this

been in a Bath, or knew anything about it, spoke successively, giving utterance to opinions and asserting
them with a confidence which could only be the result
of the reverse of knowledge. Being invited to speak,
I could do neither more nor less than say that it was
impossible for them to judge of a matter of which they
were ignorant ; but that if they desired to understand
it, which they could only do by experience, I should be
very happy to see any of them, or the whole Society, at
my residence in Hertfordshire, where they could take
the Bath themselves ; and, after that, I should be very
happy to answer any questions that they thought fit to
put to me.

This invitation was accepted : an entire day was
allotted for this purpose ; and the deputation, filling
an omnibus, and accompanied by a short-hand writer,
arrived soon after ten A.M., returning to the station
only about ten P.M. It was singular that not one of
the twelve who had spoken so decidedly on the subject
at the meeting appeared among the number ; although
I have since learnt that the most eloquent on

experimental process he will obtain results which he will convert
into instruments available to every land, so as to make science
the handmaid of daily practice ! '

" I have made that renunciation in full ; and if I claim to be
honest by pointing my finger in the direction of error, and by
denouncing false principles of action and modes of thinking,
I am no less so in inviting you to participate in the benefits of
such an act, by imposing it upon yourselves."—*Dr. Thudichum's
Paper read before the Medical Society of London.*

that occasion—Dr. Richardson—has since become a convert.

I was subjected to an examination of seven hours. Every objection put forward was met and withdrawn, and my statements were left intact. I would not venture to say so, were not the short-hand notes in existence, and available as proof if called for.

It was then that, for the first time, I saw the author of the papers now reprinted. He was one of those whose questions most indicated scepticism, and he did not leave on me the impression of a favourable result.

Soon afterwards, a company was formed for the building of a Turkish Bath. The project sprang from the alarm felt by some who knew from experience in the East what a Bath really was, lest the public favour, then culminating, should turn to disgust by the spurious and mercenary imitations arising on every side.

Whilst the building in Jermyn-street was in progress, Dr. Leared came to visit it, and thus our intercourse was renewed; several conversations succeeded, and finding that his basis of judgment was hospital results, I proposed to him to obtain a small share for himself, offering to build a Bath at once, and put it at his disposal for the patients of the Consumptive Hospital, in which he was physician. The Board (of the Turkish Bath Company) having sanctioned this arrangement, I was enabled shortly afterwards—that is in October, 1861,—to redeem my pledge. The experiment recorded in the subjoined papers thus extend beyond two years.

Whilst these cases were attending the Bath, I scrupulously abstained from so much as an observation in respect either to the degree of heat or the period of time. It was with great difficulty that I so restrained myself. These patients were barely undergoing the ablutions which I should hold to be conducive to the maintenance of health. Had these patients been in my hands, they would have been in the Bath each day twice the number of hours that they spent in it during the week, and at double the temperature,—that is, at 100 degrees above the ordinary summer atmosphere, instead of 50°.

Feeling, however, that we were only at the very dawn of a new day, and that professional men must feel their way slowly, doubtingly, cautiously, and experimentally, I held that there was more chance of ultimate success from the hesitating and almost unwilling admissions of Dr. Leared, than if this first regular experiment had been conducted by a bolder man. There is, however, no reason—now that so fortunate an issue has been arrived at by such slender means, and that his patients have absolutely themselves broken away from him, and engaged themselves as shampooers so as to get the Bath fourteen hours a day instead of two hours a week—why I should not now say that the results might have been attained in a quarter if not in a twentieth part of the time.

I give, as confirmation, a note of the treatment of a case during the winter preceding these experiments, when the patient was taken for treatment into the bleak, cold, mining regions of the county of Durham, and with no medical supervision. But he went into that desolate region to find a Bath at 200°, and to use it daily. An Ironmaster writes to me, December 26th, 1860,—

"My engineer, who has got a Bath at his own house here, has got a brother pretty far gone in Consumption : pulse 120 ; weak, and growing weaker; cough—spitting matter ; hectical, and growing worse. He has had him about three weeks in his own house, treating him daily with the Bath, and thinks him virtually cured: pulse 75 ; coughs very little ; good appetite ; good sleep; walks two miles a day, without feeling it, in the deep snow and bitter frost. Certainly, if there be any stages of Consumption which it will not cure, it is not the early stages."

I will now give an instance of one of the inflammatory attacks which may end in Consumption. Here it is a medical man who will speak for himself: the writer is a London practitioner, and the most eminent medical chemist :—

"September 30, 1861.

"On Saturday the Bath effected wonders upon my frame. I was close to an attack of pneumonia, and in presence of many dangers. I knew the feeling so well from former experience, that it is impossible to misconstrue it. I came out of the Bath a new man, that is to say, one to whom six weeks of illness have been spared. Before the Bath, I was close to faintness, sick, and weak on my legs ; I suffered agonizing headache, and could not keep my eyes open from photophobia ; I shivered and fevered in turns, and had those premonitory stitches in the right chest which are with me a sure sign of coming inflammation. Two hours in the Bath changed the aspect of affairs so completely, that I was able to walk home with Lord R. M——, and spend some hours with him in agreeable conversation. It was to me the most wonderful experiment I have yet made. I was yet weak yesterday, but not ill : to-day I am in almost perfect health."

Two days later he writes—

"Last Saturday's experience with the Bath has engendered a new feeling in my mind, which I cannot describe otherwise than as security against unnatural death."

It is painful to reflect that so many days, weeks, months, and years have elapsed since such results have been unquestionably established, without any steps to render them available for the hundreds of thousands of our fellow creatures who, in the mean time, have been dragging out lives of hopeless suffering, or have been consigned to an untimely grave. Physicians stand in the way, stopping those who would look forward, and pretending the desire of investigation, demand the production of hospital experience and results. How can such results be obtained, except by their co-operation ? Those who stand in the way of trial, and who then deny to their patients the benefit of a cleanly habit, for the Bath is no more, because the trial in one peculiar fashion has not been made, would be the first to demand that test were they not satisfied that it would be successful. Every patient has now, however, the means which he never possessed before, of testing the capacity or the integrity of his medical adviser. At all events, the friends of the patient ordered to Madeira can fairly say to medical men, " Will you not allow your patient first to try the effect of the Turkish Bath ? "

Morocco in climate resembles Madeira. Morocco is inhabited by three races : the inhabitants of the towns, who use the Bath ; the dwellers in tents, who do not use the Bath, but whose garments are open, like the *toga* of the Romans ; the Jews who do not, or rarely, use the Bath, and who cover up their bodies in clothes. The first two do not know Consumption ; the third are peculiarly subject to it.

The foregoing pages having been submitted to the medical man who has the first right to speak on this subject, his acquaintance with the Bath in the East being coeval with my own, and he having introduced it at the time of the Crimean war into one of our hospitals on the Bosphorus ; he made thereon a criticism which I am bound to quote : it was in substance this :—

" The friend or relative of the consumptive patient who reads these pages with the view of acting thereon, will of course refer them to some medical man for his opinion. Such medical man, if he is minded to dissuade his patients from using the Bath, will at once say, ' You cannot rely on the statements here put forth, and I will give you the proof of their unsoundness. The writer says that ordinary medicines cannot reach Consumption in the way of cure. *This is not true.* If you will not take my word, ask any medical man you like ; you can even consult for yourself medical works: take for instance, the highest authority on Consumption, Williams; turn to p. 193, and you will find the distinct enunciation of the curability of Consumption in certain cases.'

" Now, if you stated your case in a less absolute or in a more distinctive fashion, you would deprive an objecting physician of such advantage. I mean, that after having referred to the predisposing structure of the individual, you should have distinguished in reference to hereditary taint and in reference to predisposing circumstances, so as to show, especially in regard to the latter, that where the lungs, being themselves in due proportion, are subject to accidental lesion, then depuration may take place while the patient is undergoing medicinal treatment, and the physician will of course designate the result as cure."

Fully accepting this criticism, I will add that in referring to the passage of Dr. Williams I observe an expression of peculiar significance. In treating of the exceptional cases in which a cure is hesitatingly predicated, he says—

" Under treatment, *and favourable circumstances of air and climate,* these symptoms and signs have been gradually removed."

" Air and climate " is all I contend for as sufficient

s

to stop the progress of the disease up to the moment when the amount of working power of the lungs ceases to be equal to the sustaining of life. But then the "air" shall be admitted through the skin as well as the lungs, and "climate" shall represent heat raised to the point of efficiency.

Treatment of Phthisis by the Turkish Bath.

By ARTHUR LEARED, M.D., M.R.I.A.,

Physician to the Infirmary for Diseases of the Chest.

From the "Lancet" of November and December, 1863.

I HAVE long believed that we make far too little use of the skin as a means of depurating the blood, and that the uncertain action of diaphoretic medicines has had much to do with this neglect. The great importance of the skin will be acknowledged, if we remember that the volatile matters discharged through its pores are about double the amount of those discharged by the lungs, and that even the quantity of water expelled by the skin nearly equals that discharged by the kidneys.

When in Turkey some years ago, I had frequent opportunity of experiencing and observing the effects of the Turkish Bath. I became convinced that it was the only reliable means of causing diaphoresis, and that it might be most effectively employed as a remedial agent, as well as one of cleanliness and luxury. Gout, a true blood disease, is said to be unknown amongst the Turks; and this exemption is probably as much due to the free action of the skin caused by the Bath as to their temperate habits. In estimating the value of the Bath as a curative agent, however, the special effects of caloric on the body are to be taken largely into account. The effects of the higher degrees of heat possess a great but as yet an almost unrecognized importance.

The treatment of phthisis has made little or no progress for many years. General tonics, as mineral acids, iron, and quinine, are found highly useful in this disease, as well as in others marked by depression of vital power. But, with the single exception of cod-liver oil, none of the special remedies proposed have stood the test of experience. The utility of the oil is proved by the undoubted extension of life in the case of those patients who take it compared with those who do not. Being convinced that other valuable agents in the treatment of the disease may be discovered, this has been long a subject of my experimental inquiry. It is my present purpose to place before the reader the results of the treatment of phthisis by the Turkish or Hot-air Bath.

An opportunity of trying the effects of this treatment in the fullest manner was kindly afforded me by the Directors of the Turkish Bath Company in Jermyn street. A good deal had been said or written in a general way about the beneficial effects of the Bath in affection of the lungs, but it seemed desirable that its action upon phthisis should be patiently tested and fairly made public. Although resolved not to allow any theory to occupy my mind, it appeared to me that he Bath was likely to prove useful in phthisis for the following reasons :—

First. As the functions of the skin are promoted by the removal of effete matters which clog its pores and hinder free excretion, benefit might be expected from the Bath regarded in a purely hygienic light. Experience proves that whatever promotes the general health of the patient tends to retard the destructive changes in the lungs.

Second. If, as is highly probable, the perspirations ot phthisis are an effort of nature to depurate the blood by excretion of offending material, the substitution of sweating induced artificially might effect the same end in a better and safer manner.

Third. In cases in which sweating was a marked symptom, this, as well as the exhausting fever which precedes it, might be replaced by the operation of a process agreeable to the sensations of the patient, and one which, being completely within control, might be regulated according to his strength.

Fourth. The inhalation of heated air might prove beneficial by a direct action on the lungs, as would be evidenced by check of the cough and expectoration.

For several months at first a small private Bath was employed, but subsequently the large Bath was used by the patients. The temperature ranged from 120° to 180° F., and the patients remained exposed to it from half an hour to an hour or longer, the time being regulated by the action of the skin and their own feelings.

Great care was taken not only to observe any improvement, but also to prevent possible harm.

I regret that I am unable to bring forward a larger number of results. Several patients commenced with the Bath, and, although well satisfied with its effects, were compelled to desist in consequence of not being able to give up the necessary time to it. But the long period during which two of the cases were under treatment, and the precision with which the facts will be detailed, give these cases unusual importance.

The first patient I shall mention died unexpectedly; but, as will be seen, death was not caused by phthisis, and the rare opportunity was afforded of examining the lungs of a phthisical patient, in whom improvement of chest-symptoms was going on up to the time fatal disease of another kind set in.

J. C—— is a man of small stature and dark complexion, forty-two years of age. His father died of phthisis; also a maternal uncle, and a sister of his own. Early in 1851 the patient had cough, and felt out of health. In May of that year he had for the first time an attack of hæmoptysis. He thinks the quantity of blood brought up was not less than a pint. It continued to come up in smaller quantities almost daily for about three months. He was at length able to attend to business, although in very delicate health. In March, 1852, hæmoptysis returned, accompanied by the same symptoms, and he was under medical treatment until September. In 1854 he was laid up from May to July from the same cause. Again in August, 1858, blood was brought up in such quantities that his life was almost despaired of, and he was under treatment until April, 1859. The cough then became a little better; but great difficulty of breathing remained. In 1860 he became an out-patient at the Brompton Hospital for Consumption, and continued so for twelve months, when he left, his breathing and cough being unrelieved. In 1861 he became for many months an out-patient at the Royal Infirmary for Diseases of the Chest. He had the old symptoms, and blood made its appearance several times, the last time having been in November of that year.

Present state.—Jan. 1st, 1862: Pale and very thin, but thinks himself less so than he has been. Complains of weakness, and great dyspnœa even from ordinary walking; shooting pains in the chest, especially through the right side; night-sweats; troublesome cough, with yellow sputa. The upper and anterior part of the right side of the chest is dull on percussion, and in the same position crepitation is heard over a considerable space, as also in the right axillary region. He was ordered a hot-air bath three times a week.

Jan. 27th (fourth week of Bath treatment).—Has taken ten baths; says he felt benefited by the first bath; pain and night-sweats quite gone; cough better, and expectoration less; what he chiefly notices is improvement in his breathing; has also a feeling of improved general health, and the bad headaches from which he suffered at short intervals for years have entirely left him; bowels regular; except for cough and slight dyspnœa, would consider himself well. Weighed Jan. 1st, 9 st. 4 lb., and on Jan. 26th, 9 st. 6 lb. The crepitation that existed over the front of the right lung decidedly smaller, and in the mammary region hardly to be distinguished.

Feb. 17th. — Cough and expectoration rather better; breathing about the same; appetite good, and attends to business more closely than for a long time previously; up to present date has taken cod-liver oil and quinine as he did before commencing Baths. All internal medicines to be now omitted.

April 21st.—Health in every respect improved; cough and expectoration very slight; some dyspnœa on strong exertion, but "nothing like what it was;" lives in Long-lane, Smithfield,

and now walks to and from the bath (about six miles) without
inconvenience; could not have attempted this for a long time
previous to taking baths; the dulness on percussion over right
apex *seems* less; crepitation less marked.

June 11th.—Breathing greatly improved; cough has lately
been rather troublesome before breakfast. Sent to Dr. George
Johnson, who kindly examined the patient, and made the following note: " Slight dulness; feeble respiration and crackling
at right apex; harsh breathing at left apex."

25th.—Continues very well; removed to Bethnal-green-
road a month ago; walked twelve miles on one day this
week without trouble; has taken not less than fifty baths in
all. After careful examination, could detect no crepitation in
the right lung; in the infra-clavicular space slight crumpling
sound and a sonorous râle; dulness on percussion hardly
appreciable.

Sept. 26th.—In consequence of his improved health, has
taken no baths except two for three months; one last week,
and one the week before. Took them as he was not so well as
usual. Has on the whole gone on very favourably. Physical
signs the same as on June 25th. Seen to-day by Dr. G. Johnson, who made the following note :—" Slight dulness on
percussion; diminished expansion and feeble respiration at
right apex; no moist sound; respiration at left apex
harsh, almost tubular, with prolonged expiration; face
still pale."

Oct. 20th.—Had bath on day he last saw me; none since.
About a month ago began to make the bodies of hats, in which
process ammonia is evolved. On account of his health has not
worked at this branch of his trade since 1851. At present
does full work. Can walk any reasonable distance, but ascending tries him. Cough troublesome at times. In all other
respects doing well. Physical signs: No crepitation at right
infra-clavicular region, but a low and peculiar rumbling sound.
To resume the Baths.

Dec. 2nd.—Baths twice a week regularly since last note.
Breathing and cough considerably improved. Says his general

health is good. Physical signs unchanged. Showed me a swelling on left side of chest, about three inches below nipple, which he noticed for the first time yesterday. It could scarcely be called sore, and was not painful. Said he did not feel at all weak. Advised him to apply a poultice, and to see me again if it did not soon improve.

7th.—I was sent for in haste to visit him, but he had expired before my arrival. His wife told me that from the time of my last seeing him he had become gradually weaker until the debility was excessive. The swelling continued almost painless, although it had increased considerably in size. He had taken nothing but beef-tea to support him, as a physician formerly consulted had advised him never to take stimulants of any kind. His wife added, that he had been of late greatly depressed in mind by business affairs. There was no increase of cough or other chest symptoms. At eight o'clock this morning he managed to dress and get down-stairs; had some tea; returned to bed much exhausted, and died calmly about ten o'clock.

Examination of the body, eighteen hours after death.—Body in very good condition; sub-clavicular spaces well filled. Three inches below the left nipple was an anthrax two inches in diameter, having a very dark appearance, and on its surface several points of ulceration. Some elevated dark spots were scattered about on the surrounding healthy skin. The cellular tissue involved in the anthrax was in a sloughy condition. On laying open the thorax, a layer of fat at least half an inch thick was found beneath the skin. The heart was larger than natural, and lay more to the right side than usual. All the valves appeared healthy. The right lung was a good deal smaller than the left, which accounted for the position of the heart. There were firm adhesions in various parts, and the apex was so adherent to the opposed surface that a portion of lung-structure was torn through in separating it. Crepitation was impaired, and it had a much more solid feel than is natural; this was remarkably the case at the summit, but there was no appearance of tubercular matter.

The left lung was adherent in places, but less so than the right; and it was less crepitant than natural. At the apex there was a tubercular mass about the size of a filbert, and of a cheesy consistence.

Remarks.—It is plain that death in this case did not result from phthisis. So far from being emaciated, the patient was in good condition; and the state of the lungs, which contained neither cavities nor softening tubercular matter, precluded the idea. It is certain that death was due to the debility which is well known to occur in cases of anthrax; and it is probable that the timely use of stimulants would have averted the fatal issue. The question then arises, did the long ill-health of the patient depend upon phthisis? A review of the case admits no other conclusion. None of the leading symptoms of the disease were wanting. The case was certainly of a very chronic character; and this may be said to weaken any conclusions that may be drawn from it. But let it be remembered that, up to the time of commencing the Baths, this man's life had been for years only a succession of illnesses, with attacks of hæmoptysis, and of imperfect rallyings. From the time of beginning the Bath treatment until his death, a period of nearly a year, there was not the slightest hæmorrhage, and, until his fatal illness, he greatly improved in health. At one of his last visits he said to me: "This is the first year since 1851 that I have not had constantly to take medicine, and use blisters." It is also worth remarking, that the patient regarded the Bath treatment as very agreeable. Crepitation at the summit of the right lung was perfectly determined, not only by myself, but by the independent observation of Dr. Johnson. Both of us observed also that the crepitation subsequently ceased. No tubercles in the stage of softening, or other appearances that might have been expected, were found in the part of the lung mentioned. But the local crepitation must have depended on softened tubercle; and it can only be supposed that the tubercular matter had disappeared. I am of opinion that at the place of adhesion an abscess of the lung had existed, which having been discharged, its fundus became adherent to the adjacent surface of the chest-wall.

A. W——, aged seventeen years, a wood-engraver, became my patient in October, 1860. His sister, who had been a patient of mine, died of phthisis the previous month; and he lost his mother also from the same affection. He then stated that his health had been good until recently, when he found that he was losing flesh and strength, and had a slight cough. The treatment consisted of cod-liver oil, tonics, and sedatives, under which he soon improved, and ceased to consult me. In June, 1861, he again consulted me, and remained under treatment until he went into the country on the 17th of August, where he stayed until October 10th, since which time I have seen him at intervals. He improved at first under the same treatment, but he has lately grown weaker and less capable of exertion. Slight hæmoptysis occurred once.

Nov. 20th, 1861 (thirteen months from commencement of illness).—Much thinner than when in health; complexion of such a remarkably dusky hue as to lead to suspicion that the supra-renal capsules are diseased; feels weak and languid, especially in the afternoon; slight night-sweats; very easily put out of breath; cough very troublesome, and attended by mucous expectoration.

Physical signs.—Marked dulness on percussion, and moist crackling over the space bounded above by the left clavicle, and at a distance of four inches below by a line drawn parallel to the clavicle. Ordered the Hot-air Bath twice a week.

Jan. 24th, 1862.—In nine weeks and three days has taken eighteen baths—two per week. Stayed in the hot chamber about an hour, and was shampooed on every occasion but one. Has latterly taken the cold douche. Continued taking cod-liver oil and sulphate of quinine, as he had done for a long time previously; but the cough medicine was omitted, as he found it unnecessary; expectoration also much less. The attacks of debility in the afternoon have quite left him; he sleeps well; no night perspirations since first bath. The appetite is greatly improved, and, what is most remarkable, the dusky hue of his complexion has almost entirely disappeared.

A fortnight ago he had a severe attack of pain passing from a spot beneath the left cavicle to the back; this lasted three days. A small blister and poultices of hot bran were employed to remove it.

Physical signs.—Dulness on percussion as before; no crepitant sound whatever on deep inspiration or coughing, but a peculiar low creaking sound; no cavernous breathing or other signs of cavity.

Feb. 12th.—Shown to seven members of the Society for the Study of Diseases of the Chest, at Dr. Webb's. With one exception, all regarded the results of the Bath treatment favourably. The gentleman in question ascribed patient's improvement to his having worked at engraving two hours less since beginning baths; he works at present seven hours daily instead of nine. Chest examined by the members, and absence of crepitation admitted by all.

21st.—General symptoms good. Omit all treatment, except Baths.

March 24th.—Since last entry has had baths three times weekly, except one week, when he had them twice only. Was weighed on 9th ult., and found he had gained four pounds and a half in a month. Cough rather better; fine crepitant sounds under left clavicle.

April 16th.—Twenty-first week of Bath treatment; has had about fifty baths in all. Is now in all respects going on well. Sleeps well, and has no night-sweats; appetite good; bowels regular; cough almost gone. Has worked ten hours a day for last two months, except on days when he takes the bath.

May 18th.—Doing well. Weighed on 15th ult. 126 pounds, without any clothes, and before taking bath. (This mode of weighing is to be understood whenever his weight is afterwards mentioned.) Sent to Dr. George Johnson, who was kind enough to examine him and make the following note:—" Dulness at left apex; deficient respiration; large crepitation; bronchophony; face pale; night-sweats have ceased. Has been taking Turkish Baths three times a week; soon began to improve; has gained flesh and strength."

July 16th.—Going on well. Physical signs: Large crepitation under left clavicle. Bath closed for the present. ,

Sept. 10th.—States that he continued very well without any baths until about a month ago, when he got pain under left clavicle, night-sweats, and increase of cough. Took three baths, one per week, at an establishment in the Euston-road, with direct benefit. With the exception of about ten days, when so unwell, as stated above, and on the days when he takes the baths, has worked full time for several months. Ordered medicine for cough, as it is now sometimes troublesome. Large crepitation as before.

26th.—Taken only two baths since last date. Note by Dr. Johnson: " Dulness over left upper lobe ; gurgling under cla-vicle ; crepitation large, as low as mamma. Expectoration in morning."

Oct. 29th.—Has lately been occupied two hours in drawing, in addition to ten hours at engraving, daily, except on the bath days. Cough trifling, with a little mucous expectoration in the morning. Takes bath twice a week, with the cold plunge after it. Weight on Oct. 1st, 121½ pounds. Physical signs as in Dr. Johnson's report. To omit drawing-lessons.

Dec. 31st.—Increased two pounds in weight between Oct. 1st and Nov. 21st, and a pound and a half between Nov. 21st and Dec. 30th. Weighed yesterday 125 pounds. Cavity seems drier.

March 11th, 1863.—Is looking well, and a week ago weighed 126 pounds. Cough has given little trouble ; no night-sweats ; appetite very good ; works on an average nine hours a day ; has taken the baths and cold plunge twice and sometimes three times a week.

May 14th.—Says his cough is better than since commencing Baths ; can go up-hill much better than he could some months ago ; works and takes baths as usual. He has long been in the habit of walking to and from the bath, a distance of about six miles ; but his weight has not been sustained lately : weighs 119 pounds.

30th.—Not so well as usual for some days ; cough trouble-some at night ; working seven hours a day. Physical signs : Right side as before. Left : some dulness on percussion under the clavicle, and slight crepitation on coughing.

June 22nd,—Hæmoptysis in small amount came on early on the 19th ult., and occurred throughout the day when he coughed ; sputa more or less tinged since. Weighed, June 19th 116½ pounds. Ordered a grain of quinine three times a day, and to continue Baths.

Sept. 15th.—Has lost weight considerably; weighed on the 11th ult. 118 pounds. Has not worked at his trade for some time. Physical signs as before. Has left off the quinine. Ordered for the cough a mixture of ipecacuanha and morphia.

Nov. 19th.—Like J. C——, the Bath is a source of enjoyment to him; his fondness of it and faith in it are indeed remarkable. On Sept. 26th he took, without my knowledge, a situation as shampooer, from a conviction that *his being constantly in the Bath would prove still more beneficial to him.* Since then he has been from eight to ten hours daily employed actively in his duties. He assures me that he seldom coughs when in the Bath, and less at night than he did previously; that his "chest feels quite easy," and that his appetite and strength are improved, but that he feels a good deal fatigued at night from the labour. He takes the cold douche daily, and very often more than once. What is most remarkable is, that *his weight has increased six pounds since he has been constantly in the Bath.* Physical signs show that the cavity in the left lung has become drier; no moist sounds can be heard except on coughing, and the same is true of the crepitation at the right apex.

Remarks.—This patient has been subjected to the Bath treatment exactly two years. I have found that when he does not drink, he loses by perspiration two pounds in weight in the course of an ordinary bath. From the commencement up to September 26th he had taken not less than 170 baths. At the rate mentioned, that would give a total loss of 340 pounds from this source. Add to this four pounds a day loss (a moderate estimate) during forty-six days that he has been constantly in the bath, making 184 pounds, and the total loss of forced perspiration from both sources will be 524 pounds. This is more than four times the highest observed weight of his body—126 pounds. Some idea may be gained from these figures of the activity of the treatment.*   As to the result, it is, of course, admitted that the disease, which from the physical signs seemed arrested at first, afterwards advanced.   On the other hand, when the Baths were omitted for several weeks, the bad symptoms returned, and were to all appearance removed by resuming them.   Again, when his general health and weight had fallen off so considerably, a prolonged and daily exposure to the Bath was followed by a great improvement in both, and there is reason to hope it will be long maintained.

In testing a new remedy, it is desirable that the diseases against which it is employed should be well developed.   If the action of the remedy is favourable, it may reasonably be supposed that it would be still more efficacious in the earlier stages of the same disease.

The following is a case of phthisis in its first stage treated by the Bath :—

Feb. 3rd, 1862.—H. W——, aged twenty-seven, is an omnibus conductor, but was a butcher until twelve months ago.   Is married, and of steady habits.   His parents are living.   A brother of his father died of phthisis.   He has been out of health about thirteen months ; has lost flesh and strength ; had some cough with expectoration ; and has had slight hæmoptysis at intervals for some months, marked dyspnœa, and slight night-sweats.   Says he has at present no cough or expectora-

---

* " It may be laid down, I think, as a general rule, that large evacuations by sweating may be employed more freely, and with less disadvantage to patients, than by any other secretion."
—*Todd's Clinical Lectures*, 1860, p. 409.

tion, and that the dyspnœa is less troublesome. Physical signs : Well-marked dulness on percussion in the right infra-clavicular region; deficiency of expansion, and roughness of respiration.

He has taken cod-liver oil and quinine for about six months with advantage; and in December last he took, by my advice, three Turkish Baths, which seemed beneficial. Circumstances prevented his resuming them until the 15th January, since which time he has had seven baths.

May 3rd.—Every bad symptom has disappeared. He has taken no medicine for several weeks, but has had two baths a week, with some interruptions, since the last note was made. Except when he takes baths, he works fourteen hours and a half daily.

Nov. 13th, 1863.—Has taken the baths ever since at intervals of about a fortnight. He is constantly employed at his business, and is free from pulmonary symptoms. On carefully examining his chest, I could not detect any physical signs, except a slight roughness of respiration at the right apex.

After much careful and prolonged observation of these cases, the evidence that the Bath treatment proved beneficial is to myself conclusive. I have been anxious that every source of error should be eliminated as far as possible, and, at the risk of being tedious, any cir-cumstances that seemed to have relation to the improved health of the patients, such as going into the country, curtailment of hours of work, &c., have been carefully noted. I am well aware that the statements of patients who are subjected to any new treatment are not to be hastily accepted. There is a tendency on their parts to believe that they are deriving benefit, and if the mind of the physician is itself biassed in favour of a remedy,

T

the conditions for erroneous conclusions are complete. But even if I had not steadily held this danger in view, the length of time during which the patients were under observation must have corrected fallacies. As soon as it was plain that the Bath treatment could be safely substituted for internal remedies, all medicines were omitted in order to give the Bath a more perfect trial.

It will be convenient to consider the effects of treatment in the foregoing cases relative to the prominent symptoms of phthisis under separate heads.

Cough.—The patients who suffered from this asserted that the Bath had a decidedly beneficial effect.

Dyspnœa.—There was marked improvement of this symptom in all the cases. J. C—— especially complained of a long-standing dyspnœa when he commenced the Baths, and he attributed his power of increased exertion as much to " better breath " as to greater strength. The diminution of dyspnœa is very suggestive.

Hæmoptysis.—It might be supposed that spitting of blood would be induced, where the predisposition to it existed, by the stimulating effects of a high degree of heat. On reflection this seemed to me improbable, as, notwithstanding acceleration of pulse, the stimulating action is mainly exerted on the surface of the body. The superficial circulation being thereby promoted, blood is diverted from the internal organs. The result proved that any apprehension was unnecessary.

J. C——, who suffered so much from hæmoptysis, never had the least return of it while using the Bath; and H. W——, who had it in a milder degree, continued to take the Bath during its occurrence, not only without injury, but with apparent advantage.

Night perspirations.—*The direct action of the Bath has been more strongly shown in removing night-sweats than in any other symptom.* As already stated, this was expected on rational grounds. In several other cases I have recommended the Hot-air Bath for this distressing symptom. A patient who had been drenched by night perspirations told me recently, that after having taken a bath which I advised for him he had no return of them, and several days had then elapsed.

Debility and loss of weight.—A strong impression prevails that the Bath weakens the body; and it is not uncommonly asserted by healthy people, whose experience is confined to a single trial, that they did not recover from its effects for several days. One of the following alternatives must therefore be accepted: a mistake must be made, from prejudice or other causes, by those who in health declare the Bath to be weakening; or else the Turkish Bath is peculiarly adapted for the consumptive. As debility is a leading symptom in phthisis, patients suffering from the disease would be much more sensitive of anything having a weakening tendency than those in health could possibly be. Now, not only in the cases detailed, but in several other instances which came under my notice, the Bath was from the first pronounced by the patients to be comforting and sustaining.*   As far as all outward appearance was concerned, that was really the case.   To myself it is plain that, if not beneficial, positively bad effects must soon have been discovered.   It is impossible to suppose that patients in whom vitality was so much impaired could endure the abstraction of from two to four pounds † of sweat twice or three times each week, unless these apparent losses were in reality a gain ; that gain was evidenced by increased strength and weight of body, and improved general health.   The remarkable increase of weight in the case of H. W——— may be compared with the happiest results of the same kind from taking cod-liver oil.

One remarkable change of opinion has resulted from the introduction of the Turkish Bath.   Not five years ago it was generally supposed that to pass while in a state of profuse perspiration into water the temperature of the air in winter, must be injurious, or even highly dangerous.   The dread of the contact of cold water to the heated skin was sometimes carried to a ludicrous extent.   I well remember, when a schoolboy, having been taken to bathe with other boys, and, if heated by

* It is admitted that in exceptional cases the bath, when taken for the first time, or else at rare intervals, causes temporary debility, drowsiness, or headache ; but these effects are soon dispelled by repetition.   Sea-bathing, as is well known, frequently induces the same results in those unaccustomed to it.

† As proved by accurate weighing before and after the bath.

exercise, being compelled to wait in a state of semi-nudity until the point of regulation coolness was attained before entering the water. This refrigeration was, of course, the best possible foundation for bad results from bathing. It remained, however, for the Eastern Bath to prove that the most profuse perspiration may be suddenly checked, not only without risk, but with positive advantage.

Now, it seemed to me that since my phthisical patients endured the influence of heat as well, if not better, than the healthy, they would equally resist any bad consequences from cold. At first I took the precaution of being present, so as to watch the result of the new experiment. That result exceeded my most sanguine expectations. The patients declared the immediate effects to be agreeable, and no subsequent catarrhal or inflammatory affection could ever be attributed to the practice. Not only was this the case, but they became much less liable to catch cold than previously. This is a very encouraging effect of the bath; for, as is well known, intercurrent attacks of bronchitis and pleuro-pneumonia from changes of weather are common complications of phthisis, and too often precipitate the fatal event. Nothing is more important for the phthisical patient than that he should be as much in the open air as possible. His hope lies in living as hardy a life as his condition admits of. In selection of climate for the invalid, temperature has been far too much regarded. A dry, bracing, winter climate is to be preferred to one which is relaxing. The absence of rain and harsh winds is mainly to be considered. According to my experience, then, the hot-air bath and cold plunge in a great measure supply the deficiencies of climate by rendering patients more tolerant of our own changeable seasons.

The remarkable modifications which the physical signs underwent in two of the cases require some comment. The well-proved disappearance of crepitation in the case of J. C—— was, to say the least, a matter of the rarest occurrence; and the state of the lung under post-mortem examination went to show that it must have undergone a favourable change. In the case of H. W——, crepitation disappeared and returned, as if the vital power, aided by treatment, had gained an unsustained mastery over the disease.

I admit that the number of cases is insufficient to warrant the inference that the bath treatment arrests the depositions of tubercle, or causes tubercle already deposited to pass from an active to a passive and less injurious condition. Its good effects are, of course, to be looked for with most confidence in the first stage of phthisis, before breaking up of the lung structure has occurred; and the case of H. W—— is highly encouraging. There is enough to make us hopeful of further success in future trials of a remedy, which has the great advantage of being agreeable to the sensations, and refreshing to the mind as well as to the body of the patient. In a disease which condemns so many to prolonged suffering and death, and in which we have been powerless to save, a treatment cannot fail to be welcome which as an agent of cure promises so well, and which has been at least proved greatly to alleviate suffering.

If it, unfortunately, fell to my lot to be affected by phthisis, I should give the hot-air bath the fullest trial.

DR. THUDICHUM ON THE CONTENTS OF PER-
SPIRATION AS DISCHARGING THE MATTER
OF DISEASE.

December 26th, 1860.

MY DEAR SIR,—The secretions of the human skin may be divided into volatile and solid. For the sake of convenience, we include the water that divides the solids with the volatile portion, though it is not always entirely so.

The volatile ingredients are—1. Carbonic acid; 2. Water; 3. Some volatile acid, not yet accurately determined.

The fixed contents are—1. Urea; 2. Chloride of sodium; 3. Fatty matter; 4. Earthy salts of some fatty acids; 5. Small quantities of some other alkaline salts. Phosphates and sulphates, always present in any other secretion, I have never found in sweat.

When the contents of perspiration are so arranged as to give the first place to the greater quantity, they take the following order:—Water, carbonic acid, chloride of sodium, urea, and other ingredients. The presence of water and carbonic acid constitutes the analogy of perspiration with the excretion of the lungs; the presence of urea and chloride of sodium with that of the kidneys. While the excretions of the skin are analogous to some extent to those of the lungs and kidneys, they are not entirely so, and cannot be substituted for the others; for the kidneys are alone empowered to remove phosphates and sulphates and acid from the blood, together with colouring matter: it is a privilege of the skin to remove volatile acid; the lungs are restricted to carbonic acid and water.

The dignity of the skin as an excreting organ becomes more apparent from a study of the quantities of matter discharged by the several organs; for while the lungs in twenty-four hours discharge fifteen ounces of volatile matter, the skin discharges thirty ounces ; so that two-thirds of all volatile excretions pass by the skin. An almost equal weight of water leaves the body through the kidneys, charged with matter peculiar to that secretion, particularly urea and chloride of sodium. But a very small amount of carbonic acid leaves by the kidneys.

The lungs discharge the products of combustion, of warmth, producing food ; the lungs discharge the final products of the same, together with some mineral food, and the results of food, producing motion (muscle albumen). The kidneys discharge the products of albuminous food (sometimes called plastic, muscle-forming) in the form of urea and mineral salts, of several of which they are the sole channel of exit.

Considering that the bulk of the sweat glands in the aggregate amount to two-thirds of that of both kidneys, the quantitative importance of the solids excreted by the skin cannot be doubted.

If the evaporation prevents the sweat from collecting on the surface of the skin, the solids are deposited in a crystalline form round the mouth of the sweat gland. The urea then soon decomposes, producing carbonate of ammonia, which combines with volatile acid. Such ammonia salts constitute the smelling elements of sweat, viz., the most repugnant one. Healthy, fresh sweat from a clear skin has a most agreeable odour, or none at all.

Suppression of the action of the skin becomes fatal by the accumulation in the body of carbonic acid ; the lungs cannot do the office of the skin because they are too small, because they are only intended to ventilate the blood, and to inhale oxygen, their principal function, and not the tissues, which are so distant and ill-connected with the lungs. The ventilation of the bulk of tissue, cellular and muscular, is the duty of the skin.

Suppression of the function of the kidneys becomes fatal by occasioning the retention, as poison in the blood, of urea, and those matters which the kidneys alone can excrete. But in cholera and other diseases the skin secretes a fluid which contains *enormous quantities of urea.* Thus life is prolonged and saved.

In kidney diseases, chronic or acute, the bath will cause the skin to do extra duty, and prolong or save life. In all pulmonary diseases, the body need not succumb to retention of carbonic acid. Cholera in the algid stage need not any longer be fatal. Typhus and yellow fever may be turned in acme, now we have the means of controlling those of their symptoms or features which made them so fatal.

Cancer offers some remarkable features. I found cancer juice to be full of chloride of sodium. The bodies of cancerous persons contain an excess of this salt. Whatever the relation, cancer and excess of salt coincide. Is the kidney unable to rid itself of salt because the skin retains its portion? Is cancer of the stomach so common because this organ, surrounded in and outside with chloride, cannot escape its irritating influence? The cancerous tumours offer features only found in vegetables; alone, of all tissues of animals, it drains a juice when heated. Here are questions pregnant with results when investigated. Under any circumstances, the bath will remove conditions accompanying, favouring, or perhaps producing that awful disease, cancer. The bath will rid the body of excess of chloride of sodium in the tissues.

The effects of the bath upon the nerves must be wonderful. But these I do not touch. It was my intention only to sketch the humeral effects, as it were. The specific vital electrical effects must be legion, and equal in importance with the material or ponderable. The bath is an engine for the production and maintenance of health; and I would express my conviction that I consider it to be such, and do not desire to limit it to the destiny of a medical instrument. It is for the benefit of all men; the sick, however, will have a large share of its blessings.

I have read "The Pillars of Hercules" with a pleasure which no book has given me before. You have done justice to our silly self-love and ignorant complacency. Many thanks for all the good I have derived from it for my part.

I am, yours truly,

J. L. W. Thudichum, M.D.

D. Urquhart, &c.

CANCER, LEPROSY, HYDROPHOBIA, AND APOPLEXY.

SUCH experience as the British public has as yet had of the curative effects of the bath is confined to chronic disorders, or at all events to the acute stages of disorders with which we are familiar in a chronic state; that is to say, to gout, rheumatism, colds, stiffness of joints, sciatica, neuralgia, and the like.

My experience of it began in cases of acute and rapid malady, and these when already beyond the reach of all medical aid. Consequently my appreciation of it is in reference to the grand and triumphant march of febrile action as displayed in those maladies which suddenly overpower the individual, and which devastate communities—namely, fever in all its forms, intermittent, remittent, putrid, scarlet, typhus, the plague, the cholera, and yellow fever.

When these ideas came to be sufficiently settled for me to open the subject to others, I found no one prepared to admit so much as the possibility of having of himself recourse to such means in an acute malady—in all such cases being under his medical man ; and at the time I refer to there was no medical man who did not treat the bath as empiricism.

I was thus thrown back on the necessity of presenting the matter theoretically, and with reference rather to chronic than acute diseases. It appeared to me that, if I could challenge the faculty in reference to some particular disorders of a hopeless character, and which might on that very account afford the opportunity of submitting patients to the test of experiment, I should, if successful, be able to carry conclusions in reference to acute disorders. So it was that I selected three maladies, which were cancer, leprosy, and hydrophobia, to which I subsequently added a fourth—apoplexy.

In regard to the two first, I have succeeded in obtaining something like an experiment. As to hydrophobia, two cases of successful treatment have since been reported on as having occurred in France. As to the fourth, although no fit of apoplexy has been brought into the bath, to be there directly dealt with, still its efficiency in allaying the tendency of blood to the head must establish reasonable *à priori* grounds for the conclusion I have stated.

I have selected these four maladies as tests, because so dissimilar that if an agent can be found capable of successfully dealing with them in common, this conclusion cannot fail to be established—that by extreme alternations of heat and cold, you place that body in a condition favourable to the developing of its own resources in the combating of disease. This is all I contend for in reference to the bath. But it covers every case of disorder, whether as merely impairing health, or as bringing death from unnatural causes.

I would offer this analogy.

A hospital containing a thousand beds, including every variety of human ailment, is restricted in its ventilation, in consequence of the ideas and the habits of the country in which it is erected, which lead them either to exclude atmospheric air without thought, or to do so by maxim. A peasant, ignorant and *indoctus*, comes from a far land, and says to the learned pathologists attending at the bed-sides, " Your diagnosis is folly, your science is empiricism, your drugs are useless. I will cure for you your patients, or rather I will let them live, if only you will let me throw the windows open or break the glass if they have no hinges."

The physician would exclaim, " What! Treat cancer and dropsy, treat scarlet fever, treat consumption by one and the same remedy! This is empiricism. Do you come here to kill our patients if you fail, and to take the bread out of our mouths if you succeed ?"

Cancer is a disorder which afforded little chance of making the experiment ; being either in an incipient or an advanced state, so as in the first to preclude the trial of a new remedy by the hope of relief from the old ; and, in the second, being beyond the reach of recovery by any means.

The proposal in such a case of a new remedy was, moreover, obnoxious to strong and obvious objections so long as the discussion revolved within the theoretic circle, because of the numerous specific treatments which had arisen among the faculty itself during recent periods, all of which had proved illusory, and had been, in consequence, abandoned.

Next came the difficulty of determining true cancer. This, indeed, is an objection in terms only ; as it little matters to the patient what the name may be which is given to a disorder ; and as the remedy now proposed is a general, not a specific one, the chances of success are at least as great in the ninety-nine cases of supposed cancer as in the one case of real cancer.

When, then, a case of undoubted cancer presented itself, in which, after an operation the nucleus had been again re-formed, I conceived I had obtained the occasion so long desired.

On seeing the patient, I at once determined that these means in themselves must utterly fail, unless at the same time the patient could be aroused out of her condition of nervous atrophy, and so constrained to abandon habits of self-indulgence bearing upon the quality of her food and drink, the frequency of its repetition, and the listlessness which hopelessness had superinduced in regard to every effort, mental or corporeal. How far I was successful in the means employed to this end, the subjoined correspondence will show.

Cancer, alike individual and hereditary, alternates with consumption and scrofula and their cognates, indicating a common origin. These cognates are unquestionably resolvable by the same process as that here applied to cancer.

Cancer is unknown in countries where the bath is in use, as also in countries where, the bath being unknown, the temperature is such that excretion by perspiration is active. It is, therefore, to be inferred that cancer owes its origin, like consumption, scrofula, &c., to the habits of Modern Europe; that is to say, to the enclosing of the body in warm and close-fitting vestments, to the exclusion of air from the apartments, to the over-supply of food, and to the frequency of the efforts called for from the stomach for the purpose of digestion.

This view is further confirmed by the chemical analysis of the cancerous matter, which consists, first, of a substance analogous to vegetable pulp, and closely resembling the matter of peach; secondly, of common kitchen salt, substances in themselves destitute of any noxious qualities, and therefore presenting no visible difficulty of absorption, so that by the presence of external heat the absorbents are brought actively into play.

At the time of this experiment I was not in possession of radiating heat.

CASE OF CANCER.

CORRESPONDENCE.

Rickmansworth, August 9th, 1861.

DEAR SIR,—It is now more than four months since you accompanied me to Rickmansworth, in order that I might avail myself of Mr. Urquhart's generous and kind permission of daily admission to his bath; and believe me it is with the deepest feelings of gratitude and thankfulness to him, and likewise to yourself, to whom I am indebted for the introduction, that I now can bear testimony to the invaluable benefits I have derived from its use.

For upwards of twenty years I have been extremely delicate, but it is only within the last ten or twelve that my complaints assumed a serious character; at one time regarded as consumptive—a disease prevalent in my family; then appeared tumours, considered by many medical men to be of a cancerous nature. From these severe illnesses, however, I rallied; and it was not until about a year and a half ago that, in consequence of a severe blow received on my breast, decided cancer appeared; and so rapidly did disease manifest itself, that in less than three months from the time of the accident an operation was performed, being pronounced as absolutely necessary. After a tedious recovery, I was for a time perfectly free of pain; but within a very short period my sufferings returned, and increased during the past winter. I became fat and puffy, without strength in proportion. I could not even walk a mile, or take the least exertion without cold and clammy perspirations; and what little strength I had was rather the effect of stimulants than natural. My nights were feverish and sleepless, and the pain in my breast and arm so acute as to awaken me with a start when sleep did overtake me. When not out, I was always reclining on the sofa. I was nervous and hysterical; and, in fact, my every energy seemed dormant, although not, perhaps, actually in low spirits. I had followed the prescriptions given me, but they neither relieved pain nor reduced the disease. It was then my friends urged me to leave Jersey, where I was residing. On reaching London, I consulted the surgeon, who had performed the operation, and likewise seen me last September. He pronounced the disease not only to have returned, but to have made *certain* and *sure* progress, although not rapid, in the six months; and he candidly told me that, excepting to try some means to alleviate the pain, he could do nothing more for me. This brings me to the time of your seeing me, and by the united opinion of Mr. Urquhart and Dr. Thudichum, I was placed on an entirely new system, both as regarded the taking the bath, and a total change of diet. As regards the former, I may say that for the *first* month

the treatment seemed severe ; and so great was the prostration
I experienced on my return from the bath, that my spirits
sank ; and I was urged by many friends to give up a treatment which they expected would shorten, not prolong my
days ; but I had passed my solemn word, not only to Mr.
Urquhart and the doctor, but to my brother, that, whatever
I might feel or suffer, I would not give in or relax one iota,
unless pronounced by them a failure. And now I can indeed
rejoice that I firmly refused to yield to their solicitations, as
from that period up to the present time I have gradually and
steadily progressed towards health and strength ; and I am
now assured by Dr. Thudichum that the disease is perfectly
arrested, and that there no longer is external evidence of its
existence, the swelling and hardness having greatly diminished.
In order, however, to confirm my general health, so recently
restored, he advises me to continue the bath for some time
longer ; and I am both willing and anxious to persevere. I can
now take a good long walk, seldom lie down through the day,
rise earlier, retire later, rest better and much more calmly ;
and if pain is not yet altogether gone, it is greatly diminished,
and not constant. Instead of feeling listless, inert, and incapable of thought or action, I can now employ myself
throughout the day ; and, in fact, I feel the greatest change,
both physically and mentally. At first the bath seemed to
exhaust, but now I come out feeling stronger than when I go
in, the more so if the temperature be high. If at 130° and
upwards, and the alcove high in proportion, say 200° and above,
I experience the most benefit ; in fact, it is a *brisk heat*, and
the sudden alternations from the hot room to the cold, that
seems to be of the greatest benefit to me ; and provided I am
well heated before I use it, I experience the greatest comfort
from the free use of cold water thrown over my head, &c. ;
but if the temperature of the bath be low—that is under 130°,
and downwards, I feel the shock of the cold water, and, almost
shiver. In the first instance, it invigorates my whole frame ;
in the second, I feel a degree of languor when I leave the bath.
When I came, my right arm was much swollen, and considerably thicker than the other. By measurement every ten

U

days or so, I gradually found it diminishing; and by the 1st of June there was a very trifling difference between it and the other arm. Since then there has been no change. By the advice of Mr. Urquhart, I have bathed it night and morning in water as hot as I can bear it, plunging it alternately into the hot and cold water. At first *there was no perspiration whatever in that arm.* Now, with the exception of a narrow stripe at the back, it perspires freely. I think this statement would be incomplete were I not to say something respecting the change of diet. Having previously lived fully and freely, taking food often, and of the most solid kind, with wine and ale, I found the change to a milk and vegetable diet, with only two meals in the day, so trying during the first month, that it became necessary to allow me a little meat and a glass of wine occasionally when low and hysterical. At first I loathed the milk, and felt sick after taking it; and in the evening a species of aguish, cold shivering came on; but this last symptom has quite disappeared, and gradually I have ceased to care either for meat or stimulant, and am now taking the diet originally prescribed. In a morning I take *sour milk* instead of sweet; and this I not only relish, but it does not in the least nauseate me. Many might have thought I would be starved, but here I am, at the end of four months only, walking about as those in health, active and vigorous. Even two months ago, when I visited London, those friends who had seen me previously to my coming here were perfectly astonished at my improved appearance, and particularly at the clearness of my complexion, and the brightness of my eyes. I think I can add nothing more but to reiterate my grateful thanks to you and Mr. Urquhart for having placed in my power a means of cure so simple, pleasant, and efficacious, and of having recalled me, as it were, from the brink of the grave to the enjoyment of life. '

Believe me, &c.,

AGNES ROBERTSON.

P.S.—I may as well mention that for the first month I felt attendance on the bath as irksome, and only a duty; *now* I experience all the pleasurable sensations described by so many.

August 20th.

In the hurry of the moment I omitted two or three things in my letter, which I think it would be desirable to add as a sort of postscript, viz., that when in the bath, Mr. Urquhart recommended me to drink milk instead of water, a change which I have found beneficial as well as agreeable. Another very great change which I have made is in the clothing I wear. When I first came to Rickmansworth it was of the warmest description, and I wore much flannel. This I have entirely removed, and my dress is now of the thinnest material, and as little of it as possible. Again, in allusion to my improved sleep and nights' rest, I did not mention that I attribute this improvement in no small degree to my now keeping my bed-room window wide open all night, and having only a thin covering on my bed. Besides this, I sit in the morning and evening with but a light dress on, in my room with either a thorough draught, or as much air as possible, with perfect impunity; and I am certain that the habit is conducive to health. There are other two circumstances which I may add as a summing-up and proof of the renewed vigour of my health. In the letter I mentioned having become very fat and puffy during the past winter. Since taking the bath, although not really *thinner*, I have entirely lost that puffiness and feeling of swelling and breathlessness. The second is, that my hair, previously short and thin, has grown longer, and become much thicker since I came here. I think now I have mentioned all in my case that can be useful to others.

Rickmansworth, August 28th, 1861.

DEAR SIR,—I feel that my letter to Mr. —— would be incomplete, as far as you are concerned, were I not to mention an additional circumstance, to which I attribute much of my recovery, and for which I must ever entertain the deepest feelings of gratitude towards you individually. I allude to the effects produced on me by what you said on the first day of my coming to Riverside, and the advice you gave me then, and on subsequent occasions. At the moment I considered your opinion erroneous, and even felt hurt and disposed to resent it; but your words led me to reflect and examine into my previous state of mind; and if, *at first*, as I am ashamed to confess, my compliance with the prescribed rules, proceeded from piqued pride, and the determination to prove to you that I was not void of energy, these feelings soon gave place to a more healthy mental condition; and reason and pr nciple influenced me from that time. These reflections likewise led to the discovery, that what I had believed to be resignation to the will of Heaven was little else than an apathetic indifference arising, perhaps, from the belief that it was useless to try any further remedies for my disease.

It is, *you*, therefore, that I must regard as the chief means of my restoration to health and vigour: for I am convinced that, had you not roused my dormant energies, and shown me my *real state*, that in all probability, by a continuance of self-indulgence, the good effects of the bath would have been of little avail.

Believe me, &c., AGNES ROBERTSON.

D. Urquhart, Esq.

Riverside, August 31st, 1861.

DEAR MADAM,—Your letter has afforded me a gratification of no ordinary kind. the occasion having been one of the few great and painful efforts which I have made in my life. You know how few the moments were between my placing my eyes on you and the commencement of the endeavour. In that interval, however, my mind had been made up that your chance of life depended on the chance of my success in wrenching your spirit. Had I failed, besides that failure in itself, you would have preserved against me to your dying day an unquenchable hate, so that I should have left you worse every way than I found you. You may, therefore, now judge of the gratification you have enabled me to experience, to which is added the agreeable surprise that you have yourself followed the operation.

Believe me, &c., D. URQUHART.

Miss Robertson.

65, South Audley-street, London,
October 1, 1861.

MY DEAR MISS ROBERTSON,—When in March last you placed yourself under my care, you had suffered a relapse of the disorder, for which a severe operation had been performed upon you only a twelvemonth before. In less than five months the new tumour had increased from the size of a pea to that of a cherry. You suffered severe pain, were encumbered with a swelling of the right arm, which made it almost useless, and the disorder of the blood, of which the tumours are but a local expression, had reduced you to such a state of weakness that you could not walk a distance of one mile. Your mind, moreover, was in a condition of hopeless indifference, which made you very unhappy.

A persistent use of the Turkish bath, and the adoption of a peculiar specially adapted diet, have now, after seven months, effected such a change in your condition, that the dyscrasia of the blood has ceased to produce the amount of morbid material which is necessary for the deposition of tumours. But not only has the progress of the local disease been thus arrested, but in addition, the relapse, which had attained the size of a cherry, could at my last examination, not be perceived any longer; the tumor had evidently been dissolved. The arm had lost much of its size, and its surface had begun to share in the important function of the remaining part of the skin—perspiration. Pain had been mitigated, digestion had been restored. Strength and well-being had returned to you to such a degree that you could walk a distance of five miles, and felt called upon to give expression to your altered state of mind, in a letter to your benefactor, Mr. Urquhart.

At this juncture the question arises, whether you should continue the use of the bath and of the diet, which have effected such remarkable results. Considering that you were the subject of an experiment, that the experiment has been so far successful, but that it is not yet complete by any means, I think I am obliged to advise you most decidedly to continue the present mode of treatment. For though your disorder is arrested, and its local expression diminished, it is by no means cured. The risk of a relapse is constantly threatening you, and you would jeopardize your own safety, and the issue of the great experiment of which I want to make your case a foundation, if you were now to return to old habits of living.

I am, &c.,

J. L. W. Thudichum.

This case ended fatally, but not till after a long cessation of the means that had proved effectual, and a relapse into the habits that had been for a time amended.

CASE OF LEPROSY.

CORRESPONDENCE.

Burlington-street, Ashton-under-Lyne,
June 12, 1860.

Respected Sir,—I wrote to you some months since, stating the disorder of my skin. I gave you a full detail of the condition I was in, and you gave me some very good advice. I followed your instructions as well as I could.

Now, sir, I am happy to inform you that I am well, and free from any scurf on my body.

I have been in the Turkish bath at Staleybridge 195 times, and in one at Ashton, making a total of 207 baths. All who saw me before say they never saw such a sight.

I am, &c., Isaac Summer.

D. Urquhart, Esq.

Burlington-street, Ashton,
15th June, 1860.

RESPECTED SIR,—I am sorry to inform you that your original note is mislaid, and I cannot meet with it; but I will try to give you a detail of my condition when first I wrote to you.

There were mounds on my head like eggs. My neck was spotted with white scurf. My arms were covered with scurf from my shoulders down to my wrist. My back was like fishes' scales, and my belly very red. My thighs were nearly all of a scurf, and the calves of my legs very bad. Indeed, I was afflicted in every part of my body with this malady. It has been about seventeen or eighteen years in making this progress.

You advised me to refrain from all intoxicating drinks, and coffee (if not tea). Also you wished me to live making an experiment of one month on milk, which I tried to do. You desired me to refrain from animal food; so I did for some months.

I had wet bandages on my arms, thighs, and legs, with oil silk over them, and renewed the bandages three times a day; also, that on my belly for some months, I had fresh bandages nearly every morning, and found the oftener I had clean ones on the better.

I am now without the wet bandages. I have continued the above process for nearly two years. Added to the above, I have had two dripping sheets every morning as soon as I have got out of bed, one warm and the other cold.

All last winter I had three Turkish baths per week, and continued this practice till the beginning of this spring. After that I took two, and now I only take one.

I have had many crises during this time. I have been so sore at these times that I could not bear to be touched. During this period I have had dropsy in my legs, but soon mended from that. Now I am quite free from any scurf on my body, and can walk as well as ever. But before it was very painful for me to walk, and especially to go up steps. I generally soaped down two or three times while in the bath, and went under the shower bath four or five times before I dressed. I was only once lounging between the sheets. I dressed immediately after coming out of the bath, and never took cold but once. I found my own towels.

The scurf has come off me in such large flakes during the night that we have had to sweep the bedroom every morning, and a large quantity has come for a long time this way. Indeed, it has bristled like leaves. My duty to you.

I am, respected Sir,
Your humble and obedient servant,
ISAAC SUMNER.

P.S.—Have stopped in the Turkish bath two hours and one and a-half hours at one time. Tried to stop in as long as I could.

Riverside, June 17th, 1860.

MY DEAR SIR,—I do not know if you are aware that in the course of last year leprosy broke out in Norway. I learnt the circumstance in Berlin. The Swedish Government having desired the attendance of a distinguished physician from that city to examine, treat, and endeavour to arrest the malady. Dr. Virchow was the physician selected, and, before his departure, I earnestly entreated him to try the effect of the bath, which is in use in Norway, but failed to make any impression upon him. I mentioned to him that there had been a case in England, which I had not seen, but in respect to which I had been consulted. He inquired what the results of the treatment I proposed had been, but I could give him no answer. Since that period I had heard nothing of this case, and had dismissed it from my mind, supposing either that my advice had not been followed, or that it had been followed without beneficial results.

I have now received a communication from the patient announcing his perfect restoration to health from a supposed incurable disorder by which he had been afflicted for seventeen years. I enclose two letters, which cannot fail to be of interest to you. I much regret that my first letter of instructions has not been preserved, but I can sum them up in these words. Exposure of the body as far as practicable to air and to the sun. The total disuse of stimulants, of animal food, and of every aliment excepting milk. Whilst taking the bath as often, for as long a period of time, and as hot as he could endure it.

In the "Arabian Nights," (Lane's translation), vol. 1, page 75, you will find a curious incident of a similar cure,—a tradition of the times, when Easterns knew the bath as a curative agent, which they have now forgotten.

Are we never to have a talk on this subject? The talk when we have it must be here. London atmosphere kills conversation, and you must have a bath here before you can know what a bath is.

I cannot conclude with one of our meaningless endings, but to you must say—Roman-like—"Health and farewell."

D. URQUHART.

To Erasmus Wilson, Esq.

17, Henrietta-street, Cavendish-square, W.,
June 28, 1860.

MY DEAR SIR,—All honour to the bath. I am not surprised to hear that a seventeen years' malady has been cured by it. It is a mighty power, easy of control, but needing control and judgment; certainly not fitting to be entrusted to everybody and anybody. You will soon learn the difference between the physician and the quack; you are the physician, and can estimate the mischievous propensities of the quack. Augustus said, "that at thirty all men were physicians or fools." Alack, how few physicians there be. The seventeen years' case is either one of chronic eczema, in other words, psoriasis, or lepra vulgaris, the common lepra of Europe. Both are curable complaints, but there is this difference between them, viz., that the former being cured remains cured; but the latter is certain to recur. So that supposing the latter to be the disease, we shall hear more of it by-and-by, or probably so. The old leprosy, the elephantiasis of the Greeks, that stalked its hideous way from the shores of the Nile, through Syria, Greece, Italy, and France, to England; then turned about, and marched northward, to Scotland and Scandinavia; that still lingered in the Hebrides, at the close of the last century; and has ever since

been revelling in Norway, Sweden, Iceland, and the north of
Russia, is a totally different disease, and, happily, never seen
in this country now, except when imported. A capital treatise
on this dreadful disease was published in Sweden in 1848, and
it was to suggest a treatment for it that Virchow's assistance
was doubtless wanted. I fear that in consequence of the
dreadful organic mischief existing in the ancient leprosy ; even
the bath would fail. I have at present under my care a young
girl suffering under this dreadful malady, and hopelessly
doomed.

May God send you health and wisdom.

ERASMUS WILSON, C.B.

David Urquhart, Esq.

Riverside, Rickmansworth,
June 29th, 1860.

MY DEAR SIR,—Your letter has acutely revived in me a long
and somewhat self-reproach, that of not having pursued leprosy
in the East ; but this I can tell you, that the malady that is
there held to be such, is perfectly distinct from elephantiasis,
it is the same in the remote part of the East as in India. ·

I have had leprosy in my mind as the *beau idéal* of a neglected skin, and that will account for the peculiar interest I
took in a case within reach ; conceiving it to be an extreme
test of the means by which we propose to purify the skin.

In the East it is held to be incurable, but there it is not subjected to the action of the bath. In the ceremonial laws of the
Jews, leprosy is not assumed to be incurable, but the contrary,
as sacrificial ordinances are ordained ; but this is remarkable,
that the means of cure are indicated in the disposal of the
leper ; not shut up within walls, as practised now in the East,
but sent forth into the wilderness, that is to say to be treated
by means of the rays of the sun, the breath of heaven, the
waters of the sky, and the alternations of heat and cold.

You say nothing of the hoped-for enjoyment and instruction
which my letter to you was intended to propose and expected
to hasten.

If the order of the bath is to be re-instituted, your grade must surely be Grand Cross.

And believe me to be,

Yours faithfully,

DAVID URQUHART.

Erasmus Wilson, Esq.

Up to the present time (June, 1864) nothing more has been heard of this case, so the cure would appear to have been permanent.

CASE OF HYDROPHOBIA.

I should not mind my own child being bitten by a mad dog, so certain am I that the bath would cure him. Some time since I asked a medical man to find me a case of hydrophobia, as I was convinced that that disorder must yield to the bath. He told me that my idea had been anticipated in the only known case of cure. A French physician, having been bitten by a mad dog, and suffering from the first symptoms of the disorder, knowing that medicine was of no avail, and thinking only how he could die most easily, had himself carried into a vapour bath, there to remain till death. He remained until life. He was carried out cured.—*D. Urquhart at Cork*, August, 1856.

Case reported in Galignani's Messenger, Oct. 1863.

Dr. Buisson has addressed the following communication to the *Abeille Médicale :*—

A single vapour bath is sufficient to prevent hydrophobia by eliminating the virus; nevertheless, for the sake of greater security, I caused seven to be taken in as many days, at a temperature of from 42° to 48° Réaumur (127° to 140° Fahrenheit. Care should be taken to press the wound well while in the bath, in order to promote the expulsion. If the disorder has declared itself, I only prescribe a single bath, and leave the patient in it till the cure is effected, taking care to raise the temperature gradually. Hydrophobia may last three days. Experience has proved to me that the cure is certain on the first day of the outbreak; on the second it is uncertain, and on the third impossible, from the difficulty and danger there would be in conveying the patient to the bath, and keeping him in. Who would wait for the third day, knowing my treatment? Nor should one wait for the outbreak; it ought always to be prevented. Hydrophobia never breaks out before the seventh day, so that there is time to perform a long journey to obtain what is called a Russian vapour bath.

TENDENCY OF BLOOD TO THE HEAD AND EPILEPSY.

It is generally supposed, and naturally enough I admit, THAT PERSONS WHO HAVE A TENDENCY OF BLOOD TO THE HEAD WOULD RUN GREAT RISK IN TAKING THE BATH. I suffer much from a high temperature when dressed, being inconvenienced and oppressed by a hot day or hot room; but I can and do stand in the hot room of a Turkish bath, without any inconvenience with the thermometer at 170°.

Oct. 1st, 1862. J. WELLS.

I used this kind of bath as a remedy for fulness of blood in the head. I find not only relief at the time of taking the bath, but a permanent amelioration of the symptoms of determination. The profuse perspiration on the forehead and hair takes away all sense of weight and heaviness consequent on a surcharge of blood in the brain, and makes it circulate evenly throughout the frame. This I can testify from experience.

Nov. 16, 1861. JOHN COOKE.

I write to corroborate my former statement of Nov. 16, 1861, as to the efficacy of the Turkish bath as a remedy for fulness of blood in the head, from which many middle-aged persons of the learned professions are apt to suffer. I am still in the habit of taking the bath twice a week to ensure a cool forehead. I am aware that an erroneous impression exists about the Turkish bath causing rushing of blood to the head and eyes, whereas my experience is that the warmth of the bath causes an even circulation, a circulation which is felt even before the heaviness affecting head and eyes begins to go off.

Nov. 19, 1863.   JOHN COOKE.

What is the chief danger in the various forms of Bright's disease of the kidneys ?   Is it not non-elimination of urea ?

But it may be said that apoplexy is very common in this disease; and the Turkish bath should not be used when there is a tendency to apoplexy.   But what is the chief cause of the apoplexy here ?   Is it not uræmia ?   And will not the skin, under the influence of heat, eliminate urea; and thus, in preventing further toxæmia, if not removing that already present, prevent also the apoplexy which depends upon it ?—" Turkish Bath," by Dr. Cummins, M.D., Edinburgh.

SPECIAL CASES.

IMMUNITY FROM POISONS BY A HIGH TEMPERATURE IN COPPER MINES.

Extracts from Reports of Commissions, Session 1842.

Diseases of the heart and great vessels might, *à priori*, be expected to be of frequent occurrence under the above circumstances (inhalation of carbonaceous and mineral particles). My own experience leads me to believe that they are rare, if we except such degrees of hypertrophy and dilatation as are usually found in those who have followed laborious occupations during a long series of years. Vascular disease is very uncommon. The unplethoric condition of the miner, and *the very free perspiration* maintained during his labour, will serve to account for his not being the subject of disease of the great organs of circulation to the extent which might have been anticipated.—(Dr. Barham, in Appendix to First Report.)

One peculiar feature attendant upon copper works is the devastating influence of the smoke they emit upon the vegetation of the country around them, over which it appears to throw a species of poisonous deposit, at once destructive to the herbage and the animals which graze upon it; and so great is its influence felt in the immediate neighbourhood of the works, that the verdure of the land is completely destroyed, and the most fertile meadows converted into sterile wastes, on which scarcely a trace of vegetation appears.

Notwithstanding the deleterious effects of the copper smoke upon vegetable and animal life, as above described, the inhalation of it does not appear to operate prejudicially upon human health, as will be observed by the testimony of the workpeople and agents who reside around the works, and of the medical gentlemen in the neighbourhood, that those dwelling close to the works are generally the most healthy. The doctor attends these people at one-third less per month than the colliers pay. This statement is borne out by the evidence of Mr. W. P. Evans, the surgeon of the works, and of G. G. Brice, Esq., M.D., of Swansea, who has extensively practised in the immediate neighbourhood of copper works for the last fifteen years.

I may observe that the heat endured by the furnace-men of copper works is, both in intensity and duration, fully equal to the scorching temperature experienced by the founders or puddlers of the iron works.

I have seen the copperman skimming his furnace (a process of fifteen or twenty minutes' duration), standing within six feet of its open door, exposed to the reflective heat of the large body of molten metal within, and the scum or slag which he was abstracting flowing in a stream of liquid fire at his feet—a position of elevated temperature which could not be approached within many yards by unpractised persons. In this position I have seen him go through his laborious operation, stretching his heavy iron rabble or skimmer into the furnace, until the perspiration ran off his person like drops of rain, and the few clothes he wore became dripping wet; and it is not, the men say, until this profuse perspiration appears, or, as they term it, they become "wringing wet with sweat," that they can easily bear the smarting influence of the fire.

During these severe operations the men usually carry a towel on their shoulders to wipe the perspiration off their faces; and as soon as the labour is over, they not unfrequently run to a jug of cold water, and drink off a pint or two with impunity—a practice which, to them, does not seem to be attended with any ill effects.—(Report of R. W. Jones on the Employment of Children in the Copper Works of Glamorganshire, p. 679.)

INGUINAL HERNIA.

Oct. 22nd, 1862.

While residing at Tripoli some years ago, I witnessed an Arab mode of reducing inguinal hernia. The Arab doctor placed some lighted charcoal into a small iron shovel, and then kept moving this about in a circular manner over the seat of the tumour, at a short distance from it, and without touching any part of the patient's person. The swelling seemed at first to increase a little; a gurgling sound was then heard; and, finally, the swelling disappeared entirely.

E. D. DICKSON,
Physician to the British Embassy.

CATARACT CURED WITHOUT AN OPERATION.

Case communicated by Dr. Bryce.

In the month of September, 1859, I had an attack of ophthalmia, with severe inflammation in right eye, and was under Dr. Macmurdo as my medical attendant, who reduced the inflammation in about six weeks; and I was enabled to do without any further medical attendance till about August, 1860, when it came on again; and on applying to Dr. Macmurdo, he told me I had cataract in both eyes, and he strongly advised me to undergo an operation on the left eye, and have it removed at once before I entirely lost my sight. At this time my sight was very bad. I arranged to undergo the operation, but was unable to fix the day; and before I could do so, Mr. Barnes was taken seriously ill, which prevented my being able to leave business for the purpose. In December I was suffering very acutely from rheumatism, and expressed a wish to Dr. Macmurdo to try the Turkish bath, which at first he objected to, but afterwards consented; and about the middle of December 1860, I took the first Turkish bath, and found so much benefit to my general health, that I have continued it to the present time, more or less. On taking the first bath, I left off all medical treatment; and on calling, in July 1861, on Dr. Macmurdo, at his request, he was astonished to see the alteration in the eyes; and instead of advising an operation, he advised the contrary, and to keep on as I was going, and allow no one to do anything to my eyes. My sight improved on first taking the baths, and has continued so to this time, except for a short time last summer, when I got a severe cold in the right eye; but on applying to Dr. Macmurdo again, he got rid of that, but said nothing about the cataract.

IMPROVEMENT OF THE SIGHT.

Extract from a Private Letter.

He also said, " My sight is a good deal affected sometimes, and I cannot see even with two pairs of spectacles. I then go off to the Turkish bath, and when I come home my eye-glass is quite sufficient for me, and I feel I could walk miles. I often go to the Turkish bath, for I feel that nothing but that will do for me when I require two pairs of spectacles."

DISEASES OF THE KIDNEYS.

From a London Practitioner.

October 2nd, 1861.

An old case of kidney disease comes to the bath daily; and with the assistance of nitrous acid, exercise, milk diet and regimen, I have brought the albumen in the renal secretion down from forty to four grains per day.

A colonel, retired, also a sufferer from the kidney, with a most irregular heart, and martyred by neuralgia, had for

x

months been frightened that the bath would damage him.
I accompanied him myself to the bath. He bore it exceedingly
well. His heart continued as fitful as before, but no symptom
occurred; and he is now a staunch advocate.

EXTRACT FROM CASE REPORTED IN THE "BRITISH MEDICAL JOURNAL," BY DR. ROBERTSON.

M. W. (No. 720) was admitted at Hayward's Heath on February 23rd, 1863.

State on admission. a. Bodily.—He was very weak. The
tongue was furred and tremulous; the whole frame in a state
of tremor. He was restless and did not sleep. *b. Mental.*
The mind was quite confused; he was unable to understand or
answer questions. There was difficulty of articulation. He
was unable to tell his name; and was disposed to be destructive
and dirty.

February 25.—Want of sleep and restlessness continued.
He was very nervous and tremulous. Pulse feeble, 90 ; pupil
contracted. He ate slops. He was ordered to have a glass of
whisky at bed-time, and to be packed in the wet sheet for two
hours, with two cold pails afterwards.

*   *   *   *   *   *

May 10.—He had lost ground; the restlessness and incoherence continued. He was noisy at night; his habits were
dirty; he was feebler. Œdema of the legs had set in. The
urine* was found laden with albumen, abundant in quantity,
specific gravity 1025, clear, no deposit. The heart was healthy;
pulse 110. He was rambling in his conversation; he spoke
also of his strength and ability, and that he would build me a
carriage and provide four horses for it, and drive it himself.

---

* Unfortunately, the urine was not microscopically examined.

He was very troublesome, secreting things, &c. He was ordered to have the bath at 150°; to omit the sedative mixture. He was so feeble that he could hardly stand. He had to be carried to the bath. The skin acted feebly ; pulse 70, on his return.

May 21.—The bath was continued twice a week at 170°. The skin acted better. He was still very feeble. The œdema of the legs was less. His mind was no better ; he had delusions, and was incoherent. The albumen was less in quantity.

June 17.—He was in every way better. His conversation was more rational. He was gaining strength daily. He still entertained rather an exaggerated idea of his ability and strength, and had a propensity to secrete and collect trash as before. He was ordered to continue the bath twice a week, and to go to the carpenter's shop. The œdema of the legs was quite gone. His appetite was hearty. Albumen was slightly present only.

October 5.—A steady improvement had taken place. There had been no trace of albumen for some weeks in the urine. He was convalescent. The mind was clear and rational. He worked steadily in the carpenter's shop, and was allowed to go about the premises alone, satisfied with his position and care, and prospect of discharge.

November 30.—He was discharged on trial for a month. During the month, he came to Hayward's Heath to ask for a bath. I found him sound in mind and body, and working for the Brighton Railway Company, in their carriage factory, at thirty-three shillings a week.

December 30.—He was discharged cured.

REMARKS.—The therapeutic uses of the bath have yet to be studied. I believe them to be very great. Of its curative power in the early stage of phthisis I have had several examples, and I can confirm all that Dr. Leared reports of its action in the early stage of that disease. I long to see the bath fairly tried in zymotic diseases. I believe, if used in sufficiently high temperatures (170°-200°), that the results will astonish us all. If anything ever can cure hydrophobia, it will be the bath, at 200°, continued for many hours.

Yet, strange to say, although three years have elapsed since it was fairly and fully brought to the notice of the profession by Mr. Erasmus Wilson, and although the public are building baths, and using them eagerly and ignorantly, no London hospital has thought it worth while to add this potent agent to its armoury. The Newcastle Infirmary and the Sussex and Devon Lunatic Asylums are the only hospitals in England (so far as I know) provided with a bath.

In the *Journal of Mental Science* for July 1861, I gave an account of the bath at Hayward's Heath. In the same journal, for July 1862, I published some cases of melancholia (with refusal of food) successfully treated by the bath, and I have since then regularly used the bath in my practice at Hayward's Heath.

In the case above recorded, I have little doubt that the bath saved the patient's life and restored him to reason. He steadily lost ground until he began its use; the delusions increased; the bodily health gave way; œdema of the limbs set in, and he was so weak that he had to be carried to the bath, and could hardly stand when he came up from it. In six weeks he was at work at his trade, and in six months he was discharged from the asylum sound in mind and body, and able to earn a comfortable living. This cure was the only possible result which I did not foresee. I thought first that the case was tending to permanent dementia; then it looked as if general paresis of the insane would be the end; then it seemed as if he were to die from dropsy and albuminuria. I cannot but think that the bath was the agent which rescued him from all these perils, and restored him to health of mind and body.

SCARLATINA.

Brighton, March, 1864.
I have been laid up with scarlatina, infected, no doubt, during my attendance at St. Mary's Hall, where it has

abounded. It is my belief, and so proclaimed, that the severity of my attack was favourably influenced—in bed three days only—by the skin-cleansing which you so kindly effected for me immediately *preceding* my attack.

CHARLES BRYCE.

CHILD-BEARING.

A manufacturer's daughter had been married some few years, and was wishful to have a child to live. She had had several, but all never came to maturity. The father of this lady prevailed upon her to try the bath. She was then four months in the state of pregnancy. She took the bath twice a week up to a fortnight of her confinement. I should have stated that in the former cases of pregnancy she never was able to move about or do anything; but after she commenced using the bath she could assist in any household work she thought proper, and went through her confinement as well as it was possible any one could have done—the child a fine, healthy boy; and at the three weeks' end she came to enjoy her bath, quite lively, and spoke of the bath in great praise, such as I never heard any one before nor since.

This occurred in Bradford, in 1858.

HAIR RESTORED TO ITS ORIGINAL COLOUR.

A gentleman of the name of Booth, Barnsley, Yorkshire, who erected a small bath for his own and family's use, whose hair had gone grey, "with the use of the bath for several weeks, twice and three times per week, restored it to its original colour." This circumstance was communicated to me by the gentleman himself, when I called upon him to look at his bath in 1859. This was found out by the daughter at the dinner-table a day or two before he related the circumstance to me.

John Thistlewhaite was afflicted for many years with scrofula all over the face, and the eyesight to such an extent he could scarcely see his way along the street without assistance. Being in humble circumstances, I brought his case before the committee; and they granted him a free ticket for a quarter: He took the bath every other day; and after the second week he could see to read bills posted on the walls as he came along to the bath. He now enjoys good health, and is pretty good in his sight, so that he can follow his employment, the bath restoring him after every other means had failed. He had been under the Eye Infirmary in Manchester, Leeds, New-castle-on-Tyne; and other treatment, medical and non-medical, had been recommended to him. This case I had under my charge in Bradford. He is now living in Victoria-street, Manchester-road, and belongs to the Sick Club to which I belong; so that I can testify to his case.

AGUE.

Worthing, December 3rd. 1862.

I wish to give you an episode of yesterday in illustration of the benefit of the bath in a household.

I am liable to extreme and prolonged suffering from the cold easterly winds of this period.

Yesterday I took a long walk. It was a cold, bleak evening, and the easterly wind was in my teeth. The well-known but long-suspended pain came on in the region of the stomach; and it was with difficulty I reached home at eight o'clock.

I had an important letter to write for the post. My symptoms of ague had declared themselves. An arm-chair was wheeled before a blazing fire in the dining-room, and brandy and hot water ordered. Mrs. Urquhart said to me. " You had better go for five minutes into the bath, as you are, and so get heated." I did so. The fire had just been put on. The thermometer stood only at 140°. I laid down, feeling indisposed, and unable to get up again, and disembarrassed myself gradually of my clothes. The heat rose rapidly: within a quarter of an hour it was up to 160°. I was in profuse perspiration, and the pain had ceased. Within another quarter of an hour, the heat having risen co 180°, all sensation of suffering had disappeared, except a scorching of the mouth, as if the tongue was blistered. It took one hour more before I got rid of this ; in all, an hour and a half; and the heat at last rose up to 214°. Instead of the brandy-and-water, I had about two quarts of icy-cold water, besides being soused in the same. Instead of a night of suffering, to be followed by weeks, if not months, of the same, as during the three former years, I sat down at a quarter to ten to dinner, which was followed by a good night's rest; and this day I look forward to be quite able for my journey to town to-morrow, and am free from any inconvenience, save the sensations of one who has recovered from a severe ague.

My letter last night was also written, being able to dictate it during the intervals when I had to come out of the furnace within to get the cold blast outside.

You have noted the small platform outside at the door of the hot-chamber, between the window and the door, in the angle of the garden-wall, so that every blast from the sea, or from the north, comes through and falls on it. During the hour and a half I must have come out there seven or eight times, from three to five minutes each time. Without this facility of alternating the temperature, these startling results cannot be obtained any more than they can without the very high temperature (requiring a rapid circulation of air) and the heat by radiation.

The place where I lay you must have remarked. It is closer to the furnace than the thermometer, the difference being at least 10°. I was there exposed, at a distance of four feet, to the radiation from the red-hot metals ; so that 20° more may be added for the difference between radiating and transmitted caloric ; so that during the last hour of experiment the heat may be well reckoned at 250°; alternately, five minutes in that heat, and five minutes under the cold sea blast, when not under the water-cock.

Had I been at Riverside, with my model bath there, no such result could have been obtained.

Still less would it have been obtained in the Jermyn-street Hammam. The latter I could only think of as a soup served up in a golden tureen, and without salt. I trust, however, that this will be remedied before long. The obstruction I have had to encounter as an amateur from professional men will probably now disappear; and the success of the undertaking (as they consider it) will unite for future operations the practical and professional man.

While undergoing this experiment, the words of Mr. Ruskin, which I mentioned to you, were constantly ringing in my ears : " What can be more loathsome than a man stewing in his own perspiration ? " There is a specimen of the dominion over men of words. He fortified this by saying, " You know these are your own words, and you cannot deny them." My words were, "A man cannot be cleaner than his own perspiration;" thereby, to show the necessity of getting out the filth of his own perspiration, that itself should become clean. But he had no notion beyond this, that perspiration was, and must be, filthy ; and, therefore, like all foul things in the notions of this age, to be kept and concealed inside.

The case will not be complete unless I add, that during the night I was awakened with a twinge of gout ; and at the same time I perceived a troublesome indication of an eruption on my fingers. The latter had gone in again before morning, and the indications of gout had ceased. I was clearly in for a most serious attack.

25th February, 1862.

On the night of the 23rd I underwent the premonitory symptoms of an attack of ague, which with me brings on inflammation of the bladder. I am liable to these attacks in the spring, as regularly following on cold easterly winds. They have hitherto prostrated me for weeks and months.

Yesterday morning I went into the bath at half-past eight. The heat was low. It gradually rose to 150°. When I came out, at eleven o'clock, I was then so much relieved that I was able to breakfast as usual. Gradually the effect wore off, and I went in again at a quarter-past three. The heat was then 195° by the thermometer. By sensation, the heat (radiating) must have been equal to 230° or 240°. I came out at a quarter-past four, again entirely relieved, and was able to dine as usual.

After dinner I went through all the sensations that follow a severe fit of ague, and could at times scarcely credit that I had not had one. At a quarter-past ten I went in again. It was then at 180°. I came out at a quarter-past eleven, went to bed almost immediately, fell asleep, and woke at half-past seven, without having stirred all that time, and with a feeling of health, freshness, and vigour which I have not known for years. My nights are always disturbed. After an hour this morning, beginning at 150°, and rising to 180°, I went out to walk, enjoying the blast of that cold, bleak, easterly wind, which otherwise would have stricken me down as a scythe.

A friend who went into the bath yesterday after me, and who was unacquainted with my illness, afterwards, on meeting me, said, " So you have had a fit of the ague ; but I suppose, from the smell I found there, that you have left it in the bath."

CASE OF CHOREA (ST. VITUS'S DANCE).

I was requested to see Catherine Carroll, æt. 10 years, about the middle of last October. For twelve months previous the parents had noticed something peculiar about the girl, extreme restlessness, &c. This had gone on gradually increasing until she reached the state in which I found her. At this time all the symptoms of chorea were fully and strongly developed. The spasmodic irritability of all the voluntary muscles was extreme and incessant. When standing, she seemed every

instant about to throw herself down; when sitting, she was
continually rolling and twisting herself about. At night her
restlessness was so great that they had to place her in a
separate bed apart from the rest of the family. If she lifted
anything—a plate, or cup, or dish, no matter what—she would
generally let it fall; and not only that, but occasionally it
would be sent half way across the room, showing the great
muscular spasmodic irritability that existed. The expression
of her countenance and general appearance led to the idea that,
if she was not *then*, she was verging towards becoming an
imbecile.

The digestive functions were much disordered, the pulse
small and quick, appetite bad, and general debility very considerable. Her temperament is of the nervous type—that is,
of a pale and somewhat sallow complexion, large black eye,
and spare habit.

Her treatment consisted, first of all, in a course of purgatives,
to remove any cause of irritation which might exist in the
intestinal canal, such as worms, &c. This was succeeded by
quinine and a liberal diet, warm body flannel having been
already ordered. The spinal column was then rather severely
blistered throughout its whole extent, and she was put upon a
course of the chloride of iron, anodynes in the form of morphia,
and, as an anti-spasmodic, the ammoniated tincture of valerian.
This treatment was continued for about a month, and to a
certain extent was beneficial. Her tongue became clean, her
appetite better, and the anodyne gave her better nights; still
there was little improvement in the general symptoms.

I then thought of the Turkish bath; and the parents being
in poor circumstances, I mentioned the case to Mr. Attwood,
who, with his usual and considerate kindness, at once allowed
me the free use of the bath which he has erected here. The
first three baths had little effect: the fourth, however, excited
a free perspiration; and good results began to show themselves,
the first sign of which was her passing better nights without
the anodyne. So the case went on, the general irritability
gradually subsiding, until it altogether disappeared. About
three weeks ago I advised them to discontinue the baths; and

at the present date I may say that she is in perfect health, and as strong as any girl of her age and natural constitution. She took the baths for about six weeks; generally two in the week. In all, she had either thirteen or fourteen, the temperature being about 120°.

She was exceedingly weak when she first commenced with them, but only in one instance had she to be taken out before the usual time. This occurred at the second bath. With that exception, she remained in each about half an hour, and seemed to experience great comfort.

I look upon this case as being an extremely satisfactory one, and affording unquestionable testimony of the efficacy of the Turkish bath as a remedial agent. Many cases of chorea undoubtedly arise from the presence of worms; and when such is the case, unquestionably the first obvious indication must be to dislodge them; but then in those instances the bath would be proper; for so great a constitutional disturbance as chorea to be caused by the simple presence of worms, to which all children are more or less subject, is sufficient evidence that there must be something abnormal present in the system or in the blood, the removal of which, and the consequent purification of the blood, can be readily and efficiently effected by means of the Turkish bath.

I may add that not only the parents, but the neighbours about, have again and again expressed to me not only their pleasure to see such an improvement in the girl, but their surprise at the rapidity with which it has been accomplished.

ROBERT LANG, Surgeon.

Tow Law, January 15th, 1863.

SWELLING OF THE JOINTS, ETC.

Case of a Sergeant of Police.

Paddington, Nov. 2nd, 1863.

SIR,—The following are the particulars of my illness from March, 1859, to September, 1859:—

I had for many months previous to March, 1859, felt great pain in the back and legs, great swelling of the veins and feet, and contraction of the muscles of the legs; the fingers would swell to an unusual size in an instant, and as quickly disappear. I walked, or rather hobbled, in very great pain, which was chiefly in the feet. The colour of the skin below the knees and round the loins was of a parchment-like colour, and I frequently felt the sensation in the legs and feet which is termed "going to sleep," and violent throbbing in the calves of the legs. My appetite was very good, but still I wasted so rapidly that I was reduced almost to a skeleton in May, 1859. I could scarcely wear a boot or shoe, and when walking I felt a burning sensation round the feet. I thought at this time that if I could take some kind of bath which would produce a free perspiration, it would have a beneficial effect. With this view, I consulted a medical gentleman, who spoke of sulphur, vapour, and lamp baths, saying that he had no doubt such baths would prove beneficial. I was speaking to a friend a few days later, and he recommended me to try the Turkish bath in Bell-street, which was conducted by Mr. Evans, and the only public bath of its kind then in London. I entered the bath, and perspired from the face, neck, and shoulders, *but not one drop of perspiration came from the loins or legs.* I continued to bathe daily. The swelling increased, the pain becoming more acute, chiefly in the feet; and as I was then performing eight hours' duty nightly, it was with great difficulty and pain I reached home in the morning. After partaking of my breakfast, it was with still greater difficulty (owing to the contraction of the muscles of the knee) that I could get upstairs to bed. When I rose up, my feet would be swollen to such an extent that the shoes (for at this time I could not wear boots) which I had taken off in the morning could not be worn by me for an hour or two until the swelling had gone down. About the third week a rash came out on the insteps of both feet, and disappeared in a few days. About the fourth week the feet, for the first time, began to perspire. The loins and legs at this time perspired rather freely. During the fifth week large lumps began to descend the legs from the body. I felt no pain in these lumps except that the pain, when they entered the feet, was much greater, and a contraction of the muscles when they reached the bend of the knee.

Eight or ten lumps descended each leg during the fifth week. About the sixth week several small boils began to gather on the insteps of both feet, from which a large quantity of matter was discharged. As soon as the discharge had ceased I felt very great ease, and in a week or two was quite free from pain. I took the bath till Christmas, gradually reducing the numbers from six to one bath per week. I still frequent the bath, and have enjoyed very good health up to the present time, and firmly believe that the bath was the means of saving my life.

I remain, Sir,

Your obedient Servant,

BENJAMIN VARNALS.

Mr. Johnson.

J. S., aged 33 years, afflicted with chronic rheumatism for five years, finding no relief from medicine, took the Turkish bath daily for three months at Mr. Cusden's, Canterbury-terrace, Kennington, S.W., and for the last three years have continued so doing twice a week. I am now perfectly cured, and enjoy good health. When I first went to the bath my joints were swollen, rheumatic pains in all my limbs, had partially lost the use of my left arm, and my head was fixed, so that I could not turn it. I consider my cure is entirely due to the use of the bath, and have found my general health so much improved since I have taken the bath regularly, that I shall, D.V., continue its use while I live.

Construction of a Bath.

Mr. Urquhart to Sir John Fife.

WORTHING, *November* 3, 1863.

My dear Sir,—

I HAVE to announce to you an event which, taken in conjunction with the opening you have made in hospitals, promises to lead to the introduction of the Bath into the parochial and county establishments throughout the land.

I have just returned from a visit to the Lunatic Asylum of Sussex, where the Bath has been in operation for about a year. I went to it expecting to find low temperature, repulsive filth, and unventilated cellars. I found these chambers light and airy, and a temperature of 180°!

Dr. Robertson, the physician and manager, had indeed, begun with the "130°" of the judicious men, brick flues and the common prejudice against iron.

Employing, however, in some repairs, a builder who had formerly worked for me, he offered, at his own charge, to change the flues, substituting iron ones, and to replace the others if not approved of. Dr. Robertson was glad to have the opportunity of testing the other process. To his surprise, he found the higher temperature so obtained was more bearable and more agreeable to the patients and to himself. Thus has the radiating element been partially introduced; and whilst the temperature is so much raised as to be more than doubled (taking as point of departure the general temperature), the cost in fuel is diminished one- half.

Dr. Robertson had already seen my Bath, but not before his own had been constructed. Having experienced the difference in effects between 130° and 180°, he was prepared to accept my suggestion as to raising the temperature to 200° and to 220°.

I was struck by the importance he seemed to attribute to the mention I made of having *never known a case of injury arising from any amount of heat.* From this it would appear that people still continue to believe that they have got something to fear. The same illusion may prevail at Newcastle, and prevent you from making in the Infirmary due use of the means you possess. What I said at Hayward's Heath may, therefore, be also serviceable for you.

Just as I was leaving, I found, from looking over his "Case-book," that "administering the bath" meant taking it once a week! Indeed, generally, I found the words "once a fortnight:" but for this, I should have been left in ignorance of the infinitesimally small amount of power exerted to produce the beneficial results which he had to report. I begged of him not to consider the Bath as a remedial agent, unless used at least once a day at a heat of 200°; the patient being exposed to it for periods varying from five to ten minutes, so as to make up one hour.

For the present, and until his new Bath is constructed, he will not be able to get more heat; but, at all events, his Case-book will reveal the difference obtained by the frequency of the operation.

It was a most pleasurable day that I spent at Hayward's Heath: there was none of the vague, unmeaning speculation with which one is always met by medical men.

*   *   *   *   *   *   *   *

In reference to this malady (Bright's Disease), I may mention that I saw at Hayward's Heath a case of perfect cure. The patient had been entirely given over. I saw the man, and heard his own statement.*

Believe me, &c.,

D. URQUHART:

* Sir John Fife, M.D., &c. &c.

---

* This case has been since printed in the *British Medical Journal.*

SIR JOHN FIFE TO MR. URQUHART.

NEWCASTLE-ON-TYNE, *November* 21, 1863.

MY DEAR SIR,—

It is quite evident from your observations on the temperature of the Bath, and the frequency of its use, that we only have the institution in its infancy, and that a minute description of your own might be of great service in enabling others to comprehend the extent of its proper application.

I am particularly interested in your correspondent's observations on the symptoms of apoplexy or paralysis in albumenuria from retention of urea in the circulating blood; having myself recently discovered that similar symptoms occurring in the convalescence following diphtheria came from the same cause, and expecting in such cases to find the Turkish Bath the most efficacious mode of treatment.

Faithfully yours,

JOHN FIFE.

January 13, 1864.

MY DEAR SIR,—

The only satisfactory answer to your letter of November last would be to take you into my hot closet, or rather to let you take in a suffering man and observe the effect on him. This being impossible, I sit down with the

Y

intention of describing the means used, and the effects produced so minutely, that it shall be in your power to reproduce the like with certainty; although I am ready at a word to go to Newcastle for a week, which would be more than sufficient for the reconstruction of the Bath in the Infirmary.

I enclose a plan of my—let us call it—*Sweating Closet* at this seaside cottage.

There is a furnace; two couches, one raised and receiving the close and full radiation of the red-hot metal, the other moveable in the floor; also a tank, to which you descend two steps, there being a slab to prevent splashing. You may have in it hot, tepid, or cold water, as well as streams of hot or cold water, from pipes arranged so that the stream gushes out as from a rock. The water is heated simply by being in tanks close to the ceiling. The water in the tank may be three feet deep; but one foot to twenty inches is enough for sitting in, or baling over you,—an agreeable operation, and furnishing a necessary diversion, when by cause of malady the Bath has to be endured for many hours in the day.

The floor is in cement. There are no flues. From a common laundry stove, an iron pipe conveys the smoke across it. There is no plate glass, but only a double sheet of crown glass let into the wall for a window.

I use coke instead of coal, so as to keep the pipes clean, that the heat may be given off: no coal is used,

even for lighting the fire. At a heat varying from 180°
to 230°, night and morning, the fuel consumed will
not amount to more than one-half of what is required
for an ordinary fire. The ventilation is by suction
from below. The air is drawn into the furnace : there
is a constant and rapid circulation up one side and down
the other. Entering the furnace heated, the combustion is more perfect, the bad air is consumed, and
the saving of heat enormous. The fresh air being
admitted from above, it comes in its passage downwards
to the bather to-breathe.

There are three plug-holes adapted for the convenience
of the bathers ; so that when a high temperature is
required for a long time, they can refresh themselves,
or even envelope the whole head in a hood and breathe
as in the open air.

There is no difficulty whatever in thus obtaining
perfect command of the circulation. The suction being
everywhere *inward* and *downwards*, crevices are easily
stopped. The door must, however, open outwards, and
with a screw hinge, or a flap pivot out of the perpen-
dicular : the edges being bevelled, the door falls-to close
at every point. The command of the admission of
air is such, that I am independent of the use of the
damper; and when the door and plugs are closed, the
draft through the furnace and flue is stopped.

An invalid can be carried in on a bed or chair. The
platform on the outside is on the level of a window that
can be thrown open to a current of air; or the ante-room

can be closed, and by leaving the bath doors open, 120°
can be obtained.   There is but ONE STEP from the hottest
point to the open air or into the tank.

The cocks have particularly to be attended to.   The
turning part must be equal to the running part, otherwise the water will come out wabbling.   A space sufficient for washing must be allowed between the cock and
the basin : neither of these points an English tradesman
understands.   The cocks must be large, so as to admit
of a full stream.   The escape from the tank must also
be free, so as to change the water rapidly.   It is $2\frac{1}{2}$ inches
diameter.

In stating the cost to be not more than half an
ordinary fire, it has to be observed that refuse coke or
braise answers better in a stove, and does not cost more
than half.   Therefore, such a fire can be kept up for 2*d.*
a day.   But even were the expense equal to several fires,
it would be an economy: by means of it, all the passages
in the house can be heated, and even several of the
rooms, besides having always at hand a drying closet.
I have myself, not only dispensed with seven fireplaces,
but taken them out.   With our open fireplaces and
straight chimneys, fully 20 parts of the 24 of heat is
lost: managed in this way, 20 parts of the 24 are
retained.   Such an apartment would be an economy
and an advantage in any house, wholly irrespective
of the uses of which I am at present treating.   On the
other hand the incalculable benefit to the sick from the
Bath can never be otherwise realized; for the patient,

secure them, must have it under the same roof, so as to be able to go in at any hour of the day or night, and to have it within reach in case of an acute disorder.

This closet has been constructed in the rudest fashion and at the lowest possible cost. I found that my Bath at Riverside deterred rather than invited imitations, as people thought less of the advantage than the cost, and fancied that it required a thousand pounds to get a wash. This closet, with all the fittings for the supply of water hot and cold, and the building of three of the walls, has cost £37.

This is the sixth Bath I have constructed for my own use. All these have been built with a view to making experiments, or for testing ideas that had suggested themselves during the construction of previous ones. This is, indeed, the eighth, for one of these underwent three entire transformations. This one will not, however, be the last, though the most perfect of any yet built. There is still one great improvement to be made to come nearer to the rays of the sun, the type as well as the source of this means of action on the human frame.

This Bath is the only one I have constructed specially for invalids. It was made in view to the confinement of a lady:* nevertheless, it thus loses none of the utility or the charm that may be sought by the healthy. When I come back to it after absence and the use of other

---

* Lady Mary W. Montagu says, " Child-birth, so terrible with us, is regarded by the Turkish women as of no more moment than a slight cold."

Baths, even the best, it is like getting on the back of a thorough-bred after having had to ride a cart horse. It is of service at every moment and at all temperatures. You come in from a journey, say before dinner ; you go in not heated, when it may stand at 120° ; you dress in that charming temperature, with streams of hot or cold water, or the tank to revel in. So, also, you may dress in it in the morning. My regular practice, when not requiring it for health's sake, is to go in on getting up and on going to bed, dressing and undressing there. Five to ten minutes suffice to bring on the flow of perspiration. After that, a plunge in the cold water, and you come out fresh, glowing with a sense of cleanliness, health, and strength, which no other operation can convey to the body. You are then indifferent to the heat of summer and the cold of winter. If time is an object, the waste of time is thus no objection.

I will give an instance of its use as a substitute for exercise. One wintry day, feeling the want of exercise, I was deterred by the aspect of the skies ; there was sleet, and a bleak easterly wind blowing : so I bethought me of going into the Bath, instead, for half an hour. I found it particularly agreeable. Instead of half an hour, an hour and a half had flown by ; so I looked at the thermometer, and observed that the Bath stood at 176°, and the tank at 76°. I had been passing from the one to the other—say ten minutes out of the tank, and five minutes in it, alternately. I noted these points as furnishing a datum line, giving, without strain, the

contrasted enjoyments of the temperate and torrid zones.
I left the Bath invigorated as I might have been by
a gallop of fifteen miles under a bright sun on the
Sussex Downs.

When I quote the degrees of heat I use, I am dis-
believed. To be exposed to the radiation of red-hot metal
at the distance of less than four feet, seems impossible;
it must appear so even to those most conversant with
the Bath as at present in use; and this is why I commenced with saying that your inquiry could only be
satisfactorily answered by coming here and judging for
yourself.

A medical man of this place, who has been in the habit
of going in with patients, went to the Hammam in
Jermyn Street, expecting to find there something much
better. His astonishment was great when he found (as
he stated in a letter to the Chairman of the Company)
that he was more inconvenienced there in the "hot room
at 175° in five minutes," than he was in mine "at 230°
in fifteen minutes."

Now as to the relative effects in sickness of radiating
and transmitted caloric. About this time last year, I
received a letter from a medical man, informing me
that the superintendent of the Hammam, Mr. Johnson,
was dying. He has for years been unable to live out
of the Bath, from an affection of the lungs. He was
suffering from a bronchial cough, which had become
spasmodic, and so constant as to deprive him of all
rest and sleep. This came on whilst daily in a Bath,

and in spite of it, he being in it all day long. This would appear to be conclusive that the Bath was incapable of affording relief. The medical man thought so. I knew that the heat in Jermyn Street was insufficient in itself, and, besides, was not radiating. I went up to town, and, after seeing him, promised that if he could only bear the journey, I should send him back in a week able to resume his work. This promise was fulfilled to the letter. On the eighth day he did resume work.

He arrived here about half-past 5 p.m., was put into the bath at 6, remained there till 11, and then slept an unbroken sleep for eight hours. The thermometer ranged from 200° to 220°.

This great heat is here endurable for the following reasons :—

1. The heat is radiating. I cannot pretend to treat of this great secret of Nature : to work out this problem, a Liebig is required. This I can say, that such heat is more endurable than common heat. There is a liveliness about it which transmitted heat lacks. You are conscious of an electrical action. It is to transmitted heat what champagne is to flat beer.*

2. The rapid circulation of air. This depends on the

* In Jermyn Street, in the hottest chamber, there is a partial radiation. When the other chamber was raised to the same degree (there being there no radiation at all), that is, 175°, it was felt to be more oppressive than the other when 20 degrees higher.

great heating power; and the saving of that heat by the air escaping below, and not above.

3. The extreme dryness. This is obtained by the great heat itself; by the rapidity of circulation; by the water operations being carried on at a lower line, so that there is very little evaporation; and finally, by great care in preventing any evaporation whatever beyond the indispensable escape from the body.

Of this latter, the quantity is greatly diminished by passing out and in every five minutes, so that half the body evaporation takes place outside. Also by carrying out the clothing, on which you have lain whilst per- spiring.

Perfect dryness of the air is indispensable to the enduring of a high temperature.

This dryness of the air is also of service for absorbing and drawing out of the body the miasmiata of disease. Relief is obtained only in so far as those miasmata flow in a liquid or gaseous form. When the Bath is abso- lutely dry and very hot, there will be, as it were, a sudden discharge from the patient of fetid odours.

The practice of the Bath refines the olfactory nerves, and renders them capable of perceiving smells other- wise imperceptible. A wide field of observation is thus opened in the quality of their odours and their fluctuations. Nor is this all: the state of the body can be known beforehand for hours and even days. You may thus get warning of an impending attack, just as a sailor is warned of a hurricane by the barometer or the storm-glass. The sailor can, indeed, only make his vessel snug, and so await the blow; but the real physician, with caloric as his servant, can ward off and disperse the storm.

This dryness is further requisite for electrical isolation. With vapour in the chamber, an atmosphere is created injurious to health, and conducive to disease. It is the very condition in which low putrid and typhus fevers flourish. The electrical spark will not ignite in such an atmosphere, and the magnet will lose its attractive power. We all know the difference of our own sensations on a dry and on a damp day.

This point is so plain and simple, that it is sure to be misunderstood and perverted among those who cannot see, but will object, and who refuse to accept unless they can invent. Each must have something new to say in regard to anything he speaks about, so that a self-evident truth is either disregarded or falsified.

Some thirty or more years ago, a certain " fire-king " raised much wonder by exhibiting himself, going into an oven with a beefsteak and cooking it,—it was believed that no mortal being could endure 300°. When, in one of the Midland counties, an old working chemist managed to put a saucer filled with water into the oven. Long before the beefsteak was cooked, the " fire-king " rushed out in wild dismay. The moisture from the beefsteak had not supplied a dose of moisture sufficient to render the 300° unendurable. The evaporation from the saucer had supplied it.

The difficulty of keeping the chamber dry is very great. You will perceive it to be so, if you reflect for a moment on the amount of fluid that may be drawn from a man at 200° or 250°.

The ordinary loss through the skin (lungs inclusive) is about 2 oz. an hour. I have increased it ninety fold, that is, 3 oz. per minute, or 11 lb. an hour. This amounts to nearly the whole of the aqueous portion of the blood in circulation. I speak of the *rate* at which sweat can be obtained : of course, this heat can be endured only for a few minutes at a time.

Before mentioning the plan I adopted for rating the flow of perspiration, I must first observe that the greatest accuracy is requisite as to the thermometer. Also the word "Bath" must be discarded. If you spoke in the abstract of "calomel," no sense would be conveyed as to your treatment of any case where that substance was used, as it might equally mean a grain and a hundredweight. So, instead of "Bath," we must speak of *heat* by *degrees*, and of *time* by *minutes*. Then, to ascertain the heat, the thermometers must be placed so as to discriminate between the levels, the distances, and be in sufficient numbers (always detached from the walls) to give certain knowledge of the varieties of temperature pervading the whole area. The difference in level of one foot may give a difference of 20 degrees in the thermometer. When radiating caloric is employed, the discrimination is still more difficult, especially as here there is a difference between the real and the apparent heat.

On the first occasion of testing the amount of perspiration, the thermometer stood at 232° behind the
couch where I lay, the heat radiating so that the real
heat must have been a certain number of degrees above
the apparent heat, say 15°. I used a large folded
sheet to collect the sweat. In five minutes the sheet
taken out weighed 2 lb. 5 oz. : the sheet dried weighed
1 lb. 5 oz. To test the loss by evaporation, the sheet
was hung up in the Bath double, so as to represent the
evaporating surfaces of skin and cloth. In five minutes
the sheet lost 5 oz. Thus in five minutes the sweat
and evaporation amounted to 21 oz., independently of
the loss by the lungs. In my case the constant use of
these high temperatures has superinduced a facility of
percolation ; but it will not be too much to set down 2 oz.
per minute as the *rate* at which perspiration can be
obtained, although it is impossible to maintain it for
more than five or ten minutes at a time.

Taking the watery part of the blood to amount to
12 lb., that quantity has to be got rid of for the purification of the body. But this quantity cannot be sweated
out, as the blood would become incapable of circulation
and the heart be overpowered : water must then be
progressively supplied; which being polluted in turn, it
will require for the washing and rinsing of the particles
of the blood an evaporation of at least a score of pounds.
Such an operation will occupy a whole day. It is on
this ground that I consider the only treatment by the
Bath rational, complete, and not empirical, to be the

putting the patient into the Bath to remain there until cured.

This, however, has reference to diseases to which physicians now apply the term " Blood-poisons." No doubt, a very slight diminution of the amount of this polluted fluid will afford immense relief, and often allow nature to work her own way to the throwing off of the disease : but it being in our power thus easily to cleanse the whole body, it stands to reason that we should employ it.

I have further satisfied myself by this long and daily experience that the currents are constantly depositing their contents, as we see in streams and rivers, at the points of weakest circulation—that is, at the extremities of their course, and especially where the configuration of the body involves returns of the currents on themselves, as in the fingers and toes. These are the parts chiefly liable to gout. With us, indeed, the feet are more subject to it than the hands, which was not the case with the Romans : but while our hands are exposed to the sun and air, our feet are shut up in leather cases. The Romans suffered more from cheiragra (hand-ache) than podagra (foot-ache). The feet of the Romans were as much exposed to the light and air as their hands.

Were there no such deposit of the poisonous matters (urea, &c.), relief would not be afforded under ten or twelve hours' perspiration ; but relief is often afforded in a quarter of an hour, or even in five minutes.

The healthy body is not inodorous. It is endowed with a sweet odour, described, by those whose organs are sensitive enough to detect it, as resembling fresh-sawn fir boards.

At the common ordinary temperature, the body may be inodorous in all its parts, and the breath also; and yet, on going into a temperature of 220°, in five minutes a slight smell of gout will come out in the feet and the breath. (I am describing what has occurred to myself a few hours ago.) Half an hour later, and after being in at the high heat ten minutes more, the smell of gout may become very strong in the feet, legs, thighs, breast, stomach, breath, and back. The smell of herpes may have *come out* in the hands, the arms, and shoulders. Half an hour later, and after having been twice under the great heat, the smell may have been *taken out* everywhere. Now this result could not have been obtained if the whole circulation had to be purified, as for this, there has not been sufficient time. The result can only be attributed to there being a local deposit towards the surface and in the skin itself.

Supposing the experiment had been carried further ; then, after the inodorous zone has been passed through, we would come to the aromatic one, or that of perfect health. I have observed that when, from the presence of malady, I have spent eight or ten hours in the Bath, and the sweet odour has come out, then I have had the sleep of an infant, light, continuous, and refreshing, lasting for eight hours, and unaccompanied by any change of position.

In these experiments I should be wholly at sea without this guidance of smell; without it, it would be impossible to tell when the effect was produced, or when you had to stop, for sensation is no guide. It would, indeed, be impossible to sustain the attention. By means of the nose, which detects at once all the varieties and variations of the morbid state, and notes and rates the action thereon of the cleansing power, you proceed with that certainty of intellectual sight by which the steersman, magnet-led, feels his way in the darkest night.

Nor is the use of this guide restricted, as that of the needle, to each passing moment of time. It is endowed with the prophetic power. It will tell what is to come as well as what is, and with equal certainty. The future is brought up in the present, not as a coming dread superadded to present suffering, but as a prospective evil which, by being anticipated in the mind, can be averted from the body.

Before pulsation was discovered, it would have appeared a fantastic notion, had any one announced that the day would come, when wise, staid, and learned men would sit down, with watch in hand and finger on the wrist, to discover therewith the working of the concealed agencies of the man within. Still more fantastic will appear the notion to-day, that the time will come when the pulse will be reckoned but as a trifling index, and that the grave and veteran leech, no longer able to train his own nose, will have to be accompanied by a child to scent his patient and inform him of his state.

This is the third and last of my discoveries, and, like the previous ones, was not fallen on by chance. In regard to the effect of pure heat on disease, I had reasoned to a conclusion before commencing to experiment. So also in regard to radiating caloric. Again I had concluded before I had obtained the practical confirmation that each malady must be possessed of its emanation in smell, and that the human organs, if retained in their sensitiveness, must be capable of distinguishing it.

I watched in a child nurtured in the Bath for this result. It came about his fifth year; at his eighth (the present time) he can be relied on entirely as if the eye, not the nose, were at work. I have had other boys similarly trained, with results, not indeed equal, but at all events encouraging. But what is most so, is that the adult can be so trained. This has happened in the case of the servant who has for some years served me as bath-man.

There is scarcely a visitor of mine, during the last three years, who cannot bear testimony to what I now assert. Hundreds have witnessed the same at the Hammam, in London. Conscious, however, of the incredulity with which such a statement will be received, and as is always at first evinced by medical men, I will quote some instances both of the detection of actual disease, and of its announcement before-hand.

During the past summer, I was one day at the Hammam. There were about a dozen persons conversing together, members of both Houses. General K—— entered and joined the circle. He complained of great suffering, and said he had come up from the country for a Bath, in the hope of getting one night's rest. I called the boy, who had not heard a word of what had passed, and told him to pick out any one in the circle who was ill. He walked round, not approaching nearer than two feet, and stopped short at General K——, pointing, as it were;—I should rather, however, say, turning away and making wry faces.

Some weeks afterwards, I was again at the Hammam. Again there was a circle formed. Mr. Huntley (who has built the Bath at Sydney) was complaining of a severe attack of gout which had flown to the stomach; he laid his finger on the spot where the pain prevailed. I stopped him, again called for the boy, instructed him as before. He pointed at Mr. Huntley. I then told him to find the part. He smelt him all over, and pointed his finger at the very spot to which Mr. Huntley's own finger had just before been pointed.

In November last, I was again at the Hammam. Mr. Copping, a farmer from Spalding, one of the most remarkable cases of cure of "Bright's Disease," was describing his former state and sufferings, and his present relief: he was proceeding to say that the pains

z

lingered only in one part. I stopped him there, saying, "I will tell you where your pains are seated." I called the boy, and pointing out Mr. Copping, said, "Tell me if he is ill, what is the matter with him, and where he suffers." After running his nose up and down, he answered, "He is ill; but it is not gout, nor herpes, nor ague (the only diseases with which he is familar): it is something different. I don't know it, and it is very bad here," pointing to the region of the left kidney. Mr. Copping, in amazement, exclaimed, "That is the very spot!" Two eminent medical men were present.

Gout attacked me first two years ago. It took me unprepared. The odour was as yet unknown; at least by its name. It was, therefore, fully developed before I yielded credence to the assertion of my medical man. I had not yet got into the free use of high heats, nor to the full alternations, as at present, of hot and cold. I was, indeed, then in the infancy of these matters. However, by such means as I then employed, the positive suffering was stopped after six hours.

The second attack came in a month. I was still without forewarning; but otherwise I was better prepared, and the malady went through its phases (laying me up for ten days) without pain endured or rest lost. Two medical men watched closely the operation. One of these, Dr. Collet, writes in reference to it—"What has particularly to be observed is, that the attack has been gone through under this great heat without the ordinary accompaniment of pain, and its consequent depression." The other, Dr. Sharpe, in commenting on the case, further observed that the attack was un-attended "by loss of sleep or of flesh."

I now arrive at the period of *prevention*. The boy on whose nose I relied, had learnt to discriminate the peculiar smell, and to give to it a name. The two former attacks had followed at the interval of a month. The period in the month was coincident with an extra demand on me for labour, occasioned by a periodical publication coming on the top of regular and continuous work. With the third and subsequent months, I have, at the corresponding periods, received notice of approach-ing gout; and thereupon I have at once dealt with myself as if the malady had been already developed, — that is, remaining daily in the Bath for hours, as much as six and a half, and never coming out until the smell has disappeared. In every case the attack has been averted, and no sensation of my own had indicated so much as its approach.

I have, however, to cite three exceptions. Never was there such an illustration of the maxim, "The exception proves the rule."

These occurred when away from the Bath. Twice I got back after the symptoms had appeared during twenty-four hours. On both occasions two or three days sufficed completely to restore me. On the third occasion these symptoms had lasted forty-eight hours; and though the pain was stopped so soon as I got into the high heat, still I was disabled from using my foot freely, either for walking or riding, for seven or eight days.

From this you will see the grounds I have for believing that I hold my tenure, not of health only, but of life also, by heat; and that tenure would be of little value if I had to wait until my own sensations informed me of a supervening malady.

I cannot conclude this letter, inordinate as is the length to which it has already grown, without at least one word on the important matter of absorption.

Taking the Bath regularly as I do, I can always tell the quantity I perspire by the quantity I drink. I can also estimate by the same means, in an approximate way, the heat, and the time I have been exposed to it. When, however, I came, in fighting the gout, to use the cold water, my calculation was disturbed. So also, when, being already thirsty, I went into the cold tank and remained there some time, the thirst subsided. Proceeding thereupon to observe closely, I discovered that I had not only to deduct the time spent in the cold water from the sum of drink, but that I had to reckon that time the other way, in this fashion: that five minutes in the tank, the water being at 65°, compensated, in so far as drink was required, for five minutes in the chamber at 230°.

Up to this time the whole question of absorption had been to me a puzzle. No medical man with whom I had hitherto spoken, had gone beyond the assertion that absorption was always going on; this opinion being based on the effect on the evacuations of Baths, and lotions containing chemical ingredients. I had refused to accept this solution, attributing such effects to endosmose and exosmose, by reason of which the *contents* of fluids are exchanged, although the fluids themselves remain unaltered in volume. I spoke, however, to persons who had never heard of endosmose, or who fancied it meant a transmission of fluids.

It now appeared to me that I had discovered the law of absorption, viz., that it was correlative with exudation, depending on the alternations of temperature ; the vessels expelling the fluid at a high temperature, and absorbing it at a low temperature. Also, that their faculty of absorption was equal to their faculty of exudation : consequently, that both functions were performed by the same vessels. Otherwise, indeed, absorption would require a distinct set of vessels in the skin, which are wanting.

At first I apprehended that the cold would diminish the discharge of poisonous matter : the reverse appeared to be the result. This explanation suggested itself.

The pain, the malady, the gout, the urea, or whatever term may be given to the undischarged residue of digestion, must, though chemical, have a corporeal existence, and occupy space. When compared with the minutest vascular and cellular lining, this space will stand as mere specks on an outstretched plain. To remove these noxious particles is the duty of perspiration ; but the currents of perspiration (though numbered by millions) are but partial and finite streams, with difficulty searching for, finding, and cleansing out these particles. If these currents be at times reversed, the particles will be stirred up, and be more easily carried out by the returning stream.

Excuse my venturing to speak thus on such matters. Ignorance, as a rule, renders speech presumptuous. In this case, however, it is ignorance alone that furnishes to me the right to speak, or can supply to you the inducement to listen. Had I been learned, I should not have travelled beyond the circle of received ideas. It is what I have experienced in myself, not what I know of what others have done, that can alone be of value to you.

In every line I have been writing, I have had a design against yourself. I want to constrain you into making the resolve to have in the Newcastle Infirmary the counterpart of what I have here, and so gain for your 12,000 yearly sufferers what I myself possess. If you did so, it is not tens of thousands, but tens of millions who would be benefited; for the results obtained by you, extending over such numbers, and coming with such authority, must at once put down alike the interested or the prejudiced opposition of medical men, and the weak illusions of patients and the public. After all, it would only be going back a century, when "*Sweating Rooms*"* (look at the sensible and indigenous name, compared with the "Roman Bath," the "Oriental Bath," "Thermo-Therapæa," &c., of the would-be schemers and imita-

---

* The "Sweating Houses" of the Irish still exist. A man of ninety-two, in the county Louth, told me that in his youth every respectable farmer had a "Sweating Room."

tors) were attached to infirmaries, and these heated to 250°. For in Sir Joseph Banks's experiments that heat is mentioned, without comment, as obtained in the Sweating Room of the Liverpool Infirmary.

For the treatment of disease, the Bath and the patient must be under the same roof.

This can be obtained only in Hospitals, Infirmaries, Unions, Asylums, and Barracks, or in the mansions of the wealthy.

The Newcastle Infirmary, if it does not take the lead, will be left behind. The process in its perfect form will start up in unheard-of places, and new medical men, and most probably from the number of the present opposers and scoffers, will suddenly spring to eminence on the very scaffolding raised by those first pioneers whom they at present revile.

Not only at Newcastle is the matter in your own hands as regards the Infirmary, but you have further this great facility, that the whole faculty there are with you. Compared with other medical men engaged in the same cause, you repose on a bed of down—a position superinducing slumber at times.

I have had for some time in my mind a plan which I desire to submit to you; and that is, a *Consumptive Hospital*, not only to be endowed with a perfect Bath, but one in which the rays of the sun shall be called into play, and the whole directed to the correction of the vicious habits in the individual which are conducive to the development of that disorder.

This idea arose from my having been induced by Dr. Pollock to visit the Consumptive Hospital at Brompton. We were engaged there in discussing how a Bath might be added; but I came away, not with the desire that this should be effected, but with a far different one. It became my ambition to build a Consumptive Hospital. I should almost regret to see a Bath introduced in such establishments on their present footing.

It is not to be expected that, until the knowledge of the benefit becomes general, the money could be raised on philanthropic grounds; but the way might be opened for it by a proprietary Consumptive Hospital, intended for the wealthy, who at present send, or desire to send, their sick relatives to Montpelier and to Madeira. The pecuniary results of the Hammam in London, and its rapidly-extending use by the higher and wealthier classes, hold out inducements to make the attempt, if any earnest and sincere persons would make a beginning, being themselves moved by worthier considerations.

In a recent letter, you regretted that the Bath was not more generally known. Unfortunately, since Baths have been opened, the sense of their importance has decayed. This is, of course, attributable to the spurious imitation. We have prevented a general disgust by getting one proper Bath built. But what is one Bath, when, for anything deserving the name of public benefit, they should be counted by tens of thousands; and these not proprietary ones, but charitably and munificently endowed for the public use,—at least, of the working classes ? What we have accomplished is but a sample. Having a whole people to cleanse, that building stands, in reference to the national need, as would do the landing of a bushel of wheat at Gloucester in reference to the public hunger, were there famine in the land.

Believe me,

Faithfully yours,

D. URQUHART.

P.S.—I find I have omitted to say, in reference to the cited cases of gout (as in all other cases), that no medicine of any kind was administered.

(EXTRACT.)

SIR JOHN FIFE TO MR. URQUHART.

Newcastle-on-Tyne,
February 14, 1864.

Perhaps your pamphlet might go forth to the world with greatest effect independent of any introduction by me. But if you think otherwise let me know.

It seems to me that the faith, and hope, and zeal which shine through your style may make a better impression on the public mind than the qualified and guarded statements of sceptical science.

ANTICIPATION BY DR. W. STOKES OF THE DETECTION OF MALADIES BY SMELL.

A pupil of Dr. W. Stokes informs me that, in his course of lectures at Dublin, in 1848, after pointing out that the discovery of Laennec, in reference to auscultation, had only realised the anticipation of Hippocrates as to thoracic dropsy (when a sound as of boiling vinegar could be detected by applying the ear to the chest) went on to remark that "pathology, when carried to greater perfection, would probably enable us to detect the existence and conditions of many maladies, no less than auscultation did in reference to those diseases in which the disturbance of mechanical processes in connection with the fluids enabled that organ to become perceptive. Thus, at some future period, the nose may, from the mere surface of the body, be able to detect the difference between pneumonia and bronchitis —that is, disease of the substance of the lungs as distinguished from disease of the ducts."

Introduction of the Bath into the Lunatic Asylums, and the Naval and Military Hospitals.

There are two peculiarities of insanity which point to the Bath as a remedy. These are inertness of the skin, and a disagreeable odour. The power of heat to remove both being established, we may infer a powerful and beneficial action through the symptoms on their causes. We are, however, no longer restricted to the region of à *priori* reasoning; we have entered on the field of experiment.

SUSSEX LUNATIC ASYLUM.

LUNATIC ASYLUM, HAYWARD'S HEATH,
February, 1863.

MY DEAR MR. URQUHART,—I gladly comply with your request that I should send you a few lines regarding my experience of the use of the bath in the treatment of mental disease. In the "Journal of Mental Science" for July, 1862, I published a short paper "Cases illustrating the use of the Turkish Bath in the treatment of Mental Disease," in which I endeavoured to give an account of my use of the bath (recently erected here) during the previous six months. The temperature at which my observations (about thirty in number) were then made was 145° to 150°. The results as detailed in that paper were most encouraging, and such as to have induced me to continue the use of this powerful remedial agent in my practice here. Another year's experience has, however, modified, as one might expect, my views on several points connected with the remedial use of the bath. Thus I have passed the test you have often spoken of, of 150°! I now as often use the bath at 170° as at 150°, and I am slowly feeling my way to your temperature of 200°; and I have no manner of doubt that, *until I arrive at the use of these higher temperatures, I am not in a position to learn or judge what the bath can accomplish in the curative treatment of disease.* Next, I have abandoned the expensive fire-brick channels, by which I, in the first instance, heated the bath, and have substituted the direct radiation from iron smoke-pipes, the furnace also being in the hot room. I find that much higher temperatures can now be borne by the patients than with the former brick flues. I am also gradually using the bath for longer periods. I began with twenty minutes once and twice a week. I have now got to an hour's length, and am progressing herein also. I fully realize how much I have to learn yet of the therapeutic uses of the bath; how little I know of its operations.

As regards the use of the bath in the treatment of mental disease, I continue to entertain the most favourable opinion. As yet we have no specific in the cure of insanity, such as quinine is for the cure of ague; and I for one do not look for such. Insanity is a disease depending on, and associated with, various functional disorders, and especially with the perverted nutrition of the organ of the mind. The treatment of these pathological conditions consists not in the mechanical administration of specifics, but in the rational application of the principles of medicine to the special symptoms of each individual case. Thus to illustrate my meaning by a case. A patient is suffering from an attack of mania, with great restlessness and incoherence of thought and violence, with increased action of the heart, and congestion of the head and suppression of the catamenia, and of the secretion of the skin, which is rough and dry. The indications of treatment here are to restore the balance of the circulation, and thus to regulate the secretions and the supply of blood to the brain, and so to restore the healthy action of the uterus, the skin, and the brain. Experience teaches us that such a result will only follow the slow and steady use of remedies influencing the action of the heart and of the nervous system. Of such remedies, few are more powerful in their action than the bath; and I find that the continued use in such a case of this remedy will, through its soothing action on the nervous system, and the relief it affords to internal congestion by determining the blood to the surface, modify, if not cure, the symptoms of mental disease present.

My experience of the use of the bath has hitherto been chiefly limited to cases of chronic mental disease. In one instance of acute mania, depending apparently on recent small-pox, I found immediate relief of the maniacal symptoms follow the administration of the bath. My great success has been with cases of melancholia, with refusal of food, and loss of strength and flesh. I have a record of more than a dozen such cases of melancholia which have materially benefited by the use continued over a period of two or three months of the bath twice a week.

In several cases of melancholia, complicated with phthisis in its earlier stage, a great improvement both of the mental and physical symptoms has followed the treatment.

In irregularity of the uterine functions, which in young girls is sometimes complicated with mania, I have found in several instances a cure follow the restoration through the agency of the bath, of the healthy uterine action.

Setting the mental symptoms aside, I would here say, that if the bath had only this one remedial power of restoring suppressed menstruation, its value in reducing the ills resulting from our high civilization would still be great. I have within the last two months discharged two young girls cured, who for many months suffered from maniacal symptoms, connected with irregular menstrual action.

When you were at Hayward's Heath the other day I showed you a patient, M. W., who was admitted here on the 23rd of February, 1863, apparently in a state of confirmed dementia, unable even to tell his name ; restless and destructive. He was much reduced in health, and there was dropsy of the lower limbs, with albuminous urine of a marked character. The patient gradually got worse, and after he had been a month in the asylum, I sent him to the bath almost as a forlorn hope. The result of a month's treatment of the bath, twice a week, was that the dropsy disappeared, that no trace of albumen is now to be found in the urine, and that the man is apparently convalescent. You will remember seeing him here at his work as a carpenter.

These few words on the use of the bath in the treatment of the insane would be incomplete were I to omit to notice a specific power to remove the noxious secretion of the skin so frequent with the insane, and which, in the asylums of twenty years ago, one could recognize as distinctly as the smell of a dog-kennel, and which still sometimes refuses to yield to ordinary ablution. The bath entirely removes this unpleasant complication.

Lastly, the bath is a remedial agent grateful to the feelings of the insane, and which they do not, like other means of washing, associate with the idea of punishment. Were the bath at Hayward's Heath large enough for the purpose (which, unfortunately, it is not, having been built at a small cost, £40, as an experiment), I should entirely replace the ordinary hot-water baths used twice a week for cleanliness—with "*the bath*" as you always term it.

Believe me, sincerely yours,

C. L. ROBERTSON, M.D. Cantab.,

Medical Superintendent.

D. Urquhart, Esq.

In the Fifth Annual Report of the Sussex County Lunatic Asylum, just issued, Dr. Lockhart Robertson publishes some important remarks on the Turkish bath as a curative agent. He relates a case in which a patient was admitted with symptoms of mania, complicated with dropsy and albuminuria of the most severe character. The patient was in a desperate state, menaced with madness and paralysis, and apparently dying from the extent of kidney-disease. Dr. Robertson states that the bath saved the patient's life and restored him to reason. Dr. Robertson observed that the medical uses of the bath have yet to be studied. He believes them to be very great. Of its curative power in the early stages of consumption he has had several examples. He longs to see the bath fairly tried in other diseases. He believes, if used at sufficiently high temperatures (170°—200°), the results will astonish us all. If anything ever can cure hydrophobia it will be the bath at 200° continued for many hours.—*The Lancet.*

Dr. Power, in answer to a question, stated that the success of the Turkish bath in the house was even greater than he expected, and he was almost afraid to state his opinions of the success that would attend the use of it, for fear, in the event of any subsequent failure, his opinion might be quoted against the bath as having been founded on a very short trial. Out of four patients, however, regularly exercised on by it, one had been dismissed cured, and the other three were working regularly, which they have never done before.—*Cork Examiner.*

COLNEY HATCH.

Other asylums are now following the example of those in Sussex and Ireland. I subjoin an extract from a letter which I addressed to the medical superintendent of the asylum at Colney Hatch, bearing on the peculiar adaptation of the Bath to such establishments.

I may here mention that a similar bath for the Great Naval and Military Hospital at Netley is shortly to be constructed. It cannot fail thence to spread to the other Government hospitals, as also to the barracks and to vessels afloat.* Thus, in a short time the British army may be in possession of this cleanser of the armies of Rome formerly, and of the Turks to-day; and the British navy enjoy the luxury which was shared in by those of Syracuse, Carthage, of the Ptolemies, and of Mithridates.

23rd May.

DEAR SIR,—Since Monday last I have at every interval of leisure been engaged in planning an adaptation of the bath to the purposes of your institution. The bath, and that by radiating heat, must of course be there; but, in addition, you require a large available space for the daily washing of your patients, with abundant supply of hot and cold water, in a hall with an Indian temperature.

* A bath on board passenger vessels will probably be found to have the effect of stopping *sea-sickness.*

I have on Saturday entered fully on this matter with Mr. Wood, and he has carried away the dimensions so as to be able to have a plan proposed for submission to your Board to-morrow.

I consider the advantages so self-evident, that no words are required : still there are economic considerations which I would urge, as these may assist the Board in coming to a decision on the point now raised, which involves an increased expenditure in one way, but brings a very large reduction in another.

The plan originally submitted to you was based on an expenditure of £300. The present is for £500.

For this you will have a structure which will become the model for the asylums, hospitals, unions, and barracks of the three kingdoms.

You will have your present washing rooms (30 or more) set free for other uses, and no need of constructing more.

You will discharge yearly not 25, but 75 per cent. of your patients. You will save nine-tenths of your hospital charges.

You will dispense entirely with stockings.

You will reduce by one-third the amount expended on clothing and blankets.

You will reduce the amount of food consumed.

It is not, therefore, an increased charge of £500 that is proposed, but a reduction of yearly expenditure to the amount of tens of thousands.

With the prospect brought before you of such benefits in respect to the objects of the Institution,—the treatment of insanity, and with the evidence by which it is even already supported, you can scarcely put aside its consideration, nor escape from the necessity of a trial in a more or less efficient manner.

Such an edifice cannot be obtained without cost, and labour, and care.

The Hammam in Jermyn-street, which by the best judges— the Turks—is held to be the most perfect in existence, affords you the model, and if yours required an equal outlay, it would be but natural. I offer you, however, a far different prospect.

During the last four years, and while engaged on this and similar buildings, I have fallen on expedients by which the results can be obtained in a far higher degree, and at infinitely less cost. I could construct the same to-day at a third less.

The Hammam, however, has cost for the building part £10,000 (£20,000 in all). The area is 7000 square feet. I propose to give you a building with an area of 1,500 feet, at a cost of £500, and will undertake to pay the difference in case of excess of expenditure.

In this is, however, not included the swimming basin, which you will see in the outlines taken away by Mr. Wood, and to which I suppose you can devote the spare labour of your people.

You will thus have a place of recreation and exercise for your patients, such as the Gymnasia of the Greeks, and the garden prepared for himself by Pliny in the villa of Tusculum.

You will also have a bath, which, like that of Etruscus, will be visited by the sun during every hour of the day.

> " Multus ubique dies radiis ubi culmina totis
> Perforat, atque alio sol improbus uritur æstu."

As you dispose of the patients' time, and can arrange relays from six in the morning till eight at night (and herein lies your facility), you can pass 700 patients through the operation of the bath daily. For mere washing you can pass them through it at the rate of 250 an hour.

The charge for fuel will not exceed 1s. 6d. per diem. I will not speak of soap or linen, as those charges you bear already.

As to the effect in lunacy, we have, besides inductive reasons, the results obtained in the lunatic asylums of Cork and Sussex, which show a greatly increased proportion of cures. But in neither of these establishments is the bath of a power in any degree approaching in efficacy or accommodation, in cheerfulness and enjoyment, to that of which I now submit to you the plan.

In the Report of the Newcastle Infirmary the saving of drugs is particularly insisted on as one of the benefits obtained by the introduction of the Turkish Bath. Although theirs is of the paltriest and meanest construction, yet they expressed themselves in these terms :—" The bath became a species of Elysium, where ache and pain vanished as if by magic."

The whole will be arranged panoptically, so that a superintendent, himself unseen, can, with the exception of one apartment, watch every patient. With the resources of your establishment, the whole may be completed in four weeks.

I have the honour to be, Sir,

Your obedient Servant,

D. URQUHART.

E. SHEPPARD, ESQ., M.D.

P.S.—I have referred back to a report I received some time back from the Medical Superintendent of the Sussex Lunatic Asylum, and find it so useful in your case that I have sent it to be printed, and you will receive copies by this evening's post.

Heat-Rays, Sun-Rays, Electricity, and Vital Power.

"Coal is but bottled Sun."—STEPHENSON.

THAT such degree of temperature in the air or in bodies as we call heat is different from the heat that travels *through the air*, everyone knows. The inquisitive mind will doubtless seek to ascertain in what that difference consists, and the very first step he makes will also be the final one. It consists not in its *nature*, but in its *motion*. Then a wholly new field of inquiry opens. The motion proceeds, not from its nature, but from something foreign to it. The ray is discharged just as the cannon ball; it is the nature, not of the bullet, but of the gunpowder with which we have to deal. Heat discharged in this fashion is said to radiate; that is, the heat is treated as rays, and is thereby assimilated to light, which is sensible to us only as rays. But the rays of heat become at a certain point illuminated, and pass into light just as the dark metal from which they flash becomes luminous. The identification is complete. Heat and light differ only in degree.

Then comes the question, "What is light?" I do not mean in its scientific character, but in its useful application to man; and among the endless variety of these uses, "What is light in its restorative capacity?"

When the difference between heat as temperature, and heat as rays, was brought home to me by my life being prolonged through the accidental substitution of the one for the other, after the efficacy of the first had failed, this question was forced upon me, and I answered it in somewhat the following manner :—

The rays of heat when they attain to brightness have the same speed as those of the sun. Electricity has an equal speed with both. Electricity can produce both heat and light. Electricity is life. The three fluids having common properties, and being interchangeable, it follows that some portions of the virtue and use of each in the economy of the universe must be present in the other, heat converting itself into projectile, and being as it were an artillery sweeping space, it follows that, having the power to produce this projectile, I gain the powers of the sun himself.

We can produce light, and consequently rays, by the combination of the opposite qualities of electricity. These rays are at once sun-rays and radiating caloric. These rays, falling on an opaque body, disappear. The light is lost; the heat also, in a greater or less degree, is lost. Striking the body of a man, they are neither (in their whole mass) transmitted, nor reflected, nor refracted, nor absorbed. They must, therefore, be transformed; that is, decomposed; that is, resolved into their elements, the negative and positive electricity. If so, they must transfer to this human body a dose of vital power. Thus, while transmitted heat raises only the tempera- ture of the body, impinging heat does something more than raise the temperature of the body.

I was one day adducing evidence on these points, when a medical man present said, "No man can treat such an idea as empirical after the experiments of Professor Tyndall."

On this, I sent for Mr. Tyndall's book, "Heat as a Means of Motion," published last year, and found how much I might have spared myself of idle argumentation.

That work, however, deals with the rays of heat only as acting on dead matter, on vegetation and healthy life. Expecting to elicit from the author what might have been in his mind respecting their action in a restorative sense, I applied to him, and received the following reply:—

" I may say that I have lived mentally on radiant heat for the last five years, but I have made no experi- ments as to its effect upon the human system. This is a matter which can be decided by experiment alone ; but if I wanted information upon the subject, you are the man to whom I would in the first instance turn. Now that you direct my attention to the subject, I will bear it in mind, and I may possibly thus obtain some strong light as regarding the *rationale* of the thing."*

Conceiving that this work establishes the scientific

---

* In another letter he says :—" The preference you give to dry over moist air is, I think, justified by philosophy as well as practice."

grounds for the results which I have gropingly obtained, I call on all those whose duty it is to find the best means of meeting disease—that is, medical men—to study it before disregarding, on preliminary or abstract grounds, the testimony I bear as to the results which I myself have obtained.

I subjoin a passage on the agency of the sun, begging the reader to bear in mind, while perusing it, that I place in his hands the faculty of calling down this power, of using it familiarly, and of applying it to the relief of his own bodily suffering, or of those of his relatives, his friends, and his fellow-creatures.

" *Precisely the same considerations which we have formerly applied to heat we have now to apply to light.* It is at the expense of the solar light that the decomposition of the carbonic acid is effected. Without the sun the reduction cannot take place, and an amount of sunlight is consumed exactly equivalent to the molecular work accomplished. Thus trees are formed, thus the meadows grow, thus the flowers bloom. Let the solar rays fall upon the surface of the sand, the sand is heated, and finally radiates away as much as it receives; let the same rays fall upon a forest, the quantity of heat given back is less than that received, for the energy of a portion of the sunbeams is invested in the building of the trees. I have here a bundle of cotton, which I ignite; it bursts into flame, and yields a definite quantity of heat; precisely that amount of heat was abstracted from the sun, in order to form that bit of cotton. This is a representative case; every tree, plant, and flower, grows and flourishes by the grace and bounty of the sun.

" But we cannot stop at vegetable life, for this is the source of all animal life. In the animal body vegetable substances are brought again into contact with their beloved oxygen, and they burn within us as a fire in a grate. This is the source of all animal power; and the forces in play are the same, in kind, as

those which operate in organic matter. In the plant the clock
is wound up; in the animal it runs down. In the plant the
atoms are separated; in the animal they recombine. And as
surely as the force which moves a clock's hands is derived from
the arm which winds up the clock, so surely is all terrestrial
power drawn from the sun. Leaving out of account the
eruptions of volcanoes, and the ebb and flow of the tides, every
mechanical action on the earth's surface, and every manifesta-
tion of power, organic and inorganic, vital and physical, is produced by the sun. His warmth keeps the sea liquid, and the
atmosphere a gas : and all the storms which agitate both are
blown by the mechanical force of the sun. He lifts the rivers
and the glaciers up the mountains; and thus the cataract and
the avalanche shoot with an energy derived immediately from
him. Thunder and lightning are also his transmuted strength·
Every fire that burns, and every flame that glows, dispenses
light and heat which originally belonged to the sun. In these
days, unhappily, the news of battle is familiar to us ; but every
shock and every charge is an application, or misapplication, of
the mechanical force of the sun. He blows the trumpet, he urges
the projectile, he bursts the bomb. He rears, as I have said,
the whole vegetable world, and through it the animal ; the
lilies of the field are his workmanship, the verdure of the
meadows, and the cattle upon a thousand hills. He forms the
muscle, he urges the blood, he builds the brain. His fleetness
is in the lion's foot; he springs in the panther, he soars in the
eagle, he slides in the snake. He builds the forest and hews it
down; the power which raised the tree and which wields the axe
being one and the same. The clover sprouts and blossoms, and
the scythe of the mower swinges, by the same force. The sun
digs the ore from our mines ; he rolls the iron ; he rivets the
plates ; he boils the water; he draws the train. He not only grows
the cotton, but he spins the fibre and weaves the web. There
is not a hammer raised, a wheel turned, or a shuttle thrown,
that is not raised and thrown by the sun. His energy is poured
freely into space, but our world is a halting-place where his

energy is conditioned. Here the Proteus works his spells; the self-same essence takes a million shapes and hues, and finally dissolves into its primitive and almost formless form. The sun comes to us as heat; and between his entrance and departure the multiform powers of our globe appear. They are all special forms of solar power—the moulds into which his strength is temporarily poured, in passing from its source through infinitude."*

To know the part the sun or any other agent has had in your formation and growth is not of the remotest value to any human being; but to know how you can use the sun, or any other agent, for the cure of your ills or the prolongation of your life, is of the very greatest value.

We have already on several occasions had to remark that the most recent scientific discoveries had been anticipated by the earliest traditions, and also that these traditions had appeared evidences of an ignorant and a barbarous condition, because the interpretation was impossible until science in these respects had become capable of understanding them.

Another instance of the kind is furnished by the discovery that space is not empty, but is pervaded by what may be termed the inert matter of light, and consequently of heat.

We have thus to the four elements of common speech a fifth to add, that fifth consisting in empyrean atmosphere, distinguished from that which we breathe. Now the number of the elements of the earlier systems,—that

* Tyndall's "Heat considered as a Means of Motion," pp. 430 —433.

is, of the astronomic religions,—was not four, but five; and the fifth is this very matter of light and heat and motion, now rediscovered.

The religious and philosophical systems of the ancient Hindus have classified these elements by their attributes, as appreciable to the five senses of man, commencing with the æther, as follows :—

Æther.	Air.	Fire.	Water.	Earth.
Sound.	Sound	Sound	Sound	Sound
	Touch.	Touch	Touch	Touch
		Form.	Form	Form
			Savour.	Savour
				Odour.

The Sanscrit name for æther is *âkâśa*, from the prefix *â*, towards, and *kâś*, shine; therefore implying "everywhere shining;" hence it also means space; âkâśa being supposed to pervade the universe.

On this point, as in so many others, we have in Greece, the reflection of Hindostan, as recorded in the adjuration placed by Æschylus in the mouth of Prometheus.

He is appealing to the powers of nature against the tyranny of Jove, and he does so in this order :—1. Æther. 2. Air. 3. Water. 4. Earth. 5. Fire (the Sun). I subjoin the passage, as wonderful in various ways. Prometheus was chained on the Himalaya,—not on the mountain range between the Caspian and the Euxine, to which the original name of the "Mountains of the Cash" (Caucasus) has been transferred. It is to the latter, however, at this moment, that apply the words or prediction of the Greek poet. To render the application literal, it suffices to alter in the last line θεός to Ἔθνος, when the sense would run, " Behold what things I, a nation, suffer from the nations !"*

* Ὦ δῖος αἰθὴρ καὶ ταχύπτεροι πνοαί,
Ποταμῶν τε πηγαὶ, ποντίων τεκυμάτων
Ἀνήριθμον γέλασμα, παμμῆτόρ τε γῆ,
Καὶ τὸν πανόπτην κύκλον ἡλιοῦ καλῶ.
Ἴδεσθέ μ' οἷα πρὸς θεῶν πάσχω θεός.

" O divine Æther, swift-winged breathings, fountains of rivers, and countless smiles of ocean waves. Earth, of all things mother; and all-seeing circle of the Sun,—I invoke Behold, what things I, a god, suffer from the gods !"

Part II.

Action of the Bath
On Horses and Cattle.

Second Part.

The Bath in the Farm.

THE use of the bath for cattle has been almost restricted hitherto to the training of horses for the race-course. The results suffice to establish a claim on the attention of the farmer, the breeder, and the landlord.

If, in the training of horses—an art perfected by the care of so many and such able men—this process is accepted as a means of rectifying errors, and of obtaining power for the animal, independently of food and exercise,* it must be for working cattle and the farm stock at least of equal value. If so, unquestionably the profits of labour and capital and the rent of the land must be augmented by the general introduction of the bath on farms.

It is now eight years since the value of this process has been fully and experimentally established, and yet I have in England and Scotland only one farm bath to cite: it is that of Lord Kinnaird. I do so with peculiar

* See note at the end.

satisfaction, as this is the only case of an idea worked out independently.

The universal difficulty I have had to contend with has been the aversion to, and dread of, high heat, by which alone you can operate on disease. To this dulness of sight is superadded defective construction. They cannot get high heats, and then they say, "Anything above 130° is injurious." Lord Kinnaird has got heat, and has dared to use it. His thermometer ranges up to 212°, and consequently he can stop disease at once if acute, and more speedily relieve it if chronic. "In Lord Kinnaird's bath for cattle, there having been no trouble either with patients or medical men, the necessity for high temperature for the cure of grave disorders has been ascertained. The words of a report in the 'Scottish Farmer,' 1862, are:—'The heat required in cases of pneumonia needs to be very great——up to 200° to 212°—boiling point, in fact. At a less temperature the curative effect was not visible.'"*

In respect to pneumonia, Alderman Mechi says, in a recent number of the "Gardener's Chronicle" (June 4, 1864), "What is wanted is attention, or the Turkish bath." The Turkish bath is "attention," and nothing more. If any one will attend to what, in the given case "a cold," ripening into pleuro-pneumonia, is wanted to relieve nature and baffle disease, he will of necessity fall on the expedient of heat, or, in other words, *a warmer climate.* If his attention is profitable, he will also discover that, by the proper use of fuel and

* Prospectus of the Jermyn Street Hammam.

the proper construction of an apartment, he can obtain at any spot, for any time, any amount of climate that he may desire.

Professor Gamgee, in either the April or May number of the "Veterinary Review," estimates the annual loss of cattle in Great Britain from pleuro-pneumonia alone at £6,000,000.

Animals that are slaughtered for the use of man, ought not to die of natural—or, more properly speaking, unnatural—death. If they die, it is through mismanagement, and the loss incurred is but the penalty attached to neglect. From the subjoined statement of the results of four years' experience on an Irish farm, it appears that no death had occurred either on the farm itself or on those adjoining it. It is not, therefore, theoretically only that I conclude, but experimentally also, that the bath would save to the country the loss at present yearly suffered in farm stock.

I owe to the courtesy of the proprietor of the *Field* the communication of as yet unpublished returns of the yearly loss in farm stock. The following passage in the appended report is from the pen of a veterinary surgeon :—

"The Turkish Bath, not only as a medicinal agent, but also as a preventive of disease, deserves consideration, and we cannot help thinking the hot-air chamber is almost as necessary an adjunct to the extensive stock-keeper as to the veterinary surgeon, and for the simple reason, that in it we have an agent which exerts more powerful influence than any derivative, ox-purge, or blister, without lowering vital power ; for it carries off, or at

B B

any rate diminishes, the amount of any virus that may circulate in the blood, and by this means cleanses the system, and renders it better able to throw off disease, and to resist the attacks of it."

Upon such data as are at present within our reach, the yearly loss appears to be, exclusive of epidemic years, two and a half per cent. on cattle, and five per cent. on sheep. Reckoning the whole of this to be saved by the general use of the bath, still it would amount but to a small part of the gain. The saving in sickness, alike in the cattle and sheep that would die as in those that do recover, must be taken into account, and can scarcely be placed at less than twice the amount of value of mere life preserved. We may estimate the saving on farm stock at ten per cent., independently of veterinary charges, which are estimated by Alderman Mechi at sixpence per acre.

Next comes the increase of animal power, whether as applied to labour or exhibiting itself in flesh and in milk, and this may be estimated at one-third. In the subjoined report, six pounds of flesh are stated as being put on under the action of the bath, for four pounds without it.

Under this head we may safely estimate at ten per cent. the increase in the value of farm stock, giving us a total of twenty per cent. on the whole amount of live animals.

These results might be indubitable and yet unattainable. Were the expense considerable or the construction elaborate, years might elapse before the mass of agriculturists could expect to profit thereby. Such would have been the prospect had I been writing four years ago. Now, however, the cost is reduced to almost nothing, and the value of the heat is multiplied many fold. I subjoin in a note a letter that went the round of the Irish papers at the beginning of this year, showing that any farm may have its bath by means of a spare loose box, an old stove, and fifty shillings in money.*

* ACCIDENT TO A HORSE IN A TURKISH BATH—A WARNING.

Carysfort House, January 5th, 1864.

Sir,—On Wednesday last the coachman hearing a disturbance in the bath in which there was a horse, opened the door. The animal showed great uneasiness, and with difficulty was got out, on which he was seized with frightful convulsions, threw himself down in the stall and stable, and in this way rolling himself over and over, made his way into the yard, where he was secured, and prevented from destroying himself, by the combined efforts of about a dozen men. The impression which was produced was that he was seized with madness. Mr. Urquhart happening to be here on a visit, pronounced at once the case to be one of asphyxia. On his inspecting the bath this was confirmed—the air entering only under the door, and so reaching the furnace below. The horse had been in two hours and three quarters, at a temperature from 180° to 190°. This was the first bath for horses constructed on Mr. Urquhart's new plan, of a furnace with the draught from within, so as to ventilate by suction, and which, consequently, requires that there should be an air-passage from the highest point, and that it should be hermetically sealed below. A cow had been in the bath some days before for a much longer t'me without injury, probably in consequence of carrying her head lower. The accident may prove a warning against such oversight in future. This form of bath, combining so much economy both in structure and fuel, is at the same time so much

The appreciation of the process has so rapidly extended during the last few months, that it may be anticipated that no long period will elapse before a bath will be considered a necessary appendage to every farm of two hundred acres and upwards, and of every veterinary establishment.

The bath commends itself to every farmer on six several grounds :—

1. Cure of sickness in cattle, sheep, and pigs.

2. Saving of mortality in young stock.

3. Fortifying the horses engaged in ploughing and draught.

4. Increasing flesh and milk.

5. Increasing the productiveness of stock.

6. Collateral advantages : drying harness, clothes, saving damaged grain and seeds, saving of sickness to farm servants, and also to the farmer himself and his family.

It was in Ireland that the experiment of heat was first tried, or rather recommenced, on man. Naturally it was there first tried on animals. It began with horses, it was extended to cattle, and the results have been made known by the reports of agricultural associations. These results, surprising as they appeared, are still wholly inadequate to represent the effects

more efficacious, that it must come into general use. The cost of turning a loose box into this sort of bath does not exceed £1-10s. for labour, and about £2 10s. for laundry stove and sheet-iron pipes.

Your obedient Servant,

B. POORE.

obtainable by heat: for these baths were at best but timid gropings in the dark. The report which I subjoin bears on a bath which originally had also but small power. Even with the knowledge in the proprietor of the necessity of a high temperature, he has not been able to raise his above 180°, and the heat is not radiating.

By the experience of this Irish farm, we have four years without death in that and the neighbouring farms, nor was there sickness. Diseases were arrested on the appearance of the first symptoms. Now this result is peculiarly instructive, from the general deterioration of Irish stock during these four years, as shown by the following extracts from the official returns :*—

Total value of live stock in Ireland :—

1859	£35,368,259
1863	29,997,546
Decrease . . .	5,370,713

While thus the farms in question in the north, as likewise other farms in the south, were emancipated from the average loss in casualties and sickness, the other farms throughout Ireland were suffering that average loss, say four per cent. yearly, or sixteen per cent. in the four years, together with a further loss on the four years of nearly twenty per cent. ; so that in this period of time, had the bath been general in Ireland, the public fortune under this head alone would

* Parliamentary Papers, " Agricultural Statistics—Ireland," for 1863.

have been increased by nearly £10,000,000, or say £2,000,000 a year.*

The same proportion would be far below the mark for England, either as regards average or stock; the number of stock being higher to the acre, and the proportion of sheep, among whom the loss is double, being only as one to six; so that, reasoning on these data, the saving in Great Britain would be £10,000,000 per annum.

The farmer would doubtless not be influenced by general considerations: he would look to his own farm, and would have to view the matter in this shape: " My stock amounts to £500. Is it worth my while to incur an outlay of £5, and a yearly charge of £10, to insure it against loss, and to increase its productiveness, together amounting to from ten to fourteen per cent.?"

Why should not every farm of 200 acres adopt this precaution? When the Turks adopted the bath, they made it a rule that no habitation should be placed at a greater distance from a bath than three miles. Yet their baths were serviceable only for the breed of men; by their process of heating, an expensive edifice was required, with expensive fuel. What the English farmer can obtain by means of a loose box (which remains as serviceable as ever) and an iron stove, a Turkish village could obtain only by the outlay of £200 or £300.

---

* This is independently of veterinary charges, which, if estimated according to Alderman Mechi's scale, would exceed a quarter of a million per annum.

TRAINING OF HORSES.

In the first Dialogue, page 1, it has been shown that the objects of training consist in *health* and *wind*. To those passages the reader is referred.

The proper treatment for a horse is the proper treatment for a man, and is to be found in the educational maxims of ancient times, viz., to accustom the body to bear the extremes of heat and cold, and to endure privations in regard to food. Our practice is the reverse for man. Naturally enough we have applied the same rule to the horse. We clothe and house him so that he shall not know the extremes of heat and cold. We feed him often. The horse, like the camel, is indigenous to the high and cold regions of the Tartarian ranges. Nevertheless, he flourishes in hot and dry zones. He has attained to the highest perfection in those into which he has been introduced. Our own breed is immediately derived from the Tafilet Barb and the Godolphin Arab.

Trainers have closed their stables and sheeted up their animals. This was seeking heat by excluding air. As men wrapped up their bodies from the sun, and closed by glass their apartments from the air, and have so brought upon themselves morbid sensations and countless diseases, so have the like practices engendered in the horse similar diseases, and the like liability to disease.

It is, then, pure heat that the horse wants, and not muffling. But cold has also its virtue. By creating an artificial climate we obtain the benefits of both, and so acquire the power of transporting a horse to the wastes of Arabia for a certain period of the day, and of restoring him to his native bracing cold for the remainder of it.

We have experienced to the fullest extent the benefits of this operation in man, even to the cure of the most hopeless and inveterate disorders. But we should gravely err if we placed, in this respect, the man and the horse on the same footing. The facility of acting on the horse is much greater in consequence of his volume relatively to that of man.

A large portion of the food is expended on the production of animal heat. The smaller the size of the animal the larger is the surface in proportion to its bulk, and therefore the greater the escape of heat. A canary in proportion to its size and weight consumes many times as much food as a man. Heat escapes far more rapidly from the man than from the horse. The effect, then, in the form of saving food, is for the horse very considerable. It is thus that the horse is enabled to inhabit the regions adjoining the limits of eternal snow.[*] Consequently heat, externally applied to him, has so much greater power than on man. In the cold regions of Tartary, or the hot ones of Persia, Mesopotamia, the Nedjd, or the African deserts, he is severally brought to the highest perfection by heat or cold.

---

[*] See Moorcraft's Journal in the Himalaya and Tibet.

*I look therefore to the Bath as capable of furnishing a
finer breed of horses than has as yet been obtained.* For
this end, however, it is not the adult animal that has
temporarily to be subject to this action, but the foal and
the colt. From the moment of birth, and during the
period of growth, it has daily to be immersed in the
torrid, and restored to the arctic zone, without protection or covering; the aim being to fortify the muscle,
develop the frame, and brace the nervous power by
balancing the double and apparently opposing agencies
of cold and heat: in a word, using the elements at once
which separately are afforded by the Plateau of Pamer,
or the Roof of the World,* and the plains of the Sahara
below the level of the ocean.

Were any trainer or proficient in stable lore asked
this question, " What has domestication done for the
horse?" he would probably answer, " We give him
regular instead of uncertain food; we protect him
against the severity of the weather; and, lastly and
chiefly, keep him in health and strength by the currycomb, supplying a requisite to well-being, of which, in
the natural state, he is entirely destitute."

I have disposed of the first two points of so-called
amelioration. As to the third—the currycomb—we
have not followed the rule we have laid down for
ourselves. We have never thought of clearing the
scarf-skin off our own bodies. We have taxed our
invention, then, in reference to the horse, and only

---

* The Turkish name for this district is " Roof of the World"
—*Bam i Duniah.*

to inflict on him an injury equal to, if not greater, than that which, through unreasoning and stupid routine, he has suffered at our hands on the two other points.

Any one may find in any popular book on the skin every detail respecting its structure and its functions; that is, whatever may be available for the acquisition of knowledge, but nothing serviceable for the correction of common and injurious habits.

I suppose the reader to have referred to some such work, and therefore to know that there is a double covering to the body, the one the skin, or, as it is called, the "true skin;" the other the cuticle, or the covering of the skin.

Now, the process of reformation or reparation of this cuticle differs entirely from that of the rest of the body, which consists in the deposit by the blood of particles, whilst the same blood carries or washes away the used-up matter.

The cuticle is reformed by exudation from the numerous papillæ covering the "true skin," and is carried off externally by friction.

Excess of friction prompts the discharge from beneath of the gelatinous matter of the cuticle. Carried to any extent, this is disease of the nature of leprosy. In the same manner corns and bunions are produced, pressure being substituted for abrasion.

The skin of the horse is far more delicate than that of man, and consequently he is supplied with a natural coat for its defence. In his natural state, the small amount of cuticle he has to get rid of is carried off by the conjoint effects of perspiration, rapid motion, and constant exposure to the air and the *wind.*

Domesticated, of course his coat becomes clogged, and means have to be taken to free it. These means have been taken in the origin by man, and they are yet to be found practised in the East. We in Europe, however, at least in modern times, have stepped beyond the object, and by inventing for the skin of the horse an iron instrument of serrated form, we produce a condition of quasi-leprosy; when we clear from its teeth the accumulation of scarf-skin—the evidence of our stupidity—we exclaim, "How clever we are to have invented a currycomb, and how happy the horse to have intelligent grooms hissing at him; instead of having to go and rub his itchy haunches against boulders of granite or stumps of trees!"

"With regard to the horse, in parts of Central Asia, where an animal is expected to gallop twelve or fourteen miles without rein being drawn, it is necessary to put it through careful training, and especially to work off the fat. For this purpose the horse is daily sweated; and the test of prime condition is the absence of acridity and viscidity in the exudation. The taste determines the former. The latter is judged of by collecting a little of the secretion between the thumb and forefinger, which are then held up to the light and slowly separated, when viscidity appears in threads long drawn out. No currycomb is used, but the horse is shampooed with the ball of the hand."

This passage, contained in a letter from Captain Burton is the only one I have got to quote from either writers or travellers conveying instruction in regard to the horse in essential matters. I know nothing more melancholy than horse literature, from the earliest essay with which I am acquainted, *i.e.* that of Xenophon, down to the monographs of General Daumas and Abd-el-Kader. The only exception that I have to make are incidental notices as regards points of natural history, such as are found in Moorcraft, Sir John Malcolm, &c. There is, indeed, a volume of Colonel Smith in the "Library of Natural History," but it is no more than a collection of materials which have themselves to be critically examined before being used. The regular works on the horse are relieved from barrenness by perversion, bringing to bear upon the animal in disease all the aberrations of therapeutic science in regard to man, and supplying instruction for his management calculated to produce the disorders upon which therapeutic empiricism · has to act. The recent protest of Admiral De Rous against the whole system has, nevertheless, been received with respect by trainers. Men unqualified by scientific acquirements have now found a royal road to the truth. A friend of mine, who was one of the first to employ the bath in the stable, thus writes, in answer to questions as to the results which he had obtained during six years' experience :—

"1. The skin is cleansed FAR more completely than by any other method of grooming.

"2. The system relieves itself, through the skin, of every kind of impurity.

"3. The animal is enabled to bear, with perfect impunity, the greatest alternations of heat and cold.

" 4. The appetite, so frequently a poor one *in training*, is increased, and digestion promoted.

" 5. The lungs are brought into strong play, *without increased action of heart and pulse*.

" 6. What is commonly called inside fat of heart and lungs is removed, and the wind consequently greatly improved ; and this without the fearful wear and tear of legs and constitution, now so universally practised to attain that object.

" 7. Aloes and other drastics become superfluous.

" 8. And lastly, whereas, in the opinion of the first trainers of the day, by the present system, it is impossible to bring a horse fit to the post more than once or twice in the year for a great race. by the use of the bath he may ever be in the highest state of condition. I have now only stated what I believe I clearly proved, in the conditioning of five horses, without physic, and with the bath, to the satisfaction of a veterinary surgeon, my groom, and myself. But a few words may be necessary to the uninitiated, as to how the bath should best be used with effect. It should never be given less than once or twice a week ; as much more frequently as you please. The temperature (*especially for disease*) should be a high one, varying from 140° to 180°. The admission of fresh air into the bath should be plentiful. The animal should be thoroughly shampooed on the muscles of the back, thighs, and arms. He should be thoroughly washed after sweating, occasionally with soap, and always with water hot and cold; and having completed the process, he should be taken into the open air (the colder the atmosphere the more beneficial to him) *without clothing*, and receive as much exercise as is necessary. Above all, he should return to a thoroughly cool and well-ventilated stable ; and if requiring warmth, by exhibiting cold in his ears or legs, he should receive it from clothing and bandages, and NOT *by the exclusion of fresh air from his box.* The benefit which a clean skin derives from exposure to fresh air, after a high temperature, is such as nobody can describe who has not experienced and felt it. The advantages of such treatment, where either the legs are doubtful or the constitution delicate, are too obvious to require further explanation. Let anybody, who is sceptical as to the effects of a Turkish bath, properly given to a horse, ride the animal as soon as he comes out of one, and judge for himself. I have repeatedly seen a veterinary surgeon examine the pulsation and action of the heart, and pronounced that there was no increase whatever of either, though the action of the lungs in the bath was greatly promoted, and I maintain beneficially, from the inhalation of pure hot air. If the horse is kept in a thoroughly cool and well-ventilated stable, grooms will object to the less shining appearance of the coat; but this objection will scarcely hold with anybody who knows that a hot stable and nitre will produce a brightness and gloss which by no means indicate perfect health. There is less cough and disease to be found by fifty per cent. in the cab-stands of London, though the horses are badly groomed and exposed to all weather, than in the choicest horse training or racing establishments. Affections of the kidneys, whether chronic or acute, are at once relieved by the bath, to say nothing of rheumatism, catarrh, and inflammatory attacks of all sorts."

THE DOMESTIC ANIMALS.

The other domestic animals, the camel inclusive, with the exception of the pig, stand in the same category as the horse. They are equally natives of the Tartarian levels, or very cold countries. So long, however, as they remained in their native seats, they were endowed with an under-covering of down or fur,* which has disappeared as they have spread over lower and more genial districts. These have all attained to greater development in hot countries, showing that heat (not that of the close stable and byre) is beneficial for them.

Cats and dogs are on the Himalaya also furnished with this down.

Barn-yard fowls of all descriptions are either migratory by nature, or natives of warmer climates than ours; so that for them the bath, on mere historic grounds, must be assumed to be highly conducive to their development and fruitfulness, in a climate the standard of which is so far below their own.

---

* Hence is derived the local name of the Himalaya—Undes—or Una desa, wool country. The same is the name of the country of the algoin and alpaca—Andes. The goats of Angora—Una gori, wool mountain—retain the under-down.

THE PIG.

The pig stands by itself, or in the same category as man. It does not belong to the Himalaya, or at least not more so than to the Atlas, the Pyrenees, the Taurus, the Alps, or the low regions of all the earth. It resembles man also in its food, in its internal structure, and in the taste of its flesh.* It has also a skin like that of man, elaborately formed, so as to be able to dispense with hair or wool. It is very cleanly by instinct, whenever it is allowed the opportunity. It is very sensitive to atmospheric influences, as all hunters of the wild boar well know.† They feel the necessity of the removal of the scarf-skin, and therefore enjoy scratching and rubbing, as no other animal does. By domestication, it has acquired rounded shapes and more succulent flesh, the scantling of the skeleton being, however, generally diminished. This change has to be attributed to a more regular supply of food, and to protection against extreme inclemency of weather. They have not, however, been subjected to the closing of doors and windows, either at night or during the day, as has been the case with horses and cows.

* In the Fecjee Islands human flesh in the shambles is designated " Long pork," the joints being similar, save that they are longer.

† On the north-western coast of Africa I have found it next to impossible to start them with an easterly wind blowing. They would allow the dogs to run in upon them, and stood at bay in their lair.

The pig, therefore, is the animal for which I foresee the greatest benefit from the bath. It is not only its maladies, more injurious to man than those of all other animals combined, to which an end is put at once ; but the sweetening of its flesh, the facilitating of the formation of that flesh, the restoration of its dimensions, and the whole at a greatly reduced expenditure of food. Now, when the prolific nature of the animal is considered, an estimate may be formed of the profit of such an appendage to a farm-yard where pigs are kept.

I trust it is not too late to point to the picturesque but thriftless old breed of Irish pigs, the large dimensions of which might be filled out to the plumpness and succulence of those of Wiltshire.

ON THE BATH FOR THE TRAINING OF HORSES.

BY THE HON. ADMIRAL DE ROUS.

(*Times*, March 26th, 1863).

"Thanks to Mr. Urquhart (to whom this country is more indebted than to any living man for the introduction of Turkish *alias* Roman baths) a new era has arisen : the present barbarous system of preparing horses to race by drastic purgatives, hot clothing, hot stables, and four and five mile sweats will be ameliorated, and we may look forward with confidence to a revolution by the aid of hot-air baths, which will enable a trainer to bring his horses to the post in first-rate condition without subjecting them to a destructive apprenticeship.

"The bath invigorates a horse's frame, gives increased action to his liver, improves his appetite, cleanses the pores of suppressed perspiration, and fortifies the skin from extreme heat and cold; the joints become more supple, the sinews more elastic ; and the heart, lungs, and kidneys being freed from fat, horses are able to take the strongest exercise, without suffering from internal fever. Rheumatism, sore shins, and cutaneous eruptions are speedily subdued by hot air. Under this system no horse ought to be exercised in heavy clothes. In my opinion, it is always objectionable to give a horse a sharp or very long gallop when he is clothed, and looking to hot air as an agent, we may keep our horses sound *for thrice the estimated period of their present efficacy ;* the veterinary surgeon and the saddler will send in diminished bills : this will balance the expenses of the bath, and will save large sums of money to the proprietors of race-horses.

"Of all animals in the world there are none better endowed by nature to endure the vicissitudes of climate than a horse. From the burning deserts of Arabia to the coldest regions of Europe, Asia, and America, they enjoy the most perfect health and vigour. Why are we, then, to treat them in this temperate clime like exotic plants? If, from the day a foal is dropped, he is never shut up with his dam in a close hovel, except during a severe frost; if the same practice be adopted after he is weaned till he is taken into the stable to receive his education, there is very little risk of his catching cold, cough, or any disease, all those indispositions arising from young stock being confined in a close, unwholesome box, and then being suddenly exposed to cold winds.

"When the yearling colt is removed to a well-built, warm stable, you would suppose that, if he enjoyed perfect health during his days of liberty, in the open air, rolling on the wet grass,—if this mode of life agree with him, and added daily to his growth and strength, that, as far as fresh air was concerned, you would allow him all the advantages which nature can bestow. From a life of freedom, housed in an open box, inhaling pure, fresh air, he is confined with his head tied up to a manger in a close stable, the windows jealously opened by day, as if the air was injurious to his health, and carefully shut on an average of 13 hours during the greatest part of the year. As a foal he roughed it in the paddock during the cold winds of February; 18 months afterwards he is clothed and shut up in a warm, close room. Before the colt is reconciled to his first lessons of servitude, a woollen rug is strapped round him, to add to the naturally inflamed state of his blood; and, to crown his misfortunes, from having always had free access to water, the trainer restricts him to two draughts per diem; it signifies nothing whether the weather is hot or cold,—the stable regulations, like the laws of the Persians, are inviolable. The trainer drinks ten times a day if his throat is dry, but he never calculates that his horses may be more thirsty than usual if the thermometer in his fusty stable rises to 90°. It has been proved over and over again that if horses in a stable have free access to water they will not drink as great a quantity as when water is offered to them twice a day (excepting in sultry weather) ; because the horses, having more sense than their master, drink a whole pailful to lay in a stock to meet the exigencies of feverish thirst, and the interior demands which nature may require in the long interval of destitution. This saves trouble, but it is in direct antagonism to the principle of training men to run or to fight, who are never allowed to take a large draught."

FOUR YEARS' EXPERIENCE OF THE BATH ON AN IRISH FARM.

BY J. E. SCRIVEN, ESQ.

My experience embraces horses, cows, sheep, pigs, dogs, cats, hens, and chickens. It extends over a period exceeding four years. The bath has twelve feet six inches square of clear standing room; it is nine feet six inches high.' The floor above is tiled, and used as a corn kiln. Here are all descriptions of grain, and such can be safely and economically dried. A similar building, including furnace flues and a double roof over all, would cost about £150.

The cost per annum for fuel, washing, attendant's wages, and repairs, is £30. The fire is never out.

I have found great apprehension entertained of the amount of water required, by persons desiring to have baths of their own. I therefore desire to state how little that expenditure amounts to.

In a report to the Board of Works, I have given the following details for one week :—

Men	-	-	-	25
Women	-	-	-	19
Horses	-	-	-	5
Pigs	-	-	-	7
Dogs	-	-	-	4
				60

At this time I had no sheep.

Water, cold	-	-	-	180 gallons
„ hot	-	-	-	80 „
Scotch coal	-	-	-	25 stone
Average temperature	-	-	-	140° Fahr.

At first my labourers declined going in, on the ground that they lost enough by work, and could not stand any more perspiration. One of them broke down on a hot day, when mowing. I said to him, "Now you are done for a week or so, you may as well try the bath." He went in, and had a vigorous shampooing. The next day he took the lead in the meadow. That night the space could not accommodate the applicants.

Cure after cure having been effected, the want was so felt, that a public bath was built in the neighbourhood, under my instructions.

The first horse I had to attend to for five days myself, as none of my men would venture in. The horse after an hour or so followed me round the apartment, and would not rest unless he had his muzzle on my shoulder, or was licking my hand. He recovered from a bad strain in the loins. Weeks after he recognised me on entering his stable, and licked my hand. I asked a friend, sceptical of the horse's attachment, to go up to him. The animal rejected his caresses, and followed me with his eye.

This is no exceptional case. Horses, cows, sheep, and pigs, all show their satisfaction, and return to it with pleasure.

At first it was supposed that it would be dangerous

to put a dog in, as not being able to perspire, he might go mad.

My first case was a water-spaniel, subject to rheumatism. It was very difficult to get him out ; when he sees anyone going in, he goes too, and lies down in the hottest corner.

I shall divide the subject into the five following heads :—

I. Treatment of disease.

II. Protection against the effects of exposure, and approaching disease.

III. Increase of power for labour and productiveness in flesh, milk, and offspring.

IV. Subsidiary uses on the farm.

V. Benefit to the farm servants.

I. *Treatment of Disease.* — Subjoined is a list of diseases in which I have obtained successful results :— Bronchitis, strangles, colic, dysentery, indigestion, dropsical swellings, distemper in pigs, sturdy in sheep, jaundice in dogs, mange in horses and dogs, sore mouth and feet in sheep, garget in dairy stock, swelling in the head of calves.

Here I would call attention to the necessity of high temperatures to effect cures. All the cases of rapid and decisive cures have been at what are ordinarily called great heat, 170° to 180°. My bath was unfortunately constructed before the discovery of the cheap expedient by which heat of a so much greater curative value can be obtained. Still, no case has arisen either on my own farm or on those of my neighbours who have applied to me, that has not readily yielded, and these cases include all the diseases incidental to horses and farm stock.

HORSES.—The most violent forms of "bats" are quickly got under. Fifteen minutes in the hot room produce relief; and a recurrence of an attack after entering is very unusual.

A horse belonging to a dealer in the neighbourhood was cured of strangles, and sold within one month : so far from being reduced by the operation, he was brought out in high condition.

Under this head, an important item is the accidents common to horses in ploughing and carting. One of my work mares, heavy in foal, fell under a load in soft ground, and after violent plunging was released with great difficulty. She was helped into the bath immediately, and in three days was at her usual work. A fine foal was born in due time.

An entire horse belonging to a neighbour becoming restive while ploughing, threw himself, and was severely strained, as well as cut. His owner brought him immediately to me; and without any dressing, he resumed his work in a few days.

Cases of this nature are so numerous, and their cure so certain, that no impression is made on my memory now.

The import of my experience has been indeed established throughout England as to running horses, but not as to working horses. It appears to me very surprising that the means employed in the one case should have been disregarded in the other, and that too where *the plough is concerned.*

Cows.—If only for the cure of one disease—distemper—this subject demands the attention of every stock owner in the country.

Lord Kinnaird's experiments on distemper in cattle are so conclusive, that I shall quote a report from the "Scottish Farmer," Sept. 1862.

"Lord Kinnaird's Bath at Millhill, designed for the treatment of cattle, is largely made use of by the people in the neighbourhood. The curative properties of the bath have already been demonstrated in a marked manner in the case of several calves suffering from scour, &c.; but still more wonderful is the influence it has had upon two or three feeding stots affected with pleuro-pneumonia. Out of three patients, two that we saw have every appearance of progressing towards perfect health. They eat well, walk about with seeming comfort and ease, the cough has lost its nasty metallic sound, the discharge from the nose is stopped, they are no more hidebound, and their coat has no longer the staring aspect of disease. The third patient, a larger animal than the other two, is not yet so far recovered, but the beast is a great deal better than it was. The heat required to produce a favourable impression in cases of pleuro needs to be very great—up to 200 to 212°—boiling point, in fact. At a less temperature the curative effect was not very visible. In other diseases, less dangerous, but, if neglected, hardly less fatal, the bath has been found a 'perfect cure.' It can be erected and carried on for a comparatively trifling cost—one that, we think, would repay large stock owners to expend."

Dysentery among dairy stock, so injurious to their milking, yields readily to heat. On the fourth day after the beginning of an attack, I have frequently had cows back to their full milk.

Heat in the skin, and loss of appetite, are got over the day they appear.

Hardness in the udder, and stoppage of the teat, are thought little of here. These diseases require careful shampooing.

I have never had a fully developed case of "black quarter" since the bath has been built. Before that, I lost several fine calves by this disorder.

In swelling of the head in calves, we have found it most effectual.

SHEEP.—Two cases are worthy of record. One was a wether suffering from dysentery for three weeks, emaciated at times, suffering intense pain, and bleating pitifully. When put in, the thermometer ranged from 150° to 180°: he chose the hottest part of the floor, and lying down seemed quite happy. He was left there several hours daily, and when turned out with the flock, rapidly put on flesh.

The second is a case of "sturdy" (water on the brain)—the most intractable, if not incurable, of all diseases. To say a sheep has it, is to condemn it to the knife.

One animal evinced the ordinary symptoms, going violently round in a ring, moping by itself, and neglecting its food. It was let in, thermometer 160° to 170°, daily for three weeks, when it was turned out with the rest of the flock. Two months later, as I was going round with a friend from a celebrated sheep district, and long accustomed to examining the best flocks in the country, he pointed out this very sheep as a good specimen of my flock, both for health and condition.

Firmly convinced as my herd is of the efficacy of the bath in disease of cattle, he urged me not to make the experiment in this case, as it was sure to fail, and lose me whatever the animal might bring for mutton.

PIGS.—On no animal have I got more satisfactory and decisive results than on pigs, whether fattening or brood sows. Distemper is rapidly relieved; the spots appearing on the skin in two hours. I have had no fatal case of this scourge. And the same thing I may say with reference to those of my neighbours who have sent their pigs to me. The rule is to keep the pig in till the spots appear. Throwing alternately hot and cold water over the animal is useful in developing the spots.

When only a few hours old, the two youngest pigs of a litter of fifteen appeared to be dying. The byre-man put them in for some hours, and brought them again to the litter.

He repeated this frequently for some weeks till they were able to hold their own with their elder brethren " These two pigs were dead three times, but for the bath," was his answer to an objector.

Previous to the appearance of this litter, the sow had been repeatedly put in, for a hurt from a horse.

The first distempered pig I experimented upon was one of a litter of fatting hogs. He weighed one stone heavier than any of the same litter.

DOGS.—I have had some remarkable cases of jaundice after distemper. One pointer, during treatment, became so fond of the bath, that, when let loose, he ran to the door, and scraped at it. He was shot over for years afterwards.

A setter that had lost his scent after distemper was

sent to me for treatment. He recovered condition rapidly, being put in three times a week. His scent was quite restored.

The development of the power of scent by the bath is a subject pregnant with important results, as regards the detection of disease, as shown in Mr. Urquhart's pamphlet, "Consumption arrested by the Turkish bath."

II. *Protective against the Effects of Exposure, and approaching Disease.*—In reference to this branch, Professor Gamgee, in his work on Dairy-stock, says:—

"*So far as my inquiries have extended*, I believe dairy-stock owners, whether in town or country, may find the bath the cheapest, safest, and most desirable appendage to their premises that has yet been suggested, if only as a mere cleaning apparatus."—Page 237.

"As a *therapeutic agent*, the hot air chamber holds an intermediate position between evacuants and stimulants. It is undoubtedly a general tonic, because it fits important organs for the free and healthy exercise of their functions, and thus operates beneficially on the blood, on nutrition, and hence invigorates the body. That it is evacuant, no one can doubt, that has witnessed the kind and quantity of cutaneous secretions, whether in man or animals.

"Viewing the subject as a veterinary, I unhesitatingly say that we have in heat the most effective diaphoretic, the most active depurant, and the most efficient means of producing healthy reaction that we have yet had at our disposal. It is a great addition to our therapeutic means. We needed a satisfactory means of acting on the skin of lower animals in febrile and other diseases, and here we have it."—Page 244.

" Cows are subject to blood disorders, to fever, functional disturbance of the skin, and other secreting organs ; to organic cutaneous diseases which are apt to become chronic ; to rheumatic affections, and a large number of inflammatory disorders. In the long category of diseases included under the foregoing heads, we shall find one and all pertain to the kind likely to be much benefited by heat.* But it is to *ward off* disease, and to *preserve health*, that among dairy-stock, particularly in large towns, the bath might *prove of great service.*"

Under the head of Positive Disease, I am not able to quote an instance, on my own farm, of lung distemper. This is attributable, I believe, to the preventive power always at command ; the rule being to put every animal in on the first symptom of sickness.

The horse-dealer I referred to before, on being asked if horses accustomed to the bath caught cold readily, answered :—

" *There is not a horse sheeted in the place. The top halves of the stable-doors are always off. The horses are always ready for work. You will not hear a cough in the worst season. Whenever they are severely worked, or exposed, they are put in, and that sets them all right.*"

On one of the open nights last winter, I asked my steward, how many horses he had had in at once. He reminded me of a wet windy day that we had sent four

---

* The writer used a Greek word. I have thought it better to put the English equivalent.

horses to some distance, and kept them standing very much exposed. On their return late at night, he put the men and horses in at once. The men dried their clothes, and went home refreshed and warm. The severity of the day had no effect upon either men or horses.

When we consider the number of such days in the year, and the loss by sickness in consequence, the advantage of such a preventive will be manifest.

III. *Increase of Power, for Labour and Productiveness, in Flesh and Milk and Offspring.*—I could give numerous cases of broken-down horses trained by the new process, because they were useless, and could therefore be experimented upon, and several years added to their working lives.

The first case so treated in England was a mare that had been given up because her feet and legs would not stand the training. She was brought into a splendid condition in a few weeks without a gallop, and hunted that and succeeding winters as well as when in her prime.

We are enabled to dispense with the use of medicine in getting horses into condition off grass. The results in the availability of the horse for service are so manifest, that I do not dwell upon them.

Having been disappointed of a foal from a mare I prized, I resolved to try on her the effect of the bath. I was led to this by hearing of some cases in human beings, from which it was to be inferred that the use of the bath had removed confirmed barrenness. The result justified the expectation. Not only was a foal obtained in due course, but the foals have not ceased during three years.

In regard to muscular power, I will begin by stating, that amongst men it has been now most fully established, that the bath develops it in an extraordinary degree without any corresponding consumption of food. From this I inferred that the *condition* being improved, the effect would be no less in regard to the carcase of the animal when dead, than in respect of its power when alive.

Three years ago, I made the experiment on two cows, and found that where they had gained one stone in weight previously, they gained eighteen pounds when put in three times a week. They became quite free from heated skin, and improved in appearance and handling.

In this case I took means to measure the results. But equal results, though not accurately measured, have since been obtained. The gain being thus *one-third in flesh*, we may assume that there will be an equal gain in labour.

When the resources of nature are expended on milk, we may expect not only an economy of food, but a large increase of dairy produce, because the secreting organs of milk are so immediately affected by action on the skin, close to which the lacteal glands are situated. I have no experience to report in this respect, my attention having been but recently called to the subject ; but the grounds are so evident, and the results obtained in women so striking, that there remains no doubt on my mind that the gain in respect to milk will not fall short of that in power and flesh.

IV. *Subsidiary Uses on the Farm.* — In our damp

climate, the power of drying grain or seed, with safety and economy, is too obviously an advantage to require comment.

Last harvest, by means of the hot room and the kiln over it, I was enabled to save the produce of two acres of beans that was heating, and on its road to destruction. It was thrashed in the wet weather, and the beans carried at once to dry. In a few days a great part of a heavy crop was ground into meal, and fit for use.

Every one familiar with the ordinary mode of kiln-drying grain, knows the danger of producing diabetes in horses, arising from the admission to the grain of the fumes of burning coal. Here the process is carried on in pure air, and with equal facility.

We lose one million sterling a year in flax seed, chiefly from the difficulty of saving it. Had every farm the facility of drying flax seed at once, and without the delay of using a public kiln, we might be that much richer in feeding stuff.

So much risk attends the process of drying flax straw, preparatory to hand scutching, that it is carried on in open temporary sheds, when a wet season retards, and sometimes stops, the operation. Here it could be accomplished at the time when labour on the farm is impracticable, the produce brought to market in better condition, and many weeks earlier.

I am happy to say that some small farmers in my neighbourhood have applied to me for instruction how to convert a farm office into a bath.

The injury to horses' shoulders and backs from wet collars and saddles is avoided. The harness put into the drying room at night is gradually and thoroughly dried by morning.

Incidental to breaking in young horses, I have found their shoulders much more rapidly made by sweating them constantly during training, and the restiveness arising from soreness and stiffness avoided.

How many corn sacks would be annually saved by a convenient place to dry them in quickly?

To the laundry also it is an addition of great importance.

V. *Farm Servants.*—The preservation of health among farm labourers is no small matter. My farm servants often work willingly through wet windy days, well knowing that an hour in the hot room will send them home in dry clothes. This habit gives them also the power of enduring cold: so also amongst my visitors. Many have dispensed with flannel, some even at advanced ages. All find themselves in better health, freer from rheumatic pains, and firmer in muscle. One of my labourers was in the habit of wearing a flannel waistcoat and drawers, two waistcoats and trousers, and a heavy coat. Two years ago he left off the flannel, and now wears but one waistcoat, one pair of trousers, and seldom a coat. He says he is "suppler" than he was ten years ago, and can now resume his potato-diet, which he had left off from an enlargement of the stomach.

Improvement in digestion is one of the most marked results in man as well as in animals. More than two years ago, a man came to me suffering from disease of the stomach, inability to retain food, and dropsical swelling of the legs. His first few visits were made in a cart.

D D

After a fortnight, he walked to the bath, and is now in the enjoyment of robust health.

During a temporary absence from home, a neighbouring farmer suffering from dropsy visited the bath. He had previously requested my permission; but as the case was a severe one, I advised him to wait till I returned. On my return, my bathman told me, with dismay, that he feared the dropsical man had not reached home alive, that he had not been able to make him perspire, and his legs becoming more swollen, they hurried him out, and got him into the cart as soon as possible. The third day the cart drove up, and, leaning on two sticks, my bathman saw the object of his fears walk to the door. The night after his first visit, he had eight hours of unbroken rest, and was able to get out of bed, and sit at the fire. I took him in at 150°, and for two hours shampooed him, at first gently; by degrees he could bear considerable pressure. The swelling diminished, and his joints became more flexible. A short time afterwards, I was saluted by a tall athletic young man, in whom I recognised my dropsical patient.

A case of typhus fever is illustrative of the necessity of high temperature to *cure* disease. The patient was afraid of greater heat than 120°, and with it became worse. He became nearly incoherent. A few days afterwards he was with difficulty brought to me, when he was kept in for two hours at 180°. His clothes were purified on the heating apparatus. He described the effects by saying: "He could not help taking off his coat, and running," on his way home. He was at full work in four days.

I may here mention the account given me of the "sweating houses," by an old gamekeeper.

"In the county Fermanagh I could take you to ten or a dozen of them. They are built in the form of a bee-hive. Turf is burnt on the floor, till it is clear; then they close up the hole, and leave it for a time. When you are going to take the heat, the turf ashes are swept out, and the floor covered with rushes. You go in, and get towels and wipe the sweat off, and so on, till it is time to come out. Some knowledgable body is there that tells you when to come out, and you then jump into a stream of water; or if there is no natural stream, water is led, and a hole made for it. There was a man there, a strong (rich) farmer, and he built one for him-self, and brought water through it in pipes. These houses were first made by the ancient Milesians, long before your bath was thought of."

This rude form of bath, now only found among the mountains and islands, must have existed long before the Romans introduced into the sister country their bath, accompanied by every luxurious appliance; and when the departure of the Roman conquerors deprived the Britons of their bath, the Irish had the sense to preserve their unarchitectural, but efficient structures. What is most remarkable is, that during the English occupation no Englishman seems to have had so much as the thought of entering one of these sweating-houses. There they were, with their beneficial effects before their eyes, and they saw nothing. Now, indeed, they are written about, but· merely as an architectural curiosity, and because of the introduction from the East of a similar usage.

Since I obtained from Mr. Urquhart the knowledge on which I have acted with so much profit to myself, he has carried out his experiments to, at that time, wholly unexpected results, alike as to economy and efficiency. Having undergone the experience by being in a chamber heated up to 250°, I enjoyed a new sensation from the heat sent off in rays from the red-hot stove. It reminded me of a practice of former years, when studying engineering in Lancashire. After a day's hard work, I often went to the forge, and exposed myself to the glowing heat of the air furnaces for some half-hour; and found the stiffness and fatigue dispelled, and so much vigour supplied that I sought vent for it by throwing off my coat, and taking to the hammer and anvil.

The author of the foregoing paper is now applying himself to test by experience, in regard to labouring horses, the grounds laid down in this volume in respect to the debilitating effects of frequent feeding, allowing his horses but two feeds, and some only one feed a day.

Appendix.

No. 1.

EXPERIENCE OF SUNSHINE ON THE BODY.

(Extract from a Letter.)

I WAS first led to reflect on the probable advantage to health of exposure of the body to the atmosphere by reading the observations of Dr. Franklin in favour of this practice, which he frequently adopted.

In the water cure, Priesnitz used to say that air was quite as important an agent in the cure as water.

Some years since, after a long and debilitating illness, I went to the baths of Gastein. At these baths, Dr. Proel, a clever physician of much experience, strongly urged me to aid their action by taking, what he called, air baths in the neighbouring pine forest. He was in the habit of recommending this practice to his patients, and those who, undeterred by the seeming eccentricity of the proceeding, followed his advice, derived much benefit.

Conforming with Dr. Proel's instructions, I used frequently to remain during a couple of hours undressed in the forest, carefully, however, seeking shade as well as shelter. Judging from sensations of returning health and vigour, and the instinct I acquired for this original mode of cure, I confidently assert that my health derived the greatest benefit from my contact with the open air in this primitive guise.

When last upon the Continent, I was again induced to take the air bath; but I determined on the addition of another element of power—full sunshine—which, in former instances, I had carefully avoided. The weather being seldom favourable, I was unable to make more than four trials abroad, and one on my return to this country. On each occasion their effects and results were precisely the same.

I am easily affected by the sun; the consequence being headache and derangement of stomach. I found, however, when the body was entirely exposed to the sunshine, and without even the head being covered, or the pit of the stomach, an equally sensitive part, being sheltered from the rays, that I was not in the slightest degree unpleasantly affected. But on resuming my clothes, or even a portion of my clothing, I instantly experienced the symptoms I have alluded to, and was obliged quickly to get into the shade. I reversed the experiment, and proved the fact.

The sensation of sunshine on the body is very agreeable. Genial warmth, not heat, is felt. A gentle moisture on the skin causes it to feel cool under the rays;·but I noticed, on covering any portion of it with a single fold of light clothing or linen, that the heat on that part became intolerable.

I remained in this "sunshine bath" from half an hour to an hour and a half, on different occasions, and when the temperature of the day was that of ordinary summer heat.

Within an hour after having concluded the sun bath, symptoms were manifested which were repeated every time without variation. First, pricking and itching all over the body. This was succeeded by great redness and soreness of the skin in some places, with a slightly erysipelatous appearance. At the back of the thighs the muscles became rigid and corrugated under the skin, which became sore and manifested all the appearances of nettlerash, which, on examination, it was declared to be by a medical man. To describe my sensations plainly, I felt as if I were sitting in an ant's nest.

I was not relieved of these symptoms for a couple of days. But I applied no remedy. I did not again make trial of sunshine until they had disappeared, when precisely similar results occurred.

Shortly afterwards, I was so fortunate as to meet one of the most celebrated physicians in Europe—Dr. Scanzoni, of Wurtzburg. He was much interested in my narrative, but he anticipated my statement respecting the head, &c., not being affected by the sun. He observed that the influence of the sun, so powerful on the nervous organism of the skin and consequently upon the circulation, being equally diffused over the whole frame, the action of the blood would not be determined merely to the head. Without venturing to quote the words of this intelligent and most eminent man, I would say that he gave me to understand that the greatest power is practically the most ignored by medical science—that it is unreasonable not to believe that the great centre of action in nature can exert vast influence on the human organism and develop the energies and resources of life.

I mentioned to Dr. Scanzoni that you had cured a condemned consumptive patient by exposure to the sun and without recourse to medicine. At this he appeared not in the least surprised.

D. B.

No. 2.

ANTICIPATION OF THE REMEDIAL VALUE OF HEAT, BY DR. GOSSE, OF GENEVA, IN 1826.

Geneva, Oct. 25th, 1864.

On opening with Dr. Gosse the subject of the Bath, he answered me : " Tell me that it is introduced into Europe, but tell me nothing more. I know all the rest, and have known it before you were born. I have even put it in print, though nobody attended to it."

I must also record another sentence of his :—

" Look at the armies of Rome, without sickness and . without ambulances! Had there been the hospital service of modern times, it is impossible that we should have had no traces of it, in the military as well as the political writers. Had there been such loss from sickness as occurs in our armies, we should have had references to it, as in the accounts of our own campaigns. On this point, however, it is not negative testimony only on which we have to rely. Their armies passed through the extremest trials in regard to temperature. They marched from the east to the west, from the north to the south,—from Mauritania to Parthia, and from Africa to England,—without the facilities of communication by roads as to-day. Yet the numerical force of a legion, on arriving at its destination, is not supposed to vary from that of its departure from

Rome. This wonderful superiority over our modern armies they owe to two things : first, to the use of the Bath ; and, secondly, to their wearing an animal substance—wool—next to the skin ; and not a vegetable substance, such as linen or cotton ; by which means air was admitted, and electricity not lost."

I replied : "You have forgotten a third ; which was, that they only ate once a day."   D. U.

From "*Des Maladies Rhumatoïdes,*" *by Dr. Gosse, Geneva and Paris,* 1826, *page* 59.

" But the excitant which plays the most important *rôle* in the phenomena, whether of health or of disease, is caloric—a fluid imponderable and incompressible, which pervades all bodies and vivifies all organized existences. The reduction of the quantity of this fluid brings, as we have seen, weakness and disorder, whether general or local, in all nervous functions. It is, therefore, incontestable that its increase must augment their energy and contribute to the restoration of their equilibrium. No other agent can, therefore, be compared with this one, in the treatment of rheumatoid disorders. It is, so to say, the soul of this treatment ; and all other means can only be regarded as subordinate. Who can tell if even those substances which we define as *excitant* are not indebted to its presence for their properties ? At least, we find amongst them principles eminently combustible, and which disengage a considerable quantity of light and of caloric, as also substances possessing a great affinity with the develop-

ment of electricity. However, restricting ourselves for
the present to the mere effects of the sum of its accumulation, it is clear that we should make application
of it chiefly in the intervals of congestion, and at the
spot most distant therefrom. Nevertheless, in some of
these cases—chilblains, for instance—its local and immediate application is the most powerful of means for
dissipating them. Its moderate action is equally indispensable for overcoming the consequences of inflammation. If the fibre be relaxed and humid, and the
constitution lymphatic, dry heat is preferable. If
either, on the contrary, nervous or vascular irritation,
with a temperament nervous or sanguineous, it is desirable to combine moisture and heat.

"The efficaciousness of these means *for restoring the
action of the skin* explains the immense advantages
derived by the Greeks and the Romans from the use
of the Bath—advantages possessed in our times by the
daily use of the like by the Russians and the nations
of the East. We have the more to regret the negli-
gence in reference to such establishments of the middle
parts of Europe, that our more variable climate mul-
tiplies rheumatoid affections, and renders them more
inveterate. We ought to put up prayers that the
European Governments may favour the introduction of
such public establishments, and so bring within the
reach of the citizens unendowed with fortune, this real
panacea for the larger portion of the evils that assail
mankind."

No. 3.

OPENING OF THE NEW SWEATING-ROOM AT JERMYN STREET.

FROM THE MANAGER OF THE MIDDLESEX LUNATIC ASYLUM.

Colney Hatch, Oct. 13, 1864.

My dear Sir,

We have made the great experiment at the Hammam. Mr. Johnson was good enough to invite Mr. Wood (our engineer) and myself to try the perils or delights (as the case might be) of your room heated purely by radiation. It was a great success. The room was at a temperature of 205° when we entered, and felt much less oppressive than the hot-room (of transmission) upstairs, at a temperature of only 170°.

This is a very striking circumstance, and was equally noticed by Dr. Goolden (who fortunately happened to be present) and Mr. Wood.

I cannot see the occasion for raising (except for any extraordinary cases) the temperature of the radiating-room above 180°. At about this it would be perfect. I think I shall arrange for our hottest room to be one of purely radiated heat. You will be happy to know that our plans for the Bath at Colney Hatch and the specification, are now in the hands of the contractors for the purposes of an estimate, which I may hope to obtain in a few days. We shall then commence operations without delay.   Believe me, &c.,

E. SHEPPARD.

Index.

LONDON : BENJAMIN PARDON, PRINTER, PATERNOSTER ROW

www.ingramcontent.com/pod-product-compliance
Lightning Source LLC
Chambersburg PA
CBHW030942110726
47900CB00004B/1093